Taming the Tyrant

Treating Depressed Adults

By the same author

The Depressive Spectrum
A Practical Guide to Cognitive Therapy

A NORTON PROFESSIONAL BOOK

Taming the Tyrant
Treating Depressed Adults

Dean Schuyler, M.D.

W. W. Norton & Company
New York • London

For information about permission to reproduce selections
from this book, write to
Permissions, W. W. Norton & Company, Inc., 500 Fifth Avenue,
New York, NY 10110

The text of this book is composed in Goudy with the display set in Goudy Italic.
Composition and book design by Paradigm Graphics
Manufacturing by Haddon Craftsman
Cover design by DeSalvo Design

Library of Congress Cataloging-in-Publication Data
Schuyler, Dean, 1942–
Taming the tyrant: Treating depressed adults / Dean Schuyler.
p.   cm.
"A Norton Professional Book."
Includes bibliographical references and index.
ISBN 0-393-70257-X
1. Depression, Mental.
I. Title.
RC537.S385   1998
616.85'27–dc21   97-20532   CIP

W. W. Norton & Company, Inc., 500 Fifth Avenue, New York, NY 10110
http://www.wwnorton.com
W. W. Norton & Company Ltd., 10 Coptic Street, London, WC1A 1PU
1 2 3 4 5 6 7 8 9 0

For Rachel and Amy
and for Amy and Rachel

About the Title

Many authors choose their titles after much of the book's content has been written. For me, however, a title serves to keep me on track as I write. Having decided to write about depression for the practicing clinician, I felt stuck with some sort of "Guide" that would be "Practical." Not the stuff dreams are made of, eh?

So I had no title, I was writing away, and then, one day in my car, I was listening to Trisha Yearwood sing "Little Hercules."* Country music tends to be about truth, loss, and often sadness. The song says: "It's hard to shine a light when the batteries are dead/ Nothing seems as easy as it did when you were young/ There are times when being a grownup gets to be too much, and your sense of humor seems to vanish in the crush/ Now the only tyrant that you're working for is you/ When you feel the weight of the world, put your mind at ease."

The song is not explicitly about depression, but it captures for me what the problem is about and how the clinician endeavors to help. We work, I think, to "tame the tyrant" that is depression. We try to recharge the batteries, reclaim the sense of humor, and redistribute the weight. For me, "Little Hercules" would never again sound the same.

*Trisha Yearwood, "Everybody Knows." ©1996 by MCA Records, Inc.

Acknowledgments

The gestation period for a book surpasses that for a child. Over the past fourteen months, a number of people and places have been central to the writing of this volume. I spent countless hours in two libraries: The National Library of Medicine in Bethesda, Maryland, and the Georgetown University Medical Library in Washington, D.C. The library staff in each was unfailingly helpful.

Dr. John Schwartz and Diane Turner of CME, Inc. were constantly encouraging and provided real opportunities for me to develop ideas about depression and its treatment. Dr. Kathy Phillips and her husband Dr. Ralph Albertini shared a wonderful meeting in Santa Fe, where I learned about Kathy's pioneering work on body dysmorphic disorder. Several lecture platforms shared with Dr. Bob Dupont (and one fabulous dinner in Williamsburg) taught me a lot about the P 450 controversy. Paul Weil (of the Eli Lilly Company) was instrumental to the opportunity to assemble several presentations on dysthymia. Patty Lynch (of Smith Klein Beecham) was a constant source of good information and stimulating talk.

If I ever stop treating patients, I promise I will stop writing books. My patients provide the rationale to read, to think, and eventually, to write. Their stories inform the case examples and clinical anecdotes that give this book its focus. (In each case, identities are obscured to protect confidentiality.) The friendship of my patients has sustained me, thus far, through the very real assaults aimed at the practice of providing care today.

My wife, Terry, has watched me pursue this project for over a year and adapted more than anyone else to my preoccupation with it. I am grateful for her patience and love.

My daughters, Rachel and Amy, sometimes seem to support me as much as I've tried to support them. They are, each and both, the inspiration for writing this book.

Contents

Preface
The Past Twenty-Five Years

Twenty-five years ago, Richard Nixon was President of the United States. Cold War conflict between the U.S. and the U.S.S.R. was in the news. No one knew about the Watergate break-in, or AIDS. Terrorism was confined to areas distant from the United States. *Challenger* had not yet blown up.

The Middle East was frequently a war zone. There were not yet U.S. hostages in Iran, nor had there been Camp David Accords. The Berlin Wall was intact. No one knew of Poland's Solidarity. The Soviet Union comprised a multiethnic group of defined populations, all governed by a central authority. Computers were in a toddler stage. There were no fax machines, no Internet.

Meanwhile, I was twenty-eight years old, recently married, father to an infant daughter (now a pediatric nurse) and relocated from Philadelphia to Washington, D.C. There, in 1974, I wrote a book entitled *The Depressive Spectrum*. As a psychiatrist, and moreover, Coordinator of the Depression Research Program at the National Institute of Mental Health, I had unique access to research and thinking about the depressive disorders.

The book was intended to be a concise, readable exploration of what we knew about depression and its treatment. It was written for clinicians of all backgrounds, but an educated layperson could read it as well.

It introduced the idea of depression as a "spectrum of problems" ranging from the normal ("the blues" and bereavement) to the pathological (neurotic and psychotic disorders). It reviewed the phenomenology of depression. It discussed the different ways of classifying depression, including the "new" factor pattern typologies and the recently published Feighner Research Criteria for a diagnosis of depression.

Five ways were offered to explain depression, but none deserved to stand out from the rest. I discussed *who* was likely to become depressed as well as *how* to differentiate depression from other psychopathological entities. Suicide was examined in detail. Treatment choices for the affective disorders were enumerated.

The tricyclic antidepressants were then the preferred biological therapeutic agents. Lithium carbonate, while already in use, had not established its efficacy as a "preventive" agent altering the course of manic-depressive illness. There were no alternatives to its use as a "course" drug.

In 1974, my younger daughter (today a college graduate) was born. No one spoke, in those days, of managed care. The Seventies were already referred to as the "age of depression," reflecting an upsurge of interest and research in affective disorders.

Over the ensuing twenty-one years, I entered private practice, treating mostly depressed adults in an office setting. I joined the faculty of Georgetown University in Washington, D.C. and started a program of Continuing Education in Psychiatry for clinicians. At the annual meeting of the American Psychiatric Association, I assembled a panel of clinicians with different expertises in depression to educate participating psychiatrists.

I began to offer lectures, grand rounds, and workshops around the country designed to teach clinicians about depression. My own psychotherapy model was short-term cognitive therapy, which I had learned during my residency training at the University of Pennsylvania from Dr. Aaron (Tim) Beck. I prescribed antidepressant medication for many of my patients who met current criteria for its use. Therefore, I had a need to keep up with the explosion of new available agents. I had an occasional need to hospitalize patients—usually suicidal patients—so I maintained an awareness of the changing issues and services available in hospital settings. These changes became particularly evident in the middle Nineties as managed care more and more influenced the process of psychiatric treament.

Meanwhile, our clinical understanding of the spectrum of problems we have labeled depression grew at a rapid pace over the two plus decades. New ideas of classification came to America with the publication of *DSM-III* in 1980, *DSM III-R* in 1987, and *DSM-IV* in 1994. The division of clinical depression into neurotic and psychotic subgroups was clearly no longer adequate. Attention was being focused especially on achieving a better understanding of depression's chronic forms.

There was a focus, too, on factors of gender and age and how they altered depression's presentation. Biological research went beyond the hypothesis that decreases in the brain amines norepinephrine and serotonin explain the disorder, and concentrated on events at receptor sites in the brain. Progress was made in narrowing the search to define what sorts of affective illness were transmitted genetically and, more specifically, where the offending factors were located on the chromosome.

The proliferation of managed care plans (and increased consumer subscription to them) gave new primacy to drug therapies. The emphasis in psychotherapeutic interventions for depression swung strongly in favor of brief therapy. Not surprisingly, the prescription of cognitive therapy for depression grew in popularity and demand.

Little of new direct clinical usefulness emerged in our understanding of suicidal behavior. Its link to the affective disorders remained strong. Similarly, the differentiation of the depressions from other major psychopathologies (e.g., schizophrenia and the anxiety disorders) in clinical practice changed little over twenty-one years. Despite a flurry of interest in the dexamethasone suppression test (DST) as well as in thyroid challenges (TRH test) and changes in sleep parameters associated with depression (shortened REM latency), no standard clinical diagnostic test emerged for depression.

A second, and then a third, generation of antidepressant drugs was introduced. Prozac captured the public imagination in ways both illuminating and disheartening. It ushered in a new class of antidepressants (the serotonin specific reuptake inhibitors or SSRIs), which quickly became the standard for pharmacotherapy in depression. Simultaneously, its familiarity in an era of talk show radio and television led to misinformation about the nature of depression and its treatment. (Heard on one program: "It will be unseasonably warm today. A good day to go to the beach or to sit in your backyard with a sun reflector and a Prozac.")

If chlorpromazine (Thorazine) effectively changed the way we thought about treating schizophrenia, and if lithium carbonate modified our ideas about manic-depressive illness, then fluoxetine (Prozac) was changing the treatment of the depressive episode as well as our differentiation of depressive "illness" from depressive "personality."

New approaches to modifying the unrelenting course of some depressions added carbamazepine (Tegretol) and valproate (Depakote) to lithium. Now psychiatrists had choices (even combinations) to consider in their approach to the long-term problem of treating manic-depressive illness.

Taming the Tyrant loosely follows the chapter outline of *The Depressive Spectrum*. Where appropriate, reference is made to the ideas written two decades earlier, especially when they continue to represent current thought and practice. They are juxtaposed with current clinical concepts.

Chapter one updates the idea of a depressive spectrum. Chapter two delineates the signs and symptoms of a depressive episode. Chapter three describes three common clinical forms of depression. Chapter four traces the evolution in thinking about depression that resulted in *DSM-IV* and reviews other contributions to current concepts in classification. Chapter five focuses on the various clinical entities that border depression. Chapter six reviews the epidemiology and course parameters relevant to depression. Chapter seven offers five explanatory models for the clinician approaching the depressed patient. Chapter eight considers the significant problem of suicide by the depressed person. In chapter nine, those clinical problems that may relate to depression, but don't do so obviously, are unmasked. Chapters ten and eleven cover the treatment options, after some introductory words concerning the rendering of treatment in the managed care world.

The book is written with the clinical practitioner in mind: psychiatrist, social worker, psychologist, counselor. Where appropriate, clinical cases are presented to illustrate the principles offered. This volume is intended to be used by the student of any of these disciplines as well as by an established clinician seeking an up-to-date review of current thinking and practice. Today's educated individual, although not engaged in the treatment of emotional disorders, will find the material understandable and, I hope, informative. I hope this volume will continue the education of those on the front lines providing care to depressed persons.

Dean Schuyler
Rockville, Maryland
April 1997

Taming the Tyrant
Treating Depressed Adults

Chapter 1

What Is Depression?

Depression encompasses a broad range of experience, from a normal passing sadness ("the blues") to a recurrent, debilitating illness (major depressive disorder). There are acute forms of depression in which an individual reacts to a loss (bereavement), to a situation (adjustment disorder), or sometimes to no discernible cause. There are chronic forms in which a depressive episode never ends (chronic major depression) or only partially remits. In still other cases, the symptoms are insufficient to constitute a depressive episode, but persist over lengthy periods of time (dysthymia).

The hallmark of our clinical understanding of depression is the episode. This diagnostic entity encompasses change from usual functioning in four significant life areas: thinking, feelings, behavior, and physical functions (see chapter 2). This symptom complex has been denoted "the depressive syndrome." When the *DSM-IV* committee assimilated the wealth of detail written about the depressive episode, they settled upon nine defining characteristics.[1] (These are listed in Table 1.1.) They require five or more of the nine symptoms present during the same two-week period, and they must represent a change from previous functioning.

When an individual's symptoms fall short of the full syndrome, we speak of "subsyndromic depression." Bereavement, adjustment reactions, dysthymia, and some depressions secondary to medical and psychiatric conditions often fall into this category.

Once we have established the existence of a depressive syndrome (episode) we explore the individual's past for relevant historical details. Our concern is now directed to establishing the course (pattern) of the disorder. Have there been previous depressive episodes (unipolar depression)? Has there already been an episode of mania (bipolar depression) or one of the variants of manic-depressive illness?

Comorbidity is today a popular clinical concept. It refers to the coexistence (or co-occurrence) of more than one form of psychopathology. Comorbidity is common in individuals with depression. Some form of anxiety disorder, substance abuse, or eating disorder frequently accompanies depression.

A SPECTRUM APPROACH

While some great minds have applied themselves over the years to the task of understanding depression, we are left with a proliferation of descriptions sharing some characteristics but not others. The usefulness of the term depression has been compromised by the diffusion of its meaning. "Depression" has been used to describe a feeling state or symptom, a syndrome or reaction, a character style or personality disorder, and an illness. No single definition can encompass this spectrum.

Instead of a solitary definition, I will try to describe a continuum of phenomena, all related to depression. To be useful, there must be a clear demarcation between normal phenomena and clinical problems. Occupying the

---

Table 1.1
MAJOR DEPRESSIVE DISORDER: *DSM-IV* CRITERIA

1. Depressed mood

2. Markedly diminished interests or pleasures
   (At least one of #1 or #2 must be present.)

3. Significant weight loss or gain

4. Insomnia or hypersomnia

5. Psychomotor retardation or agitation

6. Fatigue or loss of energy

7. Worthlessness or inappropriate guilt

8. Diminished ability to think or concentrate

9. Recurrent thoughts of death or suicide

normal portion of the depressive spectrum (See Figure 1.1) are the feeling state ("the blues") and the common experience of bereavement (the grief reaction). It is far more challenging to adequately encompass the pathological portion. Possible organizing themes include acuteness and chronicity, mild versus severe disturbance, unipolar versus bipolar disorder, full versus partial syndrome. It is my belief that choosing "acute-chronic" as the organizing theme would focus the clinician on a meaningful dichotomy while allowing the inclusion of all known clinical depressive disorders.

THE BLUES

Every reader has a referent for the feeling state of depression. It has been captured in song, depicted in works of art, and popularly labeled "the blues." We accept the blues as a logical companion to rainy days, annoying colds, and the like. Feeling blue is as normal as feeling angry. When a person feels blue, he or she seems sad or apathetic, may want little to eat, withdraw from other people, sleep poorly, and lack whatever it is that catapults people out of bed in the morning (*joie de vivre*). One's thoughts are often preoccupied with an expectation unmet.

While society accepts the blues in certain situations, we are less likely to do so in others. Holidays (especially Christmas and New Year's Day in the U.S.), the experience of moving, and the period immediately following childbirth have been described as particularly vulnerable times for depressive *feelings*. It seems that the expectation of joy may set the stage for disappointment. The knowledge that those around you are festive may underline a personal feeling of loneliness. While moving to a new locale may be beneficial, it often entails multiple losses—of social ties, familiar patterns, security, even income. The joy we tend to associate with childbirth belies the thoughts of new responsibilities, role and relationship changes, and effects on family equilibrium the baby brings. Some have even spoken of "the baby blues."

Yet, these reactions are normal, although by no means experienced by all whose lives are touched by the events. The blues are usually short-lived, hours to a few days in duration. They rarely disrupt ability to work and may escape the notice of significant others. Although they are on the healthy end of the depressive spectrum, their shared features with clinical depression have stimulated interest. Where does "normal" depression end and clinical depression begin? Are some people predisposed to one and some to the other, while some experience neither?

It is when duration lengthens, function is affected, and symptoms intensi-fy that we consider what seemed like the blues to perhaps be the onset of a depressive episode. No single symptom or sign marks this boundary. It is my belief that changes in thinking and behavior may be more sensitive indica-tors of a depressive episode than the degree of sadness present. When one begins to *act* depressed (withdrawal and psychomotor slowing or agitation) and *think* depressed (self-blaming, helplessness), then perhaps the border from the blues to clinical depression has been crossed. (See Figure 1.1.)

Figure 1.1
THE DEPRESSIVE SPECTRUM

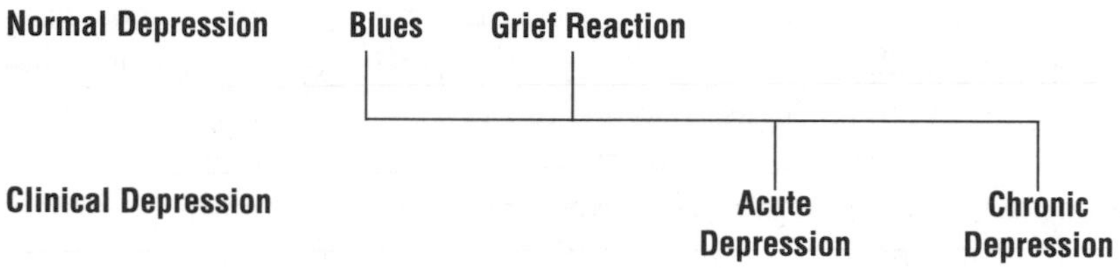

Normal Depression   **Blues**   **Grief Reaction**

Clinical Depression   **Acute**   **Chronic**
                                                                        Depression   **Depression**

GRIEF REACTION

It is also well within the realm of normal experience to sustain the loss of a significant other through death. The reaction commonly observed in some form in most survivors is grief. It is the general consensus that this grief is entirely normal, and in fact that it may be detrimental to one's subsequent mental health *not* to mourn. Parkes has found it rare for there to be no psy-chological reaction to the death of a significant other.[2]

The best description of normal grief remains that of Lindemann in 1944.[3] He studied a series of subjects that included patients who had lost a relative during treatment, relatives of patients who died in the hospital, relatives of Army casualties, and bereaved survivors of the tragic victims of the Coconut Grove fire in a Boston nightclub.

Lindemann identified *physical distress* (sighing, tightness in the throat, an empty feeling in the abdomen, lack of muscle power), *preoccupation with the image of the deceased, guilt, hostile reactions*, and *the loss of patterns of conduct* as common to normal grief reactions. Mourning consists of breaking the bonds

to the lost person, adjusting to life without the deceased, and, finally, forming new relationships. Common feelings that arise during this process and
must be dealt with by the mourner include *loneliness* (due to the actual departure of a loved one), *helplessness* (due to the irreversibility of the loss), *anger*
(related to the thought of being deserted), and sometimes *relief* (related to a
survivor's burdens associated with the deceased).

By the mid-Seventies, clinical thinking about bereavement was shifting.
Clayton reported a study of 109 widows and widowers demonstrating that
fully 35% met criteria for major depression one month after their spouse's
death.[4] Furthermore, a follow-up study found that 17% of the group remained
depressed one year later.[5] These syndromes did not fit the format of "normal"
depression; rather, they appeared identical to clinical depression.

However, some differences persisted, even in these more serious reactions
to the loss of a spouse. Clayton found few psychiatric consultations, hospitalizations, or prescriptions for antidepressant drugs in this group. Two symptoms common to clinical depression, *psychomotor slowing* and *feelings of worthlessness*, were likewise uncommon in the bereaved group. Furthermore, a family history of depression was unusual, as was a previous personal bout of affective illness.

In 1980, *DSM-III* (and in 1987, *DSM-III-R*) incorporated this landmark
study of widowhood into its new category, "Uncomplicated Bereavement." The
message to the clinician was that the grief reaction continued to be viewed as
normal and different from a depressive episode. However, bereavement carried
with it an increased risk of experiencing full or partial depressive syndromes.

Before we leave consideration of the grief reaction, it is instructive to
review some comments on the boundary between grief and depression. In
1911, Abraham noted that while both grief and depression represented a
response to loss, in *melancholia* (depression), there is "an unconscious hostility at play." [6] The implication was that the individual passed from mourning
to melancholia when his or her reaction to the lost object contained elements of anger as well as love.

Freud, elaborating on Abraham's theory, noted three signs specific to
melancholia: *decreased self-esteem, self-accusation,* and a *need for self-punishment*. Based upon this conceptualization, Freud derived a major clinical
guideline to define the boundary between grief and clinical depression: when
the mourner's focus shifts from the lost person to a preoccupation with his
own inadequacies, grief has progressed to depression.[7]

THE CLINICAL END OF THE SPECTRUM

When we divide all clinical depression into its acute and chronic forms, the focus of acute depression is on the episode itself. That episode may take one of three forms: depressive, manic, or mixed (exhibiting both depressive and manic symptoms). Milder versions—minor depression and hypomania—have been recognized that meet fewer criteria than a full syndrome.

The chronic depressive disorders are a complicated lot, and our understanding of them is at an early stage. The most useful current nosology is that of Thase and Howland.[8] The routes to a chronic syndrome are varied. In the unipolar spectrum, a depressive episode may never remit or may recur. The timing of subsequent episodes, for example, may be limited to the premenstrual period, to the postpartum period, or may be seasonal.

A subsyndromic form (dysthymic disorder) may represent partially remitted major depression (MDD-residual) or pure dysthymia (less than a full syndrome of depression, continuous for at least two years). An acute episode of depression may complicate dysthymia, producing what has been called "double depression." The term is a contribution of Martin Keller, who has done the most extensive work with these patients.[9]

In the bipolar spectrum, the disorder may feature recurrent episodes of mania and depression (bipolar I disorder), or hypomania and depression (bipolar II disorder).

Again, the pattern of recurrence may be postpartum or seasonal. There may also be a high frequency of recurrence (rapid cycling)—multiple episodes in a year. The subsyndromic form (cyclothymic disorder) may evolve into a full syndrome over time, or it may follow a chronic course of its own. (For a schematic representation of the clinical spectrum, see Figure 1.2.)

The interest shown in delineating a precipitating event for an episode of depression, so strong from 1950 to the early 1970s, has waned. As our understanding of clinical depression became more biological, the prognostic significance of the presence or absence of a life event has declined.

The publication of *DSM-IV* supported a division of the clinical territory into acute and chronic syndromes. In an initial presentation of depression, therefore, we see only the nature of the episode. It remains for time to allow the course to define itself and lead the clinician toward different approaches to treatment.

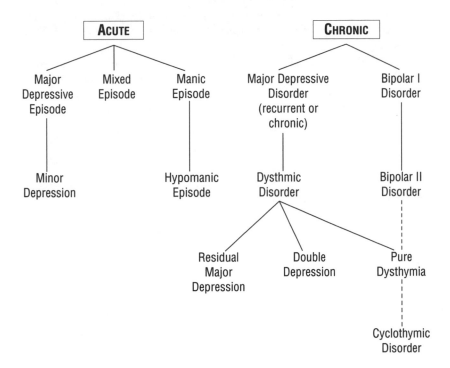

Figure 1.2
THE CLINICAL SPECTRUM

Notes

1. American Psychiatric Association (1994). *Diagnostic and statistical manual* (4th ed.). Washington D.C.: American Psychiatric Association.

2. Parkes, C.M. (1987). *Bereavement* (2nd ed.). New York: International Universities Press.

3. Lindemann, E. (1944). Symptomatology and management of acute grief. *American Journal of Psychiatry, 101*, 141.

4. Clayton, P. J. (1972). The depression of widowhood. *British Journal of Psychiatry, 120*, 71.

5. Bornstein, P. E., Clayton, P. J., Halikas, J. A., et al. (1973). The depression of widowhood after thirteen months. *British Journal of Psychiatry, 122*, 561.

6. Abraham (1911/1968). Notes on the psychoanalytical investigation and treatment of manic-depressive insanity and allied conditions. In W. Gaylin (Ed.), *The meaning of despair*. New York: Science House.

7. Freud, S. (1917). Mourning and melancholia. In J. Strachey (Ed. and Trans.), *The complete psychological works of Sigmund Freud* (Vol. 14, pp. 237–258). New York: Norton.

8. Thase, M. E., & Howland R. H. (1995). Assessment and treatment of chronic depression. *Clinical Advances in the Treatment of Psychiatric Disorders*, 9(3), 1.

9. Keller, M. B., Lavori, P. W., Endicott, J., et al. (1983). Double depression: A two year follow-up. *American Journal of Psychiatry*, 140, 689.

Chapter 2

What Depression Looks Like
Signs and Symptoms

Surveys have found that 13–20% of the United States population has depressive symptoms at any given time.[1] A depressive episode features emotional, physical, behavioral, and cognitive changes. In diagnosing a depressive episode, it is important to establish a baseline of usual functioning. The deviations from this baseline form the symptoms and signs of the depressive episode.

EMOTIONAL CHANGES

While sad mood is the anticipated feature in this category, it is not invariably present in depression. Moreover sadness, when present, can be accompanied by a variety of additional mood changes. Typically, the sadness is described as differing qualitatively from the patient's concept of "normal sadness."

A depressed patient may describe sadness in a number of ways: unhappiness, the blues, dejection, emptiness, loss of *joie de vivre*. To meet criteria established to differentiate transient reactions from depressive episodes, this sad mood must persist for at least a two-week period. Patterns of sadness are, however, variable and the mood may not be even throughout the day. The sadness may have its greatest intensity early, upon the patient's awakening, and actually brighten as the day goes on. This diurnal variation suggests a disturbance in the normal circadian rhythm. Reverse fluctuation (mood worse in the evening) has been observed as well.

Feelings of anxiety are a common accompaniment to sadness. This co-occurrence has led to controversy in differentiating an anxiety episode from a depressive episode. *DSM-IV* has provided a category to collect cases in which the criteria for neither affective episode is fully met: mixed anxiety-depressive disorder. (For a discussion about differentiating the syndromes of anxiety and depression, see chapter 5, Boundary Disputes.)

Guilt is often associated with depressive episodes. A rational view of the patient's circumstances usually finds this guilt undeserved or inappropriate. Following (or eliciting) the patient's relevant beliefs will demonstrate the symmetry between his or her thoughts and the guilty feelings.

Factor analytic studies in the 1960s by Grinker et al.[2] and Friedman et al.[3] identified a subtype of depression in which guilt is a predominant feature. In the 1970s, Roth et al. found "inappropriate guilt" associated as often with anxiety syndromes as with depression, raising questions about its specificity.[4]

The status of expressed anger in depression has been the subject of controversy. Traditional psychoanalytic formulations view hostility directed away from the external world and turned against the self as one significant etiological mechanism for depression. Therefore, the appearance of expressed anger was thought to be incompatible with clinical depression.

In 1985, Snaith and Taylor found outwardly directed anger in over one-third of their study sample of depressives.[5] In 1993, Fava noted that a depressed subgroup in his study described experiencing anger attacks that they saw as "uncharacteristic" (of themselves) and "inappropriate" (to the situation).[6]

It is useful in this regard to remember that descriptions of anger vary with culture and personality style. Irritation, annoyance, and hostility can all be found on a continuum of anger. For some depressives, anger may indeed be hypothesized to be "turned inward" and expressed anger will be rarely observed, while for others overt hostility is quite common. In fact, outwardly directed anger in depression may be an important indicator of suicide potential.[7]

Emotional changes that characterize a depressive episode are summarized in Table 2.1.

Table 2.1
SYMPTOMS AND SIGNS OF DEPRESSION: EMOTIONAL CHANGES
Sad mood • Anxiety • Guilt • Anger • Diurnal mood variation

PHYSICAL CHANGES

It is important to acknowledge the physical symptoms of depression because, when they are its sole indicators, the connection is often overlooked. Typical responses to these complaints include dismissal and minimization by family members ("You always complain about aches and pains"), elaborate medical diagnostic examinations by physicians ("There are many potentially serious causes for a thirty-pound weight loss"), and treatment aimed at symptom relief ("The red pills will improve your appetite, the white pills will help you move your bowels, and the blue pills will put you to sleep").

The somatic symptoms of depression are nonspecific. They may indeed indicate the presence of a physical disorder requiring medical diagnosis and treatment. Often, however, they do not. When the clinician encourages this depressed patient to talk about his or her feelings, other symptoms of depression are usually elicited. There is little excuse for symptomatic treatment approaches before clinical depression is *considered* as a possible underlying problem.

There has been little research on the physiological mechanism by which the somatic symptoms of depression are produced. Suffice it to say that an emotional illness (depression) can result in a person's appearing gaunt (from loss of weight), drawn (from lack of sleep), weak, and easily fatigued. The combination of insomnia, anorexia, and constipation—three commonly observed physical changes in depression—has been termed the *somatic triad.*

Sleep is disturbed in the vast majority of depressed persons. Therapeutic (purposeful) sleep deprivation has been found to alter mood in as many as 50% of depressed subjects.[8] Reynolds and Kupfer have reported that altered sleep often precedes, and may persist after, episodes of major depression.[9] Sleep and depression are, therefore, intricately linked. Polysomnographic studies have permitted the specification of altered parameters of sleep function in depression.[10]

Normal sleep is marked by recurring cycles of REM (rapid eye movement) and non-REM periods. Non-REM sleep is characterized by four stages, with stages three and four (slow wave or delta sleep) being the "deepest" levels. Most stage three and four sleep occurs early in the night. Conversely, REM (dreaming) periods are initially brief, becoming longer as sleep goes on.[10]

In unipolar depression, an episode typically manifests in difficulty initiating and maintaining sleep, interrupted sleep throughout the night, decreased total sleep time (especially decreased deep sleep), decreased REM-latency (a shorter than normal interval between sleep onset and the first REM period), and early morning awakening.[11] Decreased REM-latency has been offered as a biological marker for depression. When it persists after the clinical symptoms abate, it may even serve to predict a recurrence of the episode.[12]

In bipolar depressive episodes, more often there is hypersomnia, with an increase in daytime sleepiness.[10] The problem is compounded because patients reporting poor sleep have been found to be inaccurate in estimating their total sleep time.

Specifically designed sleep laboratories will house a patient for one or two night's sleep and enable researchers to perform a variety of studies to characterize the patient's sleep. This may help in the differentiation of *primary sleep disorders* (e.g., narcolepsy, sleep apnea, restless legs syndrome) from sleep changes seen in a depressive episode. However, typically an affective episode can be adequately diagnosed without resort to these more sophisticated techniques.

A further confound seen in depressed patients is variability in the direction of observed physical changes. For example, in addition to insomnia or hypersomnia, there are decreases or increases in appetite, bowel changes characteristic of constipation or diarrhea, and weight variations. Patients with the eating disorders anorexia and bulimia often exhibit coincident depression and may respond in part to antidepressant medications.

Less energy than usual and easier fatiguability are two common physical findings in depressed patients. Chronic fatigue syndrome and fibromyalgia may overlap, mimic, or be entirely separate entities from depression. (They are discussed further in chapter 9, Depression's Other Spectrum.)

In women, menstrual periods may cease solely on the basis of depression. In men or women, a diminished interest in sex may be an early symptom of an incipient depressive episode. A change in sexual functioning (erectile, ejaculatory, or orgasmic) is not uncommon in depression for either sex. In addition, drug treatment for depression has been found to produce sexual dysfunction in some patients. Sometimes an accurate attribution of the cause of sexual dysfunction is difficult to make. (For more on sexual dysfunction as a "side effect," see chapter 10, Treatment Issues and a Menu of Choices.)

Chronic pain disorders may have a variety of causes. Depression is on that list, and some pain syndromes respond to antidepressant treatment. In others, depression is coincident to the pain problem and arises from the debilitation and restriction imposed by the chronic suffering.

Table 2.2 summarizes the physical changes discussed for a depressive episode.

Table 2.2
SYMPTOMS AND SIGNS OF DEPRESSION: PHYSICAL CHANGES
Sleep disorder • Eating disorder
Bowel disorder • Loss of energy
Easy fatigue • Weight change
Decreased sex drive • Amenorrhea
Impotence/Frigidity • Pain

BEHAVIORAL CHANGES

The association of *crying* and depression is firm in the minds of most lay people. In Beck's landmark catalogue of depressive symptoms, 83% of the severely depressed reported crying "more frequently than usual." [13] Some patients described being so depressed they "couldn't cry." Many cry without the relief that crying typically brought in the past. It is useful in diagnosis to inquire about the patient's typical habits regarding crying prior to the onset of the episode and to compare this to their current experience.

Withdrawal in some form is typical of the depressed patient. Some stay in bed all day. Others leave the bed but not the confines of home. Some will go out, but remain absent from work. Others continue to meet their obligations, but remain distant from other people, particularly loved ones. This withdrawal may be the cardinal change that makes the depressed person so difficult for others to live with.

Psychomotor changes, though not invariably present, may be an important border between the blues or grieving and an acute depressive episode. Classically, depressed individuals "slow down" (retardation). They may walk slowly, speak slowly, and stand rigidly. Illustrator hand movements (augmenting speech with gestures) may drop out entirely. Conversely, some depressed patients exhibit increased psychomotor activity (agitation). These patients may pace, be unable to sit still, seem constantly in motion, and talk with rapid, pressured speech. There are not yet clear biological correlates of increased and decreased psychomotor activity. Changes from usual in either direction support a diagnosis of a depressed episode.

In my psychiatric residency training (1968–71), hallucinations were most often seen as indicators of schizophrenia. Earlier in the 1960s, hallucinations were commonly observed with psychedelic drug abuse. As the evaluation of the patient became more informed by biological considerations, a wide range of organic, physical illnesses were associated with hallucinations. It is important to remember that depression, too, has its psychotic forms. In these (usually) severe episodes of either unipolar or bipolar depression, hallucinations are commonly seen.

The typical behavioral changes seen in a depressive episode are listed in Table 2.3.

Table 2.3 SYMPTOMS AND SIGNS OF DEPRESSION: BEHAVIORAL CHANGES
Crying spells • Withdrawal • Agitation • Retardation • Hallucinations

COGNITIVE CHANGES

Among the emotional, physical, and behavioral changes discussed so far, none is specific to depression. To complicate matters further, no single symptom has been reliably associated with a particular subtype of depression. The study of the elements of *thinking* that change in the depressed person may produce the specificity that has thus far been missing. Schizophrenia has traditionally been described as predominantly a disorder of thinking. Depression, in contrast, has been seen as a mood disorder. Beck has been credited with focusing the clinician's attention on the cognitive changes that occur in depression. He is, however, by no means the first theorist to write about depression's effect on thinking.

For example, Bibring in 1953 called attention to the importance of lowered self-esteem in producing depression.[14] Then, in 1963, Beck wrote about systematic errors in thinking that increased in frequency and import in depressed persons: *polarization* (all-or-nothing thinking), *personalization* (an exclusive focus on the self), and *over-generalization* (reaching conclusions beyond the scope of the data).[15] By 1970, Beck had articulated a "cognitive triad" of signs in depression similar to the somatic triad noted earlier.[16] These are: a *negative view of the self* (lowered self-esteem), *a negative view of the world*, and *negative expectations for the future* (pessimism).

Closely related to a negative self-image are *self-blame* and *self-criticism*, which are common findings in depression (80% of severe depressives in Beck's 1967 study). In tandem with pessimism are the helplessness-hopelessness affects first described by Engel in 1968.[17] In his pioneering work on helplessness, Seligman described this cognitive change as an inability to act on one's environment to secure gratification.[18] In other words, there is nothing you can do to help yourself. Hopelessness is the notion that there is nothing *anyone* can do to produce the outcome you desire. Seligman blazed a trail in research, moving from helplessness in dogs,[19] to helplessness in depressed humans,[20] to helplessness and death,[21] then on to the consequences of pessimism,[22] the relationship of optimism and change in psychotherapy,[23] to the powerful effect of optimism in child rearing.[24]

A classical finding in depression is the individual's inability to decide. From the trivial ("Which shirt should I wear this morning?") to the significant ("Should I remain with my husband or leave?"), indecisiveness is a commonly encountered problem. Depressed patients have been reported to believe that their emotional state was irreversible.[25] In one older study, many patients acknowledged holding the belief that they would never recover, often despite the available data that some had recovered multiple times from depressive episodes in the past.[26] Depression can apparently render inaccessible the conclusions people would ordinarily draw from past events.

In psychotic depression, themes of worthlessness and failure, poverty and irreversibility, as well as helplessness and hopelessness, may form the basis for delusional beliefs.

The cognitive factors have been called by Grinker et al. (1961) "the core process of the depressive syndrome."[2] For example, the depressive attributes adverse experience to a deficiency in himself, then criticizes himself for the alleged defect. He may interpret positive events as neutral and neutral events as negative. He may *selectively abstract* aspects of a situation, and formulate his emotional reaction accordingly. The depressed person may see negative implications where others focus on gratifying consequences (e.g., "A promotion brings added responsibilities that will overwhelm me").

A review of the cognitive changes seen in a depressive episode can be found in Table 2.4.

> ### Table 2.4
> ### SYMPTOMS AND SIGNS OF DEPRESSION:
> ### COGNITIVE CHANGES
>
> Negative self-concept • Negative view of the world
>
> Negative expectations for the future
>
> Self-blame • Self-criticism • Indecisiveness
>
> Helplessness • Hopelessness • Worthlessness
>
> Delusions

In summary, *hope* and a *sense of control* seem significant to the maintenance of mental health. In this regard, the cognitive variables helplessness and hopelessness may be of far-reaching importance to the understanding of mental illness.

Notes

1. Kizilay, E. (1992). Predictors of depression in women. *Nursing Clinics of North America, 27*(4), 983.
2. Grinker, R. R., Miller, J., Sabshin, M., et al. (1961). *The phenomena of depression.* New York: Hoeber.
3. Friedman, A. S., Cowitz, B., Cohen, H. W., et al. (1963). Syndromes and themes of psychotic depression. *Archives of General Psychiatry, 9,* 504.
4. Roth, M., Gurney, C., Garside, R. F., et al. (1972). Studies in the classification of affective disorders: The relationship between anxiety states and depressive illness. *British Journal of Psychiatry, 121,* 147.
5. Snaith, R. P., & Taylor, C. M. (1985). Irritability: Definition, assessment and associated factors. *British Journal of Psychiatry, 147,* 127.
6. Fava, M., & Rosenbaum, J. F. (1993). The relationship between anger and depression. *Clinical Advances in the Treatment of Psychiatric Disorders, 7*(2), 1.
7. Paykel, E. S., & Dienelt, M. N. (1971). Suicide attempts following acute depression. *Journal of Nervous and Mental Disease, 153,* 234.
8. Wu, J. C., & Bunney, W. E. (1990). The biological basis of an anti-depressant response to sleep deprivation and relapse: review and hypothesis. *American Journal of Psychiatry, 147,* 14.
9. Reynolds, C. F., & Kupfer, D. J. (1987). Sleep research in affective illness: State of the art circa 1987. *Sleep, 10,* 199.

10. Neylan, T. C. (1995). Treatment of sleep disturbances in depressed patients. *Journal of Clinical Psychiatry, 56* (Suppl. 2), 56.

11. Goodwin, F., & Jamison, K. (1990). *Manic-depressive illness.* New York: Oxford University Press.

12. Giles, D. E., Jarrett, R. B., & Roffwarg, H. P. (1987). Reduced REM-latency: A predictor of recurrence of depression. *Neuropsychopharmacology, 1,* 33.

13. Beck, A. T. (1967). *Depression: Clinical, experimental and theoretical aspects.* New York: Harper and Row.

14. Bibring, E. (1953). The mechanism of depression. In P. Greenacre (Ed.), *Affective disorders.* New York: International Universities Press.

15. Beck, A. T. (1963). Thinking and depression: I. Idiosyncratic content and cognitive distortions. *Archives of General Psychiatry, 9,* 324.

16. Beck, A. T. (1970). The core problem in depression: The cognitive triad. *Science and Psychoanalysis, 17,* 47.

17. Engel, G. L. (1968). A life setting conducive to illness: The giving-up-given-up complex. *Bulletin of the Meninger Clinic, 32,* 355.

18. Seligman, M. E. P. (1972). Learned helplessness. *Annual Review of Medicine, 23,* 407.

19. Seligman, M. E. P., & Maier, S. (1967). Failure to escape traumatic shock. *Journal of Experimental Psychology, 74,* 1.

20. Seligman, M. E. P. (1974). Depression and learned helplessness. In R. J. Friedman & M. M. Katz (Eds.), *The psychology of depression: Contemporary theory and research.* Washington D.C.: Winston and Sons.

21. Seligman, M. E. P. (1975). *Helplessness: On depression, development, and death.* San Francisco, CA: W. H. Freeman.

22. Seligman, M. E. P. (1991). *Learned optimism.* New York: Knopf.

23. Seligman, M. E. P. (1994). *What you can change and what you can't.* New York: Knopf.

24. Seligman, M. E. P. (1995). *The optimistic child.* New York: Knopf.

25. Sarwer-Foner, G. J. (1966). A psychoanalytic note on the specific delusion of time in psychotic depression. *Canadian Psychiatric Association Journal, 2* (Suppl.), S221.

26. Cassidy, W. L., Flanagan, N. B., & Spellman, M. (1957). Clinical observations in manic-depressive disease: A quantitative study of 100 manic-depressive patients and 50 medically sick controls. *Journal of the American Medical Association, 164,* 1535.

Chapter 3

Three Clinical Presentations

How many kinds of depression are there? Or is there only one "depression," with the clinical entities we observe merely stages in the natural course of the development of the disorder?

How do we reconcile the psychological explanations of depression with the biological ones? When mania accompanies depression in sequence (or concurrently), is the resulting "bipolar" disorder distinct from "unipolar" depression? Does the presence of psychosis in either a unipolar or a bipolar course render the resulting syndrome distinct from other major depressions? Is dysthymia a "junior version" of major depressive disorder (just as cyclothymia may be a precursor to bipolar depression)?

Or is dysthymia a learned set of patterns better understood as a "depressive personality"? In this chapter and the next, we will examine the depressive disorders and consider the issues posed by these questions.

With the basic issues of separating the depressions as yet unresolved, my strategy will be to discuss three different forms of the clinical problem: manic-depressive (bipolar) disorder, major (unipolar) depressive disorder, and dysthymia. This is done with the acknowledgment that someday all three forms may be seen as only one, or two, discrete depressive entities.

MANIC-DEPRESSIVE (BIPOLAR) DISORDER

Cyclothymia is a disorder of subsyndromal mood swings. Once considered to solely be a personality disorder, and in fact a precursor (in some) to bipolar illness (see *DSM-II* section in chapter 4), current thinking places this entity on the bipolar spectrum of disorders. The usual pattern is short cycles of mood, interrupted by infrequent "normal" periods. Research has found that 36% of patients with cyclothymia may go on to develop manic-depressive illness.[1]

For manic-depressive disorder, there are three course patterns: *bipolar I* (episodes of depression and episodes of mania), *bipolar II* (episodes of depression and episodes of hypomania), and *cyclothymia* (subsyndromic episodes of hypomania and depression).

The bipolar disorders exhibit a course in which both depressive episodes and some form of mania each occur. Mania is typically characterized by the presence of an elevated mood. According to Goodwin and Jamison's classic text on manic-depressive illness, however, the mood in mania can be euphoric, depressed, irritable, panicky, or labile (changeable).[1] Goodwin and Jamison cite additional characteristics of mania as: more and faster speech, quicker thought, more energy (and less need for sleep), increased perceptual acuity, paranoia, heightened sexuality, and impulsivity. They classify mania into three stages by its intensity and severity: hypomania, acute mania, and delerious mania.

In hypomania, there is a rapid flow of ideas and a decrease in inhibitions, but thinking is relatively intact. The mood changes are milder than in mania, but they follow a similar format, with the exceptions of depression and panic.[1] Hypomania is a subsyndromic form of mania.

In acute mania, thinking becomes progressively fragmented; thoughts race and may be psychotic. The manic patient is easily distracted. Themes of thought may be grandiose or paranoid. The hallmark of mood is its lability. There is increased psychomotor behavior, with rapid, pressured speech and frenetic behavior that may become violent, suicidal, or homicidal. Impulsivity in decision making, money spending, and sexual behavior may occur. In psychosis, hallucinations, delusions, inappropriate affect, and disorganized behavior may be seen.[2]

In delerious mania (which is, fortunately, rare) there are, in addition, symptoms of delerium (confusion, disorientation), extremely disturbed sleep, and exhaustion (from overactivity). These may become life-threatening.[2]

For a diagnosis of a manic episode, *DSM-IV* requires "a period of abnormally and persistently elevated, expansive or irritable mood" lasting at least a week or necessitating hospitalization.[3] In addition, at least three of seven symptom complexes must be present (see Table 3.1).

In the depressive phase of bipolar disorder, the basic symptoms and signs differ little from those seen in unipolar depressions. There is a "monochromatic experience of the world," with affects including sadness, irritability (note that it may occur in manic or depressive states), anger, and anxiety.[1] Thinking is slowed, with rumination or hypochondriacal preoccupations

Table 3.1
MANIC EPISODE

- Inflated self-esteem or grandiosity

- Decreased need for sleep

- More talkative than usual or pressure to keep talking

- Flight of ideas or subjective experience that thoughts are racing

- Distractibility

- Increase in goal-directed activity (either socially, in school or at work, or sexually) or psychomotor agitation

- Excessive involvement in pleasurable activities that have a high potential for painful consequences

Diagnostic criteria from DSM-IV, *1994*[3]

observed. Activity is reduced, along with motivation. There are altered patterns of sleeping and eating, with which you are already familiar.

Goodwin and Jamison define four different patterns of the depressive state seen in the bipolar course. It may be *nonpsychotic* or *psychotic* (with hallucinations and delusions). A third, more severe form is *delerious melancholia*. Here, delusions become unclear and fragmented, hallucinations may be bizarre and frightening, and consciousness becomes clouded. In the fourth and most severe form, *depressive stupor*, there is intense inhibition of behavior and regression to the point of mutism, total inactivity, and uncooperativeness.

Mixed states manifest "the simultaneous presence of depressive and manic symptoms."[1] They may occur during a transition from one mood state to the other, or they may represent an independent phenomenon. There may be a single symptom of the "opposite" state (e.g., racing thoughts in a depressive episode) or multiple symptoms of each state. The hallmark of a mixed state is affective *lability*, at times elevated, at times lowered. A typical mixture might combine manic features like racing thoughts and grandiosity with depressed mood, hopelessness, and severe anxiety.[4] The high energy and impulsivity typically seen often create a serious suicide risk. Response to standard treatments for mania and depression tends to be poor.

The manic-depressive spectrum includes four types of episodes: manic, hypomanic, depressive, and mixed. As specified in *DSM-IV*, the features of the episode may be modified by four different elements: *psychosis, catatonia, melancholia,* and *atypical features.*[3]

Psychotic features are self-explanatory.

Catatonia consists of: immobility or purposeless motor excess, extreme negativism or mutism, voluntary posturing, prominent mannerisms or grimacing, and echolalia or echopraxia (mimicked speech or action). A catatonic picture may be seen in affective disorders as well as schizophrenia.

Melancholia applies to a depressive episode that features: loss of pleasure and lack of reactivity to pleasurable stimuli, a distinct quality to sadness (different from usual), mood worsening in the morning, early morning awakening, marked psychomotor change, significant anorexia or weight loss, and excessive or inappropriate guilt.

Atypical are generally the reverse of the typical changes seen, e.g., mood is reactive to pleasure, weight is gained, appetite increases, and hypersomnia, leaden paralysis, and extreme rejection sensitivity are present.

Factors that may influence the timing of occurrence of an episode have been specified as well.[3] These include *postpartum* (within four weeks of giving birth) and *seasonal* (a demonstrated temporal relationship between onset of episode and a time of year) depression.

When four or more episodes occur within a year, that pattern has been designated *rapid cycling.* In addition to the obvious prognostic implications, the response to treatment in this group may differ significantly from a more typical pattern (see chapter 10).

It has been known clinically that recurrence of episodes in bipolar disorder is not random. In fact, episodes typically increase in frequency with the passage of time.[1] Early episodes of bipolar illness are often precipitated by events, but later episodes seem increasingly "endogenous" (unprecipitated).

One model for this phenomenon, which has evolved from the study of seizures in animals, has been called *kindling.* Post defined kindling as a process in which a system shows an escalating response to a repetitive stimulus.[6] Eventually the stimulus is no longer needed and the response continues autonomously. It is of interest that the anticonvulsant drugs (e.g., carbamazepine) prevent this phenomenon of kindling in animals and have proven useful in altering the course of manic-depressive illness in humans. (See chapter 10 for more detail.)

Case Presentation

I was consulted by Roberta, a 39-year-old woman, divorced for six months, with two teenaged daughters. Her chief complaint was "I can't deal with being alone." She had known her husband for most of her life. They married when she was 25 years old, and had been married for fourteen years when he suddenly left her to pursue a relationship with a younger woman. He was a driven, successful attorney, and all Roberta's identity was "wrapped up in him." She had never failed before, and she considered this marital separation "the biggest failing there could possibly be."

She was, herself, a superachiever, but now anything was too much for her. She overslept, overate, stayed in bed, and was exhausted all the time. She felt helpless and hopeless, "naked and vulnerable." She had constant suicidal thoughts.

Born in Washington D.C., Roberta was an only child. She had a 4.0 grade-point average in high school. She graduated with honors from college. She started her own business, and succeeded. However, she felt that now she could never support herself at near the level that she and her husband had lived at. She was angry at him for putting her in this position.

My diagnostic impression was of a personality disorder, with histrionic and narcissistic features, and a reactive depression to the separation. My plan was for cognitive therapy and an antidepressant drug trial.

She quickly developed anticholinergic side effects to nortriptyline (Pamelor); it was discontinued and she soon "noticeably improved." This was followed shortly thereafter by a "mood crash." I started her on desipramine, another tricyclic antidepressant drug. Within one week, she reported feeling better and I stopped the drug, believing it had nothing to do with her mood shift. We continued psychotherapy sessions for one more month when she decided she wanted neither psychotherapy nor drug therapy for now.

She returned two months later, after having met a separated man who was "perfect" for her. When he decided to return to his wife, her mood crashed once again and I decided to reformulate my diagnosis. At this time, hysteroid dysphoria was being written about in the clinical literature, and I felt that Roberta fit its definition to a T. I proposed a resumption of psychotherapy and the prescription of an MAO inhibitor. She rejected the proposal for psychotherapy. "I don't want to change anything; I only need to remarry," she said. She agreed to a trial of Nardil (phenelzine). Limiting our contact to the telephone, with only occasional face-to-face visits, I prescribed Nardil for several years. She would titrate the dose to achieve mood stability, and try to limit weight gain. Her crashes occurred less often, and were briefer and less intense when they did occur. However, her weight fluctuated wildly. She had a series of relationships with ultimately unsatisfying outcomes.

At age 44, Roberta enrolled in a prestigious MBA program and graduated at the top of her class. At age 47, she met the man she would marry. About this time, she had her first prolonged depressive episode. This changed my thinking about her somewhat, and I considered the possibility that her course most resembled a bipolar II disorder. Her high-functioning periods could be thought of as hypomanic. I suggested adding lithium to the MAOI, but she refused. I agreed, however, to continue to prescribe Nardil.

Roberta called again at age 53, no longer willing to tolerate an extreme gain in weight. I had now known her for fourteen years, she was married for four years, and she had worked on and off. I arranged for a pharmacologic consultation in which the consultant diagnosed her course as recurrent affective disorder, responsive to phenelzine. He suggested replacing the Nardil with Parnate (another MAOI). When that was unsuccessful, after an appropriate washout period a trial of an SSRI (selective serotonin reuptake inhibitor), combined with lithium carbonate, was prescibed. There was no response to the SSRI. She continued to refuse a lithium trial. We returned to Nardil.

One year later, Roberta experienced the death of her father, then her mother. She weighed fifty pounds more than she had ten years ago. I asked for a second pharmacologic consultation. Following recommendations, I discontinued the Nardil once again and tried methylphenidate (Ritalin), imipramine (Tofranil), and finally desipramine (when she gave me the history of her mother's response to this drug). Now she began to develop a raft of anxiety symptoms. A third consultation produced suggestions of adding Xanax (alprazolam) to imipramine, then cytomel, and finally fluoxetine (Prozac). Nothing affected her course: periods of deep depression, panicky anxiety, short periods of hypomania.

For a while she seemed to stabilize on a regimen of desipramine, fluoxetine, and (she had consented to adding) lithium. She agreed now to resuming psychotherapy as well. After two weeks of "feeling good," she returned to an immobilizing depression. My diagnosis now was bipolar II disorder, generalized anxiety disorder, histrionic personality. Trials of carbamazepine (Tegretol), valproate (Depakote), and lithium were undertaken. There were longer periods of feeling good, but continued crashes into depression with a strong anxiety component. Nothing consistently affected the course of the disorder except the antidepressants which, in retrospect, likely accelerated the cycles of a bipolar II disorder.

If I had it to do again, I would have focused more on the course and less on the episodes. I would have insisted much earlier on a course drug (pharmacotherapy to alter the disorder's course). I would have insisted on a more consistent psychotherapeutic relationship. But, all this comes with the wisdom of hindsight, and there is no way to predict what the outcome might have been.

MAJOR DEPRESSIVE (UNIPOLAR) DISORDER

Leonhard, in Germany, first proposed the unipolar-bipolar distinction in major depression.[2] He saw a homogeneous bipolar group and a more heterogeneous unipolar group, but there were clearly two different kinds of depression. Separate research reports from Angst[7] and Perris[8] in 1966 supported this distinction on the basis of family history data.

Winokur attempted to clarify the unipolar concept by proposing narrower subgroups, once again using family history as a major criterion.[9] Those with *familial pure depressive disease* had at least one first-degree relative with primary depression. Those with *depression spectrum disease* had a first-degree relative with alcoholism or antisocial personality. Those who did not meet the family history criterion were diagnosed as having *sporadic pure depressive disease*. All had similar depressive symptoms.

What we describe today as *major* or *unipolar depressive disorder* is characterized by episodes of depression without manic, hypomanic, or mixed episodes. This diagnosis would also be made in a patient who has not yet had his or her initial manic episode, but is "destined" to do so. Since there is no way to divine this outcome, some unipolars will switch diagnostically to bipolars sometime during their course. If everyone were "destined" to have a manic episode at some distant point, there would be no need for a diagnosis of unipolar depression. This approximates the belief of the unitary theorists ("there is only one kind of depression"). For the rest of us, and for the time being, there seems to be utility in the concept of non-bipolar depression.

Is that, in fact, all unipolar depression is—"non-bipolar"? Family studies would suggest not. In 1973, Winokur outlined some unipolar-bipolar sample differences.[10] His unipolar group had its first episode of illness at an average 36 years of age; the bipolars, some eight years earlier at 28. Multiple episodes were more commonly observed in the bipolar group (57% of the bipolars had six or more episodes; only 18% of unipolars did). Only one-quarter of the unipolar depressives had affective illness in a parent; over one-half of the bipolars did.[10] Furthermore, there is a striking unipolar-bipolar gender difference, with women twice as likely to be affected by unipolar depression as men. In bipolar depression, the gender ratio is 1:1.

The NIMH-Collaborative Depression Study catalogued over nine hundred patients with major depression nationwide.[11] A significant finding was that of high rates of both relapse and chronicity. About 50% recovered from their episode of depression in one year. However, one-quarter of those who initially recovered were found to relapse within twelve weeks. After four years, nearly 20% had remained continuously ill, without recovering.[12]

The lives of people with recurrent major depression are substantially disrupted, with work absences, marital schisms, and social withdrawal commonly reported. Fully 15% of patients with a severe major depression of more than one month's duration die of suicide.[13]

Case Presentation

A primary care physician referred Peter, a 50-year-old psychologist who had served well in a career government job. He had been married for twenty years, and was the father of two daughters, who were away at college.

One week earlier, while his wife was on a long-planned visit to her parents in the Midwest, Roger took an overdose of tranquilizers with a large amount of alcohol. He left his wife a lengthy note and lay down in bed to die. He awoke sixteen hours later, "unhappy to be alive." From that point until his wife returned home two days later, he functioned "normally." When he told her what he had done, she called their family doctor, who evaluated him and referred him to me.

Roger recalled an early life dominated by nervousness, lack of self-confidence, and the sense that he was not popular. He achieved high test scores and excelled academically in college and graduate school. Two earlier marriages "ended in failure," with him feeling rejected. He had a lengthy depression after his first wife left him, and considered suicide for the first time then. When his second wife left (four years later), he made his first suicide attempt with barbiturate drugs. His current marital relationship had been "rocky," but significant similarities and pleasures helped them stay together.

His co-workers and his supervisor hold him "in the highest regard" and he has garnered multiple work awards. However, lately he had begun to think that "work was going nowhere," his "marriage was dissatisfying," and he felt "a sense of alienation" from his two daughters. In this, his third serious depressive episode, Roger made the most serious attempt to end his life.

I discussed with him the continuation of the paroxetine (Paxil) 20 mg prescription begun by his family doctor one week earlier. I presented the recommendation of a cognitive therapy model for our psychotherapeutic work. He accepted both, with little enthusiasm. He acknowledged feeling empty, sleeping poorly, eating little, having no energy and concentrating poorly. He felt worthless and continued to be pessimistic about the future. My working diagnosis was major depressive disorder (unipolar), recurrent.

Our psychotherapy work focused on helping him to reformulate his view of himself in the work setting, in his marriage, and with regard to his daughters. By week six of Paxil, there was no response. I tapered and stopped the drug, replacing it with Wellbutrin (to which he had responded once before). I added a sedative (prescribed in small amounts) to ensure that persistent insomnia wouldn't add to his burdens.

It took four months before he pronounced himself "cured." The therapeutic dose of bupropion was 400 mg per day. He had made good use of cognitive therapy to work out a *raison d'etre* at work, to reachieve closeness with his wife, and to accept the consequences of a stage of life in relating to his daughters.

I continued to see him, but at two- to three-month intervals. One year later, depression returned in the context of a severely fractured leg and the resulting immobility. We resumed weekly psychotherapy sessions, and I raised the bupropion to 450 mg per day. Within one week, he felt dramatically better.

Six months later, he attributed a loss in sexual functioning to the antidepressant drug, despite otherwise feeling well. We decided to slowly taper and discontinue bupropion, despite its reputation as a drug to prescribe when patients have sexual side effects to other antidepressant drugs. Over one month, depression recurred. After a lengthy discussion, we resumed Wellbutrin, at a lower (300 mg) dose. He remained stable and found that sexual functioning had returned to normal, until eight months later when depression reappeared in the context of a work reversal. An increase in bupropion dose to 400 mg was greeted by a remission of the acute episode.

Roger had now experienced six depressive episodes, without mania or hypomania. The acute depressions seemed uniquely responsive to bupropion, a drug that, overall, he tolerated well. There was some question about whether or not the antidepressant drug had a maintenance effect. (I suspect not.) In retrospect, the introduction of a drug (lithium or valproate) to alter the course of a recurrent unipolar disorder might have been a good idea. The psychotherapy relationship served to support the continuity of care. The psychotherapy model was useful in facilitating some changes for him that appeared to make depression as a reaction less likely.

DYSTHYMIA

Acute depression is commonly seen in clinical practice and it has a mostly favorable prognosis. Chronic depression (dysthymia) is also common, is responsible for considerable social, vocational and marital disruption, and often presents along with other psychopathology. For most of the twentieth century, chronic depression was often unrecognized and undiagnosed because it was viewed as a disorder of character or temperament (i.e., a trait) as opposed to a disorder of mood (a state). If treatment was offered, it was most commonly psychotherapy, and the so-called depressive personality was thought to have a poor prognosis.

Diagnosis of dysthymia is complicated by the disorder's heterogeneity. This condition features duration as its defining characteristic, as opposed to intensity. It is here that the unresolved but attenuated major depressions, the precursors to a full-blown major depression, and a mixed bag of characterological problems with depressive symptoms meet. *DSM-III* (1980) sought to bypass the problem by defining dysthymic disorder systematically in terms of its subsyndromic symptoms and signs, as well as by specifying that the disorder must have at least a two-year duration.

Emerging evidence suggests that active and prolonged treatment can be effective in dysthymia. That treatment combines pharmacotherapy and psychotherapy. Its premise is that chronic depression is located on the spectrum of affective disorders. (Specifics of treatment are discussed in chapter 11.)

Thase and Howland have illuminated the paths to dysthymia[14] (see Table 3.2). The first two approaches derive from the failure of a major depressive episode to resolve completely. When there are residual symptoms of depression that persist, the resulting condition (MDD-residual) may meet the subsyndromal criteria of dysthymia. Some major depressions persist with practically no improvement well beyond the two year criterion for a diagnosis of dysthymia (MDD-chronic).

Some individuals with dysthymic disorder develop a major depression at some point in their course. This condition, called *double depression*, under-

Table 3.2
TYPES OF CHRONIC DEPRESSION
MDD-residual • MDD-chronic
Double depression • Pure dysthymia
Secondary dysthymia
From Thase and Howland, 1995[14]

standably has a poorer prognosis. Some people with dysthymia have never had major depression. This is the subsample for whom the phrase, "I've been depressed for as long as I can remember," may well be an accurate rendering. This has been called *pure dysthymia*. Finally, for some the dysthymic syndrome follows the onset of a medical condition, treatment with a medication, or a habit of substance abuse. This has been called secondary dysthymia.

The undertreatment of chronic depression has been documented by Keller (see Table 3.3). Only 60% of his sample of dysthymics were offered psychotherapy. Even fewer (50% or less) received medication.

The nosologic shift catalyzed by *DSM-III* in 1980 moved dysthymia into the category of mood disorders, defining it by phenomenology, not etiology. This encouraged clinicians to consider the prescription of antidepressant medication for these patients. Attention was focused on the characteristics dysthymia and major depression shared and those that set them apart. It is sobering to realize that up to 90% of dysthymics have had a major depression at some point in their course.[15]

In *DSM-IV*, changes in mood, appetite, sleep, and energy, along with indecisiveness and inability to concentrate, were noted as common to both syndromes. Aside from duration (two weeks of symptoms to diagnose major depression; two years of symptoms for dysthymia); weight changes, diminished pleasures and interests, recurrent suicidal thoughts, psychomotor changes, and worthlessness were listed for major depression but not for dysthymia. (To visualize the shared and unshared criteria, see Table 3.4.) Befitting a subsyndromic diagnosis, dysthymia requires only two criteria in addition to depressed mood; major depression needs five.

A look at dysthymia's "roots" may shed some light on the issue of whether this is an attenuated form of major depression, or a separate entity in its own

Table 3.3 UNDERTREATMENT OF CHRONIC DEPRESSION	N	%MED	%PT
Chronic major depression	85	52.9	65.9
Double depression	113	41.6	61.1
Dysthymia	416	46.7	61.9

From Keller, 1995[18]

Table 3.4 DYSTHYMIA VS. MAJOR DEPRESSION: *DSM-IV* CRITERIA	
Shared characteristics:	**Characteristics distinct to MDD:**
• Depressed mood	• Duration
• Poor appetite/overeating	• Weight loss/gain
• Insomnia/hypersomnia	• Diminished pleasure/interests
• Anergia/fatigue	• Recurrent suicidal thoughts
• Poor concentration/indecisiveness	• Agitation/retardation
	• Worthlessness/guilt

right. The current concept of dysthymia is an admixture of three older clinical constructs, according to Klein and Kelly.[16] These are: neurotic depression, depressive personality, and chronic depression.

Neurotic depression has had a checkered history, soiled by having multiple meanings. Here is a "non-definition" I frequently employ in lectures to clinicians to make this point:

A non-psychotic, non-endogenous, non-incapacitating, non-situational, non-bipolar, non-recurring, non-severe, impure, reactive, psychogenic, characterological, pre-schizophrenic, pre-senile dementia . . . not a distinct nosologic entity.

Unfortunately, the usefulness of a term defined by "what it isn't" ran out by about 1980. Clinicians struck another telling blow. Since less of a stigma was applied to *DSM-II*'s "Depressive Neurosis, 300.4" than to the major psychiatric disorders, it was frequently employed inaccurately by some clinicians to protect the privacy of some patients. Depressive Neurosis, 300.4 has been a "stand-in" for schizophrenia, alcoholism, and manic-depressive illness.

Akiskal studied a population of patients with chronic depression in 1981.[15] He divided his early onset dysthymic population into two groups. He saw the first as a milder version of an affective disorder and called it *subaffective dysthymia*. This group had a positive family history for both unipolar and bipolar depression. Their sleep had a shortened REM-latency, as is seen in major depression. They were responsive to both tricyclic antidepressant drugs (TCAs) and lithium carbonate, again like major depression. He saw his second group as having a mixture of histrionic and antisocial personality traits. Their family history was positive only for alcoholism. Their sleep had a normal REM-latency. They were unresponsive to both TCAs and lithium.

Klein and Kelly support the argument for dysthymia as a "phase" of the major depressive process.[16] They point out that its early onset and life-long course more resemble that of a personality disorder than a mood syndrome. However, the high comorbidity with major depression tilts toward a mood disorder. The positive family history of major depression in first-degree relatives is similar to that seen in major depression itself. Finally, the high frequency of episodes of major depression in dysthymia is consistent with a status of subsyndromic depression.

In contrasting dysthymia with depressive personality, Klein and Kelly note that the *DSM-IV* diagnosis incorporates three vegetative criteria (appetite disorder, sleep disorder, and anergia or increased fatiguability), unlike the classical concept of depressive personality, which emphasizes traits like gloominess, pessimism, and submissiveness.[16] In their literature review, the overlap between the conditions is modest, and "the majority of individuals meeting criteria for one condition do not meet criteria for the other."[16]

Dysthymia rarely presents in the absence of other disorders. The "comorbidity" argument is made by Markowitz.[17] At times, the comorbid problem may mask the dysthymia. It was formerly believed that chronic depression was often a consequence of the accompanying psychiatric or medical disorder, perhaps a reaction to it. Today it is thought that the dysthymia usually comes first and, on its chronic course, predisposes the individual to the other disorders. The high frequency of comorbid conditions with dysthymia is startling. It is reviewed in Table 3.5.

Table 3.5
LIFETIME COMORBIDITY FOR DYSTHYMIA

- Major depression 38.9%

- Panic disorder 10.5%

- Bipolar disorder 2.9%

- Substance abuse 29.8%

- Eating disorder 23.0%

- Personality disorder 47.0%

- Anxiety disorder 46.2%

- Psychiatric disorder 77.1%

From Markowitz, 1993[17]

In summary, dysthymia for now appears to be a distinct entity. A portion of its population has an attenuated form of major depression. They arrive there by various routes. Some will go on to have the full syndrome at some point. Another portion seems to have a mixture of character pathology and depressive symptoms. While these cannot be separated on clinical grounds, family history and lab tests may help.

Case Presentation

I was consulted by Ralph, a 56-year-old accountant who had been depressed and in psychoanalytic psychotherapy for "all of his adult life." He was looking for an alternative approach and had read about cognitive therapy. He had never suffered an episode of major depression, but generally had been mildly to moderately depressed for as long as he could remember. He had continuing problems with concentration, fatigue, and indecision, but had never been suicidal, had no psychomotor changes, had never felt worthless. He was often sad and unmotivated. He was married, the father of a son and a daughter, and gainfully employed.

My diagnosis was dysthymic disorder. I prescribed no medication, and engaged him in cognitive therapy. He defined the problem focus as an inability to separate from an ungratifying marriage.

It took six sessions for him to learn to think about himself and life events within the context of the cognitive model. Surprising to me was the sense of commitment and hard work he brought to "getting the most out of psychotherapy," in light of his lengthy experience with a different orientation.

We focused on his self-standards and expectations for others. We discussed his tendency to be perfectionistic and to err most frequently by polarizing the options he considered. We discussed the need for him to update his resumé (integrate more recent performance and feedback into his equation of self-worth), as well as to think in terms of choices and consequences. The substance of the psychotherapy took 36 weekly sessions. Fourteen meetings, at increasing intervals, constituted a follow-up phase.

At therapy's end, he had moved out of his house, instituted divorce proceedings, handled the life changes skillfully with his children, and established a more rational (and less perfectionistic) view of himself in the work setting. His dysthymic symptoms were mostly gone, and he felt that he had an effective (cognitive) methodology to deal with future stresses.

Today, I might have added an antidepressant drug trial to his treatment, in the interest of (perhaps) shortening it. My belief is, however, that he managed to effect both a change in the disorder and substantial personal growth within a one-year time period (and a one-year follow-up).

Notes

1. Goodwin, F., & Jamison, K. (1990). *Manic-depressive illness*. New York: Oxford University Press.

2. Leonhard, K. (1957). *The classification of endogenous psychoses*. Berlin: Akademie Verlag.

3. American Psychiatric Association. (1994). *Diagnostic criteria from DSM-IV*. Washington D.C.: American Psychiatric Association.

4. Swann, A. C. (1995). Mixed or dysphoric manic states: Psychopathology and treatment. *Journal of Clinical Psychiatry, 56* (Suppl. 3), 6.

5. Akiskal, H. S., Khani, M. K., & Scott-Strauss, A. (1979). Cyclothymic temperamental disorders. *Psychiatric Clinics of North America, 5*, 527.

6. Post, R. M., Uhde, T. W., Putnam, P. W., et al. (1982). Kindling and carbamazepine in affective illness. *Journal of Nervous and Mental Disease, 170*, 717.

7. Angst, J. (1966). *The etiology and classification of endogenous depressive psychoses*. Berlin: Springer.

8. Perris, C. (1966). A study of bipolar (manic-depressive) and unipolar recurrent depressive psychoses. I. Genetic investigation. *Acta Psychiatrica Scandinavica, 42* (Suppl. 194), 15.

9. Winokur, G. (1979). Unipolar depression: Is it divisible into autonomous subtypes? *Archives of General Psychiatry, 36,* 47.

10. Winokur, G. (1973). The types of affective disorders. *Journal of Nervous and Mental Disease, 156*(2), 82.

11. Keller, M. B., Klerman, G. L., Lavori, P. W., et al. (1984). Long-term outcome of episodes of major depression: Clinical and public health significance. *Journal of the American Medical Association, 252,* 788.

12. Keller, M. B., Shapiro, R. W., & Lavori, P. W. (1982). Recovery in major depressive disorder. *Archives of General Psychiatry, 30,* 905.

13. Keller, M. B., & Hanks, D. L. (1994). The natural history and heterogeneity of depressive disorders: Implications for rational anti-depressant therapy. *Journal of Clinical Psychiatry, 55* (Suppl. 9A), 25.

14. Thase, M. E., & Howland, R. H. (1995). Assessment and treatment of chronic depression. *Clinical Advances in the Treatment of Psychiatric Disorders, 9*(3), 1.

15. Akiskal, H. S., King, D., Rosenthal, T. L., et al. (1981). Chronic depression: Part I. Clinical and familial characteristics in 137 probands. *Journal of Affective Disorders, 3,* 297.

16. Klein, D. F., & Kelly, H. S. (1993). Diagnosis and classification of dysthymia. *Psychiatric Annals, 23*(11), 609.

17. Markowitz, J. C. (1993). Comorbidity of dysthymia. *Psychiatric Annals, 23*(11), 617.

18. Keller, M. B. (May 21, 1995). Management of chronic and double depression and dysthmic disorder. In *Management of depression in today's world.* Symposium at the American Psychiatric Association, Miami Beach, FL.

Chapter 4

Classification
How Many Kinds of Depression Are There?

In 1976, Professor R.E. Kendell of the University of Edinburgh wrote a classic review article entitled: "The classification of depressions: A review of contemporary confusion."[1] In it, he bemoaned that "almost every classificatory format that is logically possible has been advocated by someone within the last twenty years, and some more or less plausible evidence offered in support." In this chapter, I will discuss the various nosologic ideas offered to explain the depressions. Let the reader judge whether, twenty years later, the "contemporary confusion" remains or has been resolved.

A useful classification scheme would point to etiology, predict outcome, suggest treatment, and increase general understanding. This is no small order.

EARLY CLASSIFICATION

Depression is described in some of humankind's earliest records. A catalogue of depressive symptoms can be found in the Book of Job. The ancient word melancholy (the black humor) has been used to describe this condition. In the second century A.D., Plutarch described the helpless feeling of the depressed as "fighting against the gods."[2] A sixteenth-century physician noted how melancholy "occupies the mind and changes the temperature of it."[3] Pinel, in 1801, described the "gloomy withdrawal of depression."[4]

In 1896, Kraepelin made an initial distinction between depressive illness and schizophrenia or dementia praecox.[5] His textbook *Psychiatry*, first published in 1896, was frequently revised and updated (eight editions by 1913). In the process, Kraepelin was defining depression as a unitary phenomenon with shared core symptoms. Those with the disorder had a family history of affective disorder, a recurrent course, and a benign outcome (compared to the deterioration seen with schizophrenia).

In 1908 in the U.S., Meyer introduced the concept of depression as a reaction to life events rather than as an illness.[6] Abraham, in 1911, established the connection between mourning and melancholia,[7] elaborated (in 1917) in the classic work by Freud.[8] Lewis, the renowned British diagnostician, compiled 61 hospital cases in 1934 to illustrate the typical clinical findings in depression.[9]

DSM-I

In the 1920s, each large teaching center employed its own system for the diagnosis of medical illness. As academicians moved from place to place, these systems were disseminated. The result was "a polyglot of diagnostic labels and systems."[10]

Spearheaded by the New York Academy of Medicine in 1927, a conference was convened, and by 1933 the first official edition of the *Standard Classified Nomenclature of Disease* was published. By 1942, the manual was in its fourth edition.

In 1951, the American Psychiatric Association's first *Diagnostic and Statistical Manual of Mental Disorders* appeared.[10] *DSM-I* took as its framework "Diseases of the Psychobiologic Unit" from the *Standard Nomenclature of Disease*. The Mental Hospital Service of the A.P.A. assumed responsibility for future publication of these statistical manuals. As a result, at the beginning of World War II American psychiatry was utilizing a system developed primarily for hospitals. The military found these concepts inapplicable to most of the psychiatric casualties they identified. By 1946, the Veterans Administration adopted a substantially revised nomenclature that reflected the war experience. In 1946, an Act of Congress established the National Institute of Mental Health. Its biometrics branch assumed responsibility for statistical reporting, permitting the A.P.A. to focus on a clinical manual for diagnosis.

In 1948, the Committee on Nomenclature and Statistics of the A.P.A. undertook to propose a new classification. They consulted the Army and the V.A. and polled the A.P.A. membership. Five years (1946–51) of work resulted in the production of *DSM-I* (see Table 4.1).

Depression appeared first under the heading *psychotic disorders*. These were defined as "disorders of psychogenic origin, or without clearly defined physi-

Table 4.1
DEPRESSION IN *DSM-I*

PSYCHOTIC DISORDERS
000–796 Involutional Psychotic Reaction
000–x10 Affective Reactions
000–x11–000–x13 Manic-Depressive Reactions
000–x14 Psychotic Depressive Reaction

PSYCHONEUROTIC DISORDERS
000–x06 Depressive Reaction

PERSONALITY PATTERN DISTURBANCE
000–x43 Cyclothymic Personality

TRANSIENT SITUATIONAL
PERSONALITY DISORDERS
000–x82 Adult Situational Reaction

cal cause or structural change in the brain." [10] The entry *affective reactions* included *manic-depressive reaction* and *psychotic depressive reaction*. Under "disorders due to disturbance of metabolism, growth, nutrition or endocrine function" was *involutional psychotic reaction*.

Psychoneurotic disorders were defined as "disorders of psychogenic origin, or without clearly defined tangible cause or structural change." In this category *depressive reaction* appeared. Note was taken of schizophrenias with "significant admixtures of schizophrenic and affective reactions." These were called *schizophrenic reaction, schizoaffective type*.

The section on personality disorders included *cyclothymic personality*. This entity was characterized by "frequent alternating moods of elation and sadness, stimulated apparently by internal factors." In sum, there appeared to be four distinct forms of depression, and one "boundary dispute" with schizophrenia.

DSM-II

In 1968, the A.P.A. published its second edition of the *Diagnostic and Statistical Manual*.[11] It offered the term *manic-depressive illness* to acknowledge the significance of biological (as opposed to psychological) factors in this form of depression. The only other category of major affective disorder specified was *involutional melancholia* (see Table 4.2).

This later-in-life depression was thought to correlate with a decline in physiological functioning (menopause in women; climacteric in men), occuring around age 50. It was described as a psychotic illness (impaired reality testing), featuring somatic preoccupations that were often delusional (e.g., "My bodily organs are rotting"). Psychological events clustering at this time period include children leaving the home and personal changes related to aging in attractiveness, stamina, and job function. So, there was ample reason to speculate about both psychological and physiological etiologies for involutional melancholia. Furthermore, this was known as a time of "stocktaking" in the culture, when one reviewed one's life and made an appraisal of successes and failures.

By 1970, however, it was written authoritatively that "there is insufficient specificity to (this entity) to warrant its separation from other forms of depressive psychosis." [12] With the publication of *DSM-III* in 1980, involutional melancholia would drop from sight.

Under *neuroses*, DSM-II described a nonpsychotic form of depression and called it *depressive neurosis*. This was defined as an excessive reaction of depression, due to an internal conflict or subsequent to an identifiable event. This diagnosis implied a clear psychological etiology, and attached itself to a

---

Table 4.2
DEPRESSION IN *DSM-II*

**296 MAJOR AFFECTIVE DISORDERS
(AFFECTIVE PSYCHOSES)**
296.0 Involutional Melancholia
296.1–.3 Manic-Depressive Illness

300 NEUROSES
300.4 Depressive Reaction

301 PERSONALITY DISORDERS
301.1 Cyclothymic Personality

307 TRANSIENT SITUATIONAL DISTURBANCES
307.3 Adjustment Disorder of Adult Life

precipitating event. As *DSM-II* evolved into *DSM-III*, this implication and this requirement each fell into disfavor.

Under *personality disorders*, the diagnosis cyclothymic personality remained to describe the premorbid personality associated with manic-depressive illness. It was now characterized as "recurring and alternating periods of depression and elation not readily attributable to external circumstances." Note the softening from "stimulated apparently by internal factors" seen in *DSM-I. DSM-II* did not yet anticipate the argument raised later about depression as a component of a personality disorder versus depression as a disorder superimposed upon a personality.

The Diagnostic Dichotomies

DSM-II reflected the dominant belief of the time (1968) that the depressions could be understood in terms of several key dichotomous elements (see Table 4.3). First among these is the *neurotic-psychotic* distinction. A key differentiating feature is the patient's ability to test reality. Hallucinations and delusions defined the psychotic form, and often somatic symptoms (e.g., sleep disorder, significant weight loss) were also associated with it. Feelings of anxiety, guilt, and agitated behavior were thought to be associated with neurotic depression. It was logical to infer then that psychotic depression was more severe, while neurotic depression was milder. At least the psychotic form had some phenomenological definition; neurotic depression was a muddle indeed. The conclusion that neurotic depression was not a distinct nosologic entity became a source of controversy that was resolved (somewhat) with its exclusion from and redefinition in *DSM-III* (it became dysthymia).

The most universally discussed dichotomy in the late 1960s and 1970s was the *endogenous-reactive* distinction. There were three working definitions of endogenous depression: (1) the absence of a precipitating event, (2) the pre-

Table 4.3 THE DIAGNOSTIC DICHOTOMIES
Neurotic-psychotic
Endogenous-reactive
Unipolar-bipolar
Primary-secondary

dominance of somatic (vegetative) symptoms, and (3) both 1 and 2. In its most literal sense, endogenous means "arising from within." In practice, endogenous had often been used synonymously with psychotic depression. Etiologically, the general assumption was that endogenous depression had a biological cause. Appropriately, biological researchers often confined their inquiry to this subtype of depression to maximize the chance of a useful discovery. Gillespie had earlier noted that a family history of depression was common in patients with endogenous depression.[13] Kallmann interpreted his genetic data to indicate that a "single, dominant, autosomal gene showing incomplete penetrance" was a likely prerequisite for endogenous depression.[14]

The psychiatric literature relevant to the endogenous-reactive distinction was reviewed by Mendels and Cochrane.[15] They found the symptom picture most often associated with the endogenous subtype to include: psychomotor retardation, "severe" depression, lack of reactivity (response) to environmental changes, loss of interest in life and, visceral (physical) symptoms. Symptoms noted by some, but not all, studies they reviewed were: weight loss, early morning awakening, guilt, and suicidal behavior. Several studies supported the contention that endogenous depressions responded well to electroconvulsive therapy.[16,17] This was interpreted to support biological causality for endogenous depression.

Ascher had argued that "reactive" depression was not depression at all, but rather a "chronic neurotic reaction accompanied by discouragement."[18] For some, the focus in reactive depression depended upon identifying a precipitating event. The depression represented a psychological reaction to, for example, the death of a loved one or the loss of a job. For others, the definition of reactive depression reflected a capacity to react positively to a rewarding life event. (A once popular television program featured a man who would come to homes to present to the unsuspecting residents a check for one million dollars. The reactive depressive would exhibit an appropriate mood elevation to such a positive life event. The mood of the unreactive depressive would remain unchanged.) Many expressed the sentiment that, while endogenous depression might be a definable entity, reactive depression was a diffuse conglomerate of differing elements (foreshadowing the later controversy over dysthymia).

The endogenous-reactive debate served as a backdrop for the ongoing argument in Great Britain, led on one side by Eysenck and on the other by Kendell (and before him by Lewis). Eysenck's *categorical* view maintained that the evidence to date (1970) supported two types of depressive disorder,[19] while Kendell advocated a dimensional approach that proposed calculating a scale of depressive factors that saw all depression as essentially alike, with only quantitative differences in severity.[20]

Motivated at least in part by the continuing lack of resolution of the endogenous-reactive debate, Perris formally introduced the *unipolar-bipolar* distinction to depression.[21] Its focus was on the course of depression, rather than on the characteristics of an episode. "Unipolar" refers to recurrent episodes of depression without mania. "Bipolar" indicates recurrent episodes of depression with at least one episode of mania. (This distinction was discussed in chapter 3, in the context of the major depressive syndromes bearing their names.)

To complete the dichotomies offered, in 1969 Robins and Guze introduced the concepts of primary and secondary depression.[22] They defined primary as an affective episode (either mania or depression) occurring in a patient who has been psychiatrically well, or has had a previous episode of only mania or depression but no other psychiatric illness. Secondary depression occurs in a person who has a preexisiting psychiatric illness other than depression.

Factor-Pattern Topologies

The advent (in the 1960s) of the capability to do factor analytic studies produced another stream of suggestions for understanding the depressions. These studies sought to differentiate clinically useful subtypes of depression based upon symptoms and signs that are clustered together.

An early attempt was made by Grinker et al. in 1961.[23] His group proposed four subtypes: empty, anxious, hypochondriacal, and angry. Overall et al., in 1966, derived three groups on the basis of response to medication: retarded depressives, anxious depressives, and hostile depressives.[24] Paykel, in 1972, utilized cluster analysis to derive a similar typology: psychotic depressives, anxious depressives, hostile depressives, and young depressives with personality disorder.[25]

Even a cursory look at the three offerings reveals their similarities. The empty, psychotic, or retarded group is reminiscent of endogenous depression. The anxious subtype reminds us of the overlap of anxiety and depressive syndromes. The hostile depressives tell us that not all depresssion can be understood in terms of anger turned inward.

DSM-III

In 1980, *DSM-III* reframed the debate on mood (affective) disorders (see Table 4.4). It distanced itself from the depressive dichotomies. It introduced the concept of "full" and "partial" syndromes by dividing depressions into three categories: major affective disorders (full), other specific affective disorders (partial), and atypical affective disorders (others).

Under *major affective disorders* were *bipolar disorder* and *major (unipolar) depression*. Under *other specific affective disorders* were *dysthymia* and *cyclothymia*. These were now, by definition, subsyndromic forms of the major syndromes. Under *atypical affective disorders* fell the variants of bipolar and unipolar disorders that did not fit the classic pictures. *Bipolar II disorders* (full depressive episodes and hypomanic episodes) were placed here, along with *brief recurrent depressions* (too short on duration and symptoms to meet criteria for major depression).

The *DSM-II* category *transient situational disturbances* was reorganized in *DSM-III* to emphasize its manifestations rather than the developmental stage

Table 4.4 DEPRESSION IN *DSM-III*
MAJOR AFFECTIVE DISORDERS 296.4–.6 Bipolar Disorder 296.2–.3 Major Depression
OTHER SPECIFIC AFFECTIVE DISORDERS 301.13 Cyclothymic Disorder 300.40 Dysthymic Disorder
ATYPICAL AFFECTIVE DISORDERS 296.70 Atypical Bipolar Disorder 296.82 Atypical Depression
ADJUSTMENT DISORDERS 309.00 Adjustment Disorder with Depressed Mood
V CODES NOT ATTRIBUTABLE TO A MENTAL DISORDER V62.82 Uncomplicated Bereavement

at which it occurred. There was now, therefore, a specific listing for *adjust-ment disorder with depressed mood*. This was defined as a "maladaptive reaction to an identifiable stressor" that did not meet criteria for major depression or dysthymia.[26]

To acknowledge reports in the literature about grief reactions aided by psychotherapy, a subcategory called *uncomplicated bereavement* was listed among the new V codes. These referred to individuals without a mental problem who nevertheless warranted examination by a psychiatrist.

As we have discussed, *DSM-III* reformulated depressive neurosis, purged it of etiological criteria, and redefined it as *dysthymic disorder*. The diagnosis required a two-year duration of subsyndromic depressive symptoms, and a sad mood or marked loss of interests and pleasures. In addition, there was a list of thirteen

---

Table 4.5
DYSTHYMIC DISORDER: *DSM-III* CRITERIA

A. Two-year duration

B. Relatively persistent (no more than a few months of normal mood)

C. Sad mood or loss of interests and pleasures

D. At least three of the following:

1. Insomnia/hypersomnia

2. Anergia/fatigue

3. Inadequacy/loss of self-esteem/self-depreciation

4. Decreased productivity

5. Decreased concentration

6. Social withdrawal

7. Lost interest/pleasure in pleasurable activities

8. Irritability/excess anger

9. Loss of reactivity

10. Less active or talkative/slowed or restless

11. Pessimism/self-pity

12. Crying

13. Recurrent thoughts of death or suicide

depressive symptoms (listed in Table 4.5), at least three of which needed to be present in order for the patient to meet diagnostic criteria for dysthymia.

DSM-III-R

By 1983, the A.P.A. took note of new research reports and some confusion or inconsistency in the use of *DSM-III*, as well as an invitation to contribute to the *International Classification of Diseases (ICD-10)*, to revise the 1980 nosology. In 1987, *DSM-III-R* was born[27] (see Table 4.6).

Mood disorders became the organizing term. The major subclassifications remained unipolar and bipolar depression. However, bipolar disorders now included *cyclothymia* (subsyndromic manic-depression) in addition to the full syndrome. Symmetrically, unipolar disorders also included *dysthymia* (subsyndromic major depression).

Fifth-digit codes (specifiers) denoted severity, psychosis, remission, melancholia, chronicity, and seasonal pattern. A new category, *not otherwise specified*, appeared for both unipolar and bipolar disorders. The bipolar category was the new home of bipolar II disorder. The unipolar category included major depression superimposed on residual schizophrenia and recurrent mild

Table 4.6
DEPRESSION IN *DSM-III-R*

BIPOLAR DISORDERS
296.4–.6 Bipolar Disorder
301.13 Cyclothymia
296.7 Bipolar Disorder, Not Otherwise Specified

DEPRESSIVE DISORDERS
296.2–.3 Major Depression
300.40 Dysthymia
311 Depressive Disorder, Not Otherwise Specified

ADJUSTMENT DISORDERS
309.00 With Depressed Mood

**V CODES FOR CONDITIONS NOT
ATTRIBUTABLE TO A MENTAL DISORDER**
V62.82 Uncomplicated Bereavement

depression. The designations for *adjustment disorder with depressed mood* and *uncomplicated bereavement* were retained.

In an appendix listing proposed diagnostic categories, a blow was struck for what had come to be called PMS or premenstrual syndrome. In some women, what *DSM-III-R* calls *late luteal phase disorder* can be so severe as to cause social or occupational impairment and can occur during a majority of menstrual cycles. This diagnosis was not yet to be included in the nosology, but was listed to "facilitate systematic clinical study and research." [26]

DSM-IV

DSM-IV arrived in 1994.[27] Little changed in the body of the nosology (see Table 4.7) relevant to depression. The classification of unipolar disorders was identical to the classification scheme in *DSM-III-R*. Under bipolar disorders, bipolar II disorder finally made it into the arena (296.89). In addition, a category for *other mood disorders* was added to accommodate affective disorders due to a general medical condition and substance-induced mood disorders. *Adjustment disorder with depressed mood* and *uncomplicated bereavement* were unchanged.

Although the body remained intact, the appendix was completely refashioned. The controversy about the separation of anxiety and depressive disorders spawned a new proposed category: *mixed anxiety-depressive disorder*. It acknowledges the nonspecific symptom presentation characteristic to some patients with concurrent symptoms of anxiety and depression. *Minor depressive disorder* (a new offering) refers to the presence of two to four symptoms of depression (the full syndrome requires five), with a duration of only two weeks (the full syndrome requires one month), in the absence of a past history of major depression, bipolar depression, or dysthymia. *Recurrent brief depressive disorder* meets all criteria for major depression except duration (two days to two weeks is specified). It must recur at least monthly for one year.

Premenstrual dysphoric disorder represents the update for the less euphonious late luteal phase disorder of *DSM-III-R*. Finally, *depressive personality disorder* confirms the new interpretation (since 1980) of dysthymia as "more biological," and offers a new category for a "pervasive pattern of depressive cognitions and behaviors that began by early adulthood." [28] (The issues raised by these appended categories will be revisited in chapter 5, Boundary Disputes.)

In closing, let us return to Professor Kendell's "confusion": is it resolved? *DSM-IV* suggests to me that there may be only two kinds of depression, and different phases of each, despite the proliferation of new terms. It no longer

Table 4.7
DEPRESSION IN *DSM-IV*

DEPRESSIVE DISORDERS
296.2–.3 Major Depressive Disorder
300.4 Dysthymic Disorder
311 Depressive Disorder, Not Otherwise Specified

BIPOLAR DISORDERS
296.0, .4, .7 Bipolar I Disorder
296.89 Bipolar II Disorder
301.13 Cyclothymic Disorder
296.80 Bipolar Disorder, Not Otherwise Specified

OTHER MOOD DISORDERS
293.83 Mood Disorder Due to a General Medical
Condition, or Substance-Induced
296.90 Mood Disorder, Not Otherwise Specified

ADJUSTMENT DISORDER
309.00 With Depressed Mood

V CODES FOR CONDITIONS NOT
ATTRIBUTABLE TO A MENTAL DISORDER
V62.82 Uncomplicated Bereavement

requires (as did *DSM-I*) that all major depression be psychotic. It no longer emphasizes (as did *DSM-II*) the neurotic-psychotic dichotomy. It remains (like *DSM-III*) phenomenologically, not etiologically, based. It accepts as the major persisting dichotomy unipolar versus bipolar disorders.

Notes

1. Kendell, R. E. (1976). The classification of depression: A review of contemporary confusion. *British Journal of Psychiatry, 129,* 15.

2. Zilboorg, G. (1941). *A history of medical psychology.* New York: Norton.

3. Hunter, R., & Macalpine, I. (1963). *Three hundred years of psychiatry.* London: Hogarth.

4. Pinel, P. (1801/1962). *A treatise on insanity* (D. D. David, Trans.). New York: Hofner.

5. Kraeplin, E. (1896). *Psychiatrie*. Leipzig: Barth.

6. Meyer, A. (1908/1957). The problems of mental reaction types. In E. Winters (Ed.), *The collected papers of Adoph Meyer*. Baltimore: Hopkins.

7. Abraham, K. (1911/1968). Notes on the psychoanalytical investigation and treatment of manic-depressive insanity and allied conditions. In W. Gaylin (Ed.), *The meaning of despair*. New York: Science House.

8. Freud, S. (1917). Mourning and melancholia. In J. Strachey (Ed. and Trans.), *The complete psychological works of Sigmund Freud* (Vol. 14, pp. 237–258). New York: Norton.

9. Lewis, A. (1934). Melancholia: A clinical survey of depressive states. *Journal of Medical Science, 80*, 277.

10. American Psychiatric Association. (1951). *Diagnostic and statistical manual of mental disorders*. Washington D.C.: American Psychiatric Association.

11. American Psychiatric Association. (1968). *Diagnostic and statistical manual of mental disorders* (2nd ed.). Washington D.C.: American Psychiatric Association.

12. Mendels, J. (1970). *Concepts of depression*. New York: Wiley.

13. Gillespie, R. D. (1929). Clinical differentiation of types of depression. *Guys Hospital Report, 79*, 306.

14. Kallmann, F. (1952). Genetic aspects of psychosis. In Millbank Memorial Fund, *Biology of mental health and disease*. New York: Hoeber.

15. Mendels, J., & Cochrane, C. (1968). The nosology of depression: The endogenous-reactive concept. *American Journal of Psychiatry, 124*(Suppl.), 1.

16. Carney, M. W. P., Roth, M., & Garside, R. F. (1965). The diagnosis of depressive syndromes and the prediction of ECT response. *British Journal of Psychiatry, 3*, 659.

17. Mendels, J. (1967). The prediction of response to electro-convulsive therapy. *American Journal of Psychiatry, 124*, 153.

18. Ascher, E. (1952). A criticism of the concept of neurotic depression. *American Journal of Psychiatry, 108*, 901.

19. Eysenck, H. J. (1970). The classification of depressive illness. *British Journal of Psychiatry, 117*, 241.

20. Kendell, R. E. (1968). *The classification of depressive illness*. London: Oxford University Press.

21. Perris, C. (1968). The course of depressive psychoses. *Acta Psychiatrica Scandinavica, 44*, 238.

22. Robins, E., & Guze, S. B. (1972). Classification of depressive disorders: The primary-secondary, the endogenous-reactive and the neurotic-psychotic concepts. In T. A. Williams, M. M. Katz, & J. A. Shields (Eds.), *Recent advances in the psychobiology of the depressive illnesses*. Washington D.C.: U.S. Government Printing Office.

23. Grinker, R. R., Miller, J., Sabshin, M., et al. (1961). *The phenomena of depression*. New York: Hoeber.

24. Overall, J. E., Hollister, L. E., Johnson, M., et al. (1966). Nosology of depression and differential response to drugs. *Journal of the American Medical Association, 195, 946.*

25. Paykel, E.S. (1972). Correlates of a depressive typology. *Archives of General Psychiatry, 27, 203.*

26. American Psychiatric Association. (1980). *Diagnostic and statistical manual of mental disorders* (3rd ed.). Washington D.C.: American Psychiatric Association.

27. American Psychiatric Association. (1987). *Diagnostic and statistical manual of mental disorders* (3rd ed., revised). Washington D.C.: American Psychiatric Association.

28. American Psychiatric Association. (1994). *Diagnostic and statistical manual of mental disorders* (4th ed.). Washington D.C.: American Psychiatric Association.

Chapter 5

Boundary Disputes

It would be clinically convenient if each diagnostic entity were clearly separated from the others, but, sadly, life does not imitate *DSM*. We are presented, therefore, with a series of "boundaries" for depression. Having an
understanding of these boundaries will aid the therapist in determining an
effective approach to the patient's problem.

Grieving and the subsyndromal depressions represent the boundary with
normalcy. The anxiety disorders are sometimes comorbid to, sometimes precede, and sometimes follow the depressions. The distinction between depression as state (affective disorder) and depression as trait (personality disorder)
has important implications for treatment. Psychotic depression and schizoaffective schizophrenia overlap depression at its most severe extreme. This
chapter will address these four boundary disputes.

THE BOUNDARY WITH NORMALCY

Clinicians have long been accused of a preoccupation with psychopathology to the neglect of an understanding of normalcy. Feeling sad is a normal
affective state, no more clinically troubling than feeling angry, happy, or
indifferent. Defining the distance between a normal reaction of disappointment and a depressive reaction to stress captures one strand of the problem
of depression's boundary dispute with normalcy.

Mood variations occur in everyone, sometimes seemingly unrelated to life
events. When a lowering of mood is sustained, however, and there are accompanying changes in behavior and thinking as well as physical symptoms,
there is little problem in diagnosing the presence of depression. Are the nor-
malcy-depression differences qualitative? Or is this boundary marked by a

quantitative difference in symptoms and signs or in duration? This latter possibility has spawned a new group of entities that occupy the space between major depression and dysthymia (itself a subsyndromal designation) on one side and normalcy on the other.

To grieve is normal and healthy, and thought to be necessary to avoid future pathological consequence. However, the bereavement period appears to confer a vulnerability to clinical depression. At what point (on the dimensions of severity and duration) is a normal reaction to a significant loss better understood as a pathological depression? Once again, are the differences qualitative or quantitative?

Finally, if these boundary states (between clinical depression and normal mood variation) are associated with significant personal, social, and vocational disability, don't they merit treatment? And, if they do, mustn't they be represented in the DSM, especially in an era of managed care?

Subsyndromal Depression

Appendix B to DSM-IV (1994) proposes several new subtypes of depression to facilitate the study of the questions raised above. Before considering these categories, let us review what we know about subsyndromal depression. Its forms include: dysthymia, cyclothymia, mixed anxiety-depressive disorder, minor depressive disorder, recurrent brief depressive disorder, and premenstrual dysphoric disorder.

Dysthymia (requiring two of six criteria for diagnosis) may be a milder form of major depressive disorder (requiring five of nine criteria), but the disorders' criteria, although similar, are not identical. The critical distinction, however, is one of duration. Major depression must last at least two weeks; dysthymia, at least two years. In summary, dysthymia involves fewer symptoms for a longer time.

Cyclothymia may be an attenuated form of bipolar disorder. (More specifically, as manic episodes are rare in this disorder, it seems to be a variant of bipolar II disorder.) Once again, the chief distinguishing feauture is duration. The definition of cyclothymia requires "numerous periods" of hypomanic symptoms and "numerous periods" of depressive symptoms that do not meet criteria for a major depressive episode and that endure for *at least two years*.

Mixed anxiety-depressive disorder represents an acknowledgment of the boundary dispute between anxiety and depression (and is discussed in detail later in this chapter). It too is a partial syndrome, meeting fewer criteria than are necessary for a diagnosis of either a depressive disorder or an anxiety disorder.

Minor depression requires a depressed mood (or the loss of pleasure or interest in most activities) as in the full syndrome. However, this diagnosis can be made when at least one depressive symptom is present, and cannot be made when more than four symptoms of depression are present. It may be a milder version of major depression. In a study by Broadhead et al., only 5.9% of their sample met criteria for minor depression, but they accounted for 8.5% of the total disability days.[1] In a follow-up study conducted one year later, fully 10% had gone on to develop major depression.

In contrast, recurrent brief depression fulfills the same criteria as the full syndrome, with duration as the only exception. This form of depression must be less than two weeks in duration, but typically may last only one to three days. It must recur on the average of once monthly for at least one year and lead to occupational impairment. In one large-scale research study of 591 subjects followed for ten years (the Zurich Study), this group demonstrated comorbidity with anxiety, a 14% incidence of suicide attempts, and a 50% rate of consultation with professionals.[2]

In addition to those syndromes identified in *DSM-IV*, Judd et al. have written about *subsyndromal symptomatic depression*.[3] It overlaps minor depression (requiring only two symptoms of depression), differing in its elimination of the need for a mood disturbance per se. In the Broadhead et al. study noted above, this syndrome accounted for even more of the disability days (16%), but rarely led to major depression (only 1.8% incidence).[1]

The significance of the subsyndromal depressions lies in their association with an increased use of health care services, an increased risk for developing full-syndrome mood disorders, and increased suicidal risk, along with demonstrated social dysfunction and disability.

The Special Problem of Bereavement

The diagnostic category *uncomplicated bereavement* (DSM-III, DSM-III-R) was offered to emphasize the status of grieving as a normal phenomenon. Zisook et al., in their review of depressive states in the bereavement period, shift the emphasis to the potentially disabling consequences of grieving.[4] They note that bereavement may be prolonged, recurrent, associated with extended suffering, disability, suicidal ideas, interpersonal difficulties, and overall poor adjustment. To bolster their claim that clinicians have a tendency to attribute depressive symptoms subsequent to a death to a "normal reaction," they note the finding that 83% of bereaved spouses who met criteria for major depression received no antidepressant medications. In their own research, they found persistent depressive symptoms (subsyndromic symptomatic depression), as well as major depression, to be prevalent throughout a two-year period following the loss of a spouse. It seems reasonable to conclude, therefore, that the bereavement period and its aftermath provide a fertile ground for the development of mood disorders. Further, a significant percentage of these may be subsyndromic, occupying that space between normal grief and clinical depression.

THE BOUNDARY WITH
PERSONALITY DISORDER

Differentiating episodic, full-syndrome depression from a personality with depressive traits usually does not pose much of a clinical problem. Rather, it is the subsyndromic disorders like dysthymia that can resemble a personality disorder, and it is at this end of the depressive spectrum that this boundary dispute may arise.

The diagnosis of depressive personality disorder has never been included in any *DSM*. The relationship between depression and personality is a complex one. Phillips et al. (1990) have explored it in their excellent review of the depressive personality.[5] Personality traits may exist prior to and may *predispose* an individual to depression, or they may *result from* the experience of a depressive disorder. Alternatively, a personality disorder or set of traits may *coexist* with depression. Personality traits may modify the appearance of depression. Some normal personality traits, like gloominess and self-criticism, may be related to depressed mood.

A proposed diagnostic category for depressive personality must meet three criteria, according to Phillips et al.: early onset, associated dysfunction or distress, and stability of traits over time.[5] The history of the concept of depressive personality covers many decades and crosses multiple different theoretical orientations. In Germany the notion of "depressive temperament" was attributed to Kraepelin (1921),[6] and later to Schneider (1958).[7] Kraepelin's description emphasized gloominess, joylessness, anxiety, depressed mood, and serious demeanor, as well as feeling burdened or guilt-ridden, being self-critical, and lacking confidence. It was not clear whether this syndrome was a subsyndromic affective disorder or whether it was unique. Schneider wrote of "depressive psychopathy." His characteristics emphasize being gloomy, pessimistic, serious, unable to enjoy or relax, quiet, skeptical, worrying, duty-bound, and self-doubting. Although his work was similar to earlier work, Schneider saw links to other personality disorders rather than to major affective disorder.

Psychoanalytic theorists have discussed the "depressive character." Kahn[8] stressed persistent low self-esteem, guilt, inability to love, hypercriticalness, self-depreciation, and self-denial. Kernberg[9] postulated a "depressive-masochistic personality disorder." His patients were noted to be overly serious, responsible, conscientious, somber, humorless, self-critical and critical of others, overdependent on others' acceptance, and to have difficulty expressing aggression. The descriptions by Kraepelin, Schneider, and the psychoanalytic writers bear a strong resemblance to one another.

While *DSM-I* and *DSM-II* were consistent with prevailing psychoanalytic thought, *DSM-III* reformulated its approach to nosology to emphasize descriptive phenomenology. Between 1968 and 1980, Klein and Davis[10] wrote about "characterological dysphorics." Their sample had chronic complaints of severe subjective distress and unhappiness. They were constantly dissatisfied, apathetic, often manipulative, and had low self-esteem. In 1975, Schildkraut and Klein[11] discussed chronic characterological depressives, and in 1977, Spitzer et al.[12] proposed three categories to supplant *DSM-II*'s "depressive neurosis." They called one of them chronic and intermittent depressive disorder. It roughly corresponded to the concept of depressive personality.

DSM-III put depressive neurosis on Axis I, called it dysthymic disorder, and accumulated within it all chronic, mild depressions. The category (like its predecessor) was criticized for being over-inclusive and heterogeneous.

Since 1980, many authors have suggested that a depressive personality disorder be defined and extracted from dysthymia and placed on Axis II. Leading the parade have been the pioneering efforts of Hagop Akiskal.

Akiskal subdivided 150 patients with characterologic depressions into *subaffective dysthymia* and *character spectrum disorder*. While the latter group was seen as a heterogeneous collection of mixed personality disorders, the former group seemed more homogeneous. The subaffective dysthymics (for their characteristics, see Table 5.1) were believed to have an attenuated form of affective (sometimes bipolar) disorder.[13] Akiskal proposed that subaffective dysthymia was the early-onset counterpart of a more symptomatic, later-onset dysthymia. He believes that this syndrome (early-onset, defined by traits,

Table 5.1
CHARACTERISTICS OF SUBAFFECTIVE DYSTHYMIA

Positive response (sometimes hypomanic) to TCAs, MAOIs, lithium

Decreased REM-latency

Family history of bipolar or unipolar affective disorder

Relatively good social outcome

Equal sex distribution

Subsyndromal, intermittent course

From Akiskal and Mallya, 1987[13]

often drug-responsive) is the depressive personality, and should be placed on Axis II.[14] He sees the later-onset, more symptomatic version of dysthymia as a separate disorder that belongs on Axis I.

The boundary between depression (especially dysthymia) and the depressive personality is unclear. Responsive to the lack of consensus, the A.P.A. proposed and defined a category for depressive personality disorder, which is presented in Appendix B of *DSM-IV*.[15] The criteria are primarily cognitive and interpersonal (as opposed to affective and somatic). Its major feature is defined as "excessive, negative, pessimistic beliefs about oneself and others." Omitted are traits suggestive of compulsive personality (excessive conscientiousness, sense of duty, need for order) and dependent personality (excessive interpersonal dependency). For the full set of criteria for depressive personality disorder, see Table 5.2.

An entity called the "depressive personality" has been described for many decades, and has remained fairly consistent in its clinical description. While the concept overlaps several other mood disorders, it is not congruent with any of them and may well merit a category of its own.

THE BOUNDARY WITH ANXIETY

To quote psychiatrist Steven Dubovsky: "In an ideal world, anxiety and depression would be clinically distinct. In the real world of clinical psychiatry, there is considerable blurring of the boundaries."[16]

Throughout the twentieth century, but especially between the publication of *DSM-II* (1968) and *DSM-III* (1980), anxiety "neurosis" and depressive

Table 5.2
RESEARCH CRITERIA FOR DEPRESSIVE PERSONALITY DISORDER

A. A pervasive pattern of depressive cognitions and behaviors beginning by early adulthood and present in a variety of contexts, as indicated by five (or more) of the following:

1. usual mood is dominated by dejection, gloominess, cheerlessness, joylessness, unhappiness

2. self-concept centers around beliefs of inadequacy, worthlessness, and low self-esteem

3. is critical, blaming, and derogatory toward self

4. is brooding and given to worry

5. is negativistic, critical and judgmental of others

6. is pessimistic

7. is prone to feeling guilty or remorseful

From DSM-IV, Appendix B

"neurosis" were seen as sharing many common characteristics. Dubovsky has suggested ways the two may be related.[16] Intense anxiety may, in some cases, mask depressive affect. Some patients may find it hard to distinguish anxiety from depression. For others, depression may be a response to psychosocial consequences of an anxiety disorder. Depression may also represent a later stage in the development of a dysregulated stress response (e.g., panic disorder). Rating scales that use anxiety symptoms among their criteria for depression may add to this diagnostic uncertainty.

Anxiety disorders may lower the threshold for depression by increasing arousal and interfering with normal coping strategies. Self-treatment of anxiety with central nervous system depressants (like alcohol) may cause depression. Some drugs used to treat anxiety symptoms (e.g., benzodiazepines) may cause depression. Changes in marital equilibrium brought on by recovery from anxiety may lead to depression. Finally, the two disorders may coexist in the same patient at the same time, independent of each other.

A now classic series of papers was published in the *British Journal of Psychiatry* in 1972. They were called "Studies in the Classification of Affective Disorders." Although first authorship was generally rotated, the senior clinician was Sir Martin Roth. In the first paper, Roth et al. began by acknowledging that the overlap of symptoms of anxiety and depressive states made differentiation difficult.[17] They saw the criteria for differentiation as "variable, subjective and unvalidated," so they designed a study to find out whether anxiety and depressive states were part of a single continuum of affective disorder or were distinct entities.

They sampled 154 patients with a diagnosis of affective disorder admitted to a psychiatric hospital in the mid-1960s. They utilized a structured clinical interview and administered the Maudsley Personality Inventory to attempt to classify patients as either anxious or depressed. Their criteria for anxiety state were: exaggerated and fearful anticipation of events; severe tension; inability to relax; and frequent somatic manifestations of anxiety in the absence of stress. The somatic symptoms they considered were: sweating, tremor, palpitations, headache, breathlessness, frequent urination, and looseness of bowels. Their criteria for depressive illness were: loss of zest, energy, drive, enthusiasm; feelings of gloom; sadness and pessimism; and inadequacy and self-reproach. They had a third (intermediate) group they called "doubtful cases." We will return to consider them later on.

Roth et al.'s findings are summarized in Table 5.3. In addition to the differences recorded on this table, they noted features specific to childhood, personality, and course that differentiated the anxiety from the depressive group (see Table 5.4). They concluded that anxiety states and depressive illness can indeed be separated into two distinct syndromes. Although they acknowledged the overlap in their group of "doubtfuls," this mixed state was not referred to again.

A follow-up study tracked 126 of the 145 patients meeting initial criteria

---

Table 5.3
SEPARATING ANXIETY AND DEPRESSION

Overlap
Episodic depression, irritability, pessimism, guilt, agitation, generalized anxiety, dizziness, mild agoraphobia

Depression
Persistent depression, unreactiveness, diurnal variation, early morning awakening, psychomotor retardation, suicidal ideas, delusions

Anxiety
Persistent tension, panic attacks, fainting, severe agoraphobia, depersonalization, derealization

From Roth et al., 1972[17]

Table 5.4
ANXIETY FEATURES
In childhood: More neurotic traits, poor school adjustment, poor social adjustment **Personality:** More easily hurt, more dependent, more immature, more "unstable" **Course:** Younger onset, shorter episode duration *From Roth et al., 1972*[17]

to be studied for a period of three to eight years.[118] The distinctiveness of anxiety and depressive syndromes persisted over time:

- Anxiety group did less well in follow-up.
- Anxiety symptoms differentiated the two groups.
- Anxiety states of long standing acquired prominent depressive symptoms.
- With new episodes, there was little diagnostic crossover.

Through the 1960s and into the early 1970s, *factor analytic studies* were a popular way of attempting to subtype the depressions. Three good examples of the genre (acknowledged in chapter 4) are the studies of Grinker et al.,[19] Overall et al.,[20] and Paykel.[21] This research also acknowledged the prominence of anxiety in depressive disorders. Table 5.5 lists the groupings that emerged from the factor analysis. Each investigation found an anxious subtype of depression.

Now, let's return to the fifteen doubtful cases of Roth et al.[17] and review the data on the comorbidity of anxiety and depression. Although statistics vary over a wide range, it is clear that major depression is a common event in

Table 5.5
FACTOR ANALYTIC STUDIES OF DEPRESSION
Grinker et al., 1961[19]: Empty, ANXIOUS, hypochondriacal, angry Overall et al., 1966[20]: Retarded, ANXIOUS, hostile Paykel, 1972[21]: Psychotic, ANXIOUS, hostile, young, with personality disorder

the course of an anxiety disorder. Zajecka and Ross reviewed the comorbidity data and stated that 21–91% of patients with a diagnosis of an anxiety disorder have a major depression along their course, and 33–85% of patients with a major depression meet criteria for an anxiety disorder at some point.[22]

These data support the existence of comorbidity, but do not explain its nature. Perhaps the co-occurrence of anxiety and depressive states represents the overlap phase of a single illness. Perhaps the comorbid state is a unique disorder, different from either syndrome. Perhaps it represents the independent coexistence of two distinct disorders.

Clayton, too, has documented the comorbidity, then tried to establish a primary diagnosis.[23] Her symptoms common to anxiety and depression (see Table 5.6) may be compared to the findings of Roth et al. (Table 5.3).

When you examine specific anxiety syndromes, the comorbidity still holds up. According to Clayton, about two-thirds of panic disorder patients have major depression at some point in their course. According to Zajecka and Ross, about one-third of depressed patients have recurrent panic attacks during a depressive episode.[22] They noted that two-thirds of obsessive-compulsive disorder patients have major depression, and for one-third of the group, that depression is comorbid with the OCD. Finally, for about one-half of social phobia patients, depression will be comorbid, with the social phobia usually predating the depression.[22]

Clayton has identified four factors she believes to be helpful in establishing a primary diagnosis when anxiety and depression coexist:

- predominant mood
- sleep pattern
- psychomotor change
- response to exercise

Table 5.6
SYMPTOMS COMMON TO ANXIETY AND DEPRESSION

Dysphoria • Sleep disturbance • Appetite disturbance

Impaired concentration • Fatigue • Irritability

Nonspecific cardio-pulmonary or G.I. complaints

From Clayton, 1990[23]

When the anxiety disorder is primary, an anxious mood, initial insomnia, no psychomotor change, and a negative response to exercise are her usual findings. When depression is primary, a depressed mood, terminal insomnia, agitation or retardation, and a positive exercise effect are seen.

Liebowitz offers some clinical questions to aid in the diagnosis of depression when significant anxiety is present:[24]

- Unipolar or bipolar?
- How many episodes?
- Is there recovery?
- MDD or dysthymia?
- Endogenous or atypical?
- Depressed or demoralized?

His concerns include: course, chronicity, full verus partial syndrome, the presence of endogenous symptoms or atypical symptoms, and the presence of demoralization (a loss of the belief in one's own effectiveness). This article provides a nice introduction to the dedicated work of Donald Klein, Michael Liebowitz and their co-workers at Columbia University in elucidating the syndrome *atypical depression*.

In 1959, West and Dally first called attention to this syndrome, which presents a mixture of symptoms of anxiety and depression.[25] It features chronic fatigue, physical complaints, and phobic anxiety. They believed it was uniquely responsive to MAO-inhibiting drugs. Klein and his group later focused on reversed vegetative changes (oversleeping, overeating, weight gain), leaden fatigue, and interpersonal (rejection) sensitivity.[26] For a time, it was referred to as *hysteroid dysphoria*, to call attention to its occurrence in patients with a histrionic personality. Liebowitz has contrasted atypical and endogenous depression (see Table 5.7).[24] The general acceptance of the usefulness of the concept of atypical depression is indicated by the presence of a "specifier" category in *DSM-IV* (see Table 5.8).

Now that we have reviewed the distinctness of the full syndromes of anxiety disorder and depressive disorder, the common comorbidity of anxiety and depression, and the concept of atypical depression, we are ready to consider the new category in *DSM-IV, mixed anxiety-depressive disorder.*

With the redefinitions brought about by *DSM-III* (1980) and *DSM-IV* (1994), Alan Schatzberg wrote, "Comorbidity (of anxiety and depression) may be the rule rather than the exception."[27] Goldberg, in an article aimed at primary care physicians, found mixed anxiety-depression to be the third

Table 5.7 ENDOGNEOUS VS. ATYPICAL DEPRESSION	Table 5.8 DEPRESSION WITH ATYPICAL FEATURES
• Middle or terminal insomnia vs. initial or hypersomnia • Decreased appetite vs. increased appetite • Weight loss vs. weight gain • Mood worse a.m. vs. mood worse p.m. • Non-reactive vs. reactive • Non rejection-sensitive vs. rejection-sensitive *From Clayton, 1990*[23]	**A. Mood reactivity** **B. Two (or more) of the following symptoms:** 1. Weight gain/increased appetite 2. Hypersomnia 3. Leaden paralysis 4. Rejection-sensitivity *Modified from DSM-IV, 1994*

most common presenting problem seen in that setting, after upper respiratory infections and hypertension.[28]

Methodological research problems have complicated our understanding of this syndrome.[29] Its diagnostic criteria define it as "the equal presence of both anxiety and depression, neither of which reaches full syndrome requirements."[15] In other words, it is a subsyndromic disorder. Subthreshold anxiety and depression are often not recorded in samples studied, whether in community or clinical settings. Furthermore, prior to 1994 there were no formal diagnostic criteria, making it hard to compare different findings in different settings. (Although *ICD-10*, published in 1993, included a category for mixed anxiety-depression, there were no diagnostic criteria.)

Differential diagnosis would have to include minor depression and adjustment disorder, raising the question of whether a new category was necessary. The sense of reports in the literature, however, is that the mixed state has an earlier onset, a tendency for patients to be more chronically ill and to respond less well to treatment, and a higher risk for suicide. So, the mixed state may represent a surprisingly severe disorder along the depressive continuum.

Katon and Roy-Byrne in 1991 called attention to significant social and vocational impairment in these patients, their high utilization of medical care, a tendency to somaticize their distress, and a heightened risk for the development of full syndromes of either anxiety disorders or depression when exposed to life stress.[30] It was clear that this syndrome may the precursor to a full syndrome or residual effects of a partial recovery.

Therefore, to acknowledge the frequently observed comorbidity of symptoms of anxiety and depressive states, to align with *ICD-10*, and to encourage further study and definition of the mixed state, *DSM-IV* in 1994 provided diagnostic criteria for the mixed anxiety-depressive disorder in Appendix B. These criteria are reproduced in Table 5.9.

THE BOUNDARY WITH PSYCHOSIS

In 1933, Kasanin described a syndrome that featured symptoms of each of the two major emotional disorders, schizophrenia and depression.[31] The episode duration was shorter than that of typical schizophrenia, with full remission often after a few months. He called the syndrome *schizoaffective disorder*. In *DSM-II*, it was listed as a subtype of schizophrenia.

When *DSM-III* published its phenomenology-based nosology (1980),

---

Table 5.9
MIXED ANXIETY-DEPRESSIVE DISORDER

A. Persistent or recurrent dysphoric mood lasting at least one month

B. Four (or more) of the following symptoms:

    1. Difficulty concentrating

    2. Sleep disturbance

    3. Anergia/fatigue

    4. Irritability

    5. Worry

    6. Tearfulness

    7. Hypervigilance

    8. Pessimism

    9. Hopelessness

    10. Low self-esteem

Modified from Appendix B, DSM-IV, 1994

there was a category for this syndrome, but no diagnostic criteria. To quote from the manual: "This category is retained . . . for those instances in which the clinician is unable to make a differential diagnosis with any degree of certainty between Affective Disorder and either Schizophreniform Disorder or Schizophrenia."[32]

DSM-III-R (1987) noted that schizoaffective disorder "represents one of the most confusing and controversial concepts."[33] It presented diagnostic criteria for the first time. The diagnosis is carried virtually without change into *DSM-IV*. The criteria are:

1. Concurrent with a major depressive, manic or mixed episode, are symptoms meeting the "A" criterion of schizophrenia (delusions, hallucinations, disorganized speech, disorganized or catatonic behavior, and negative symptoms (flat affect, alogia, avolition).

2. Acute episode features at least two weeks of delusions or hallucinations without prominent mood symptoms.

It was also specified that two different subtypes might exist: bipolar (history of mania) and depressive (no mania).

A study by Kendler et al. sought to validate the *DSM* criteria for schizoaffective disorder.[34] Nearly 12% of individuals with schizophrenia met criteria for schizoaffective disorder. And 7.5% of individuals with affective illness did so as well. This sample had more affective symptoms, fewer negative symptoms, and a better global course and outcome than did the schizophrenic patients, as well as a unique pattern of family psychopathology.[34] While there is strong evidence for a genetic factor,[35] results from family, twin, and adoption studies remain unclear as to etiology.

Therefore, the syndrome defined by the *DSM* criteria seems distinct from schizophrenia and distinct from affective disorder. The findings of Kendler et al. support the tenet that schizoaffective disorder results from the co-occurrence of schizophrenia and affective disorder. This syndrome, therefore, might represent a true boundary disorder, bridging the gap between two major emotional illnesses.

Of course, all psychotic depression is not schizoaffective disorder. In fact, studies have documented that up to 25% of hospitalized patients with depression are psychotic.[36] *DSM-IV* offers a "psychotic" specifier for both unipolar and bipolar disorders: the presence of delusions and hallucinations. The boundary question that arises is this: "Is psychotic depression a unique syndrome?" Schatzberg and Rothschild believe it is, and discuss the reasons in a recent review.[37]

Once utilized as a synonym for "severe," "psychotic" is employed by modern clinicians to indicate the presence of hallucinations and delusions. While that often presumes a more severe depression, that need not be so. Some features of depression, like guilt feelings and psychomotor disturbance, appear to cluster more frequently with psychosis. Biological changes, specifically in hypothalamic-pituitary-adrenal axis (HPA) function, are more striking and more often present in psychotic depression. Patients with nonaffective (e.g., schizophrenic) psychoses do not show, for example, the high rate of nonsuppression of cortisol on the Dexamethasone Suppression Test. There are reasons to believe that patients with psychotic depression have increases in dopamine and its metabolites as well.

Course, prognosis, and outcome of psychotic depression differ from the nonpsychotic variety. Short-term outcome is poorer, there is a trend toward a higher number of hospitalizations, and social adjustment is impaired.

When psychotic depression occurs early in life, it may be an indicator of a bipolar course.[38] If one depressive episode is psychotic, frequently future episodes are as well.[39] There is a poor treatment response to placebo or to tricyclic antidepressants (TCAs) alone, but frequently a good response to ECT. Adding a neuroleptic to the TCA increases the likelihood of a response.

The psychotic element may present subtly, with the clinician's awareness piqued only by an unexpectedly treatment-resistant patient. For now, it is probably adequate clinically to collect these cases utilizing the specifier supplied by DSM. While there are clear differences evident between psychotic and non-psychotic depression, the field does not yet appear ready to declare a new depressive entity, distinct from all others. Rather, the boundary with psychosis is a clinically significant one that may manifest as an admixture of symptoms of schizophrenia and affective disorder, or may present as depression complicated by hallucinations and delusions requiring some adjustments in treatment approach.

Notes

1. Broadhead, W. E., Blazer, D. G., George, L. K., et al. (1990). Depression, disability days and days lost from work in a prospective epidemiologic survey. *Journal of the American Medical Association, 264*, 2524.

2. Angst, J., & Hochstrasser, B. (1994). Recurrent brief depression: The Zurich study. *Journal of Clinical Psychiatry, 55*(Suppl. 4), 3.

3. Judd, L. L., Rapaport, M. H., Paulus, M. P., et al. (1994). Subsyndromal symptomatic depression: A new mood disorder? *Journal of Clinical Psychiatry,* 55(Suppl. 4), 18.

4. Zisook, S., Shucter, S. R., Sledge, P. A., et al. (1994). The spectrum of depressive phenomena after spousal bereavement. *Journal of Clinical Psychiatry,* 55(Suppl. 4), 29.

5. Phillips, K. A., Gunderson, J. G. Hirschfeld, R. M. A., et al. (1990). A review of the depressive personality. *American Journal of Psychiatry, 147,* 830.

6. Kraepelin, E. (1921). *Manic-depressive insanity and paranoia.* Edinburgh: Livingstone.

7. Schneider, K. (1958). *Psychopathic personalities.* Springfield, IL: Charles C. Thomas.

8. Kahn, E. (1975). The depressive character. *Folia Psychiat. Neurol. Jpn., 29,* 291.

9. Kernberg, O. (1987). Clinical dimensions of narcissism. In R. A. Glick & D. I. Meyers (Eds.), *Masochism: Current psychoanalytic perspectives.* New York: Analytic Press.

10. Klein, D. F. & Davis, J. M. (1969). The diagnosis of affective disorders. In D. F. Klein & J. M. Davis (Eds.), *Diagnosis and treatment of psychiatric disorders.* Baltimore: Williams & Wilkins.

11. Schildkraut, J. J., & Klein, D. F. (1975). The classification and treatment of depressive disorders. In R. I. Shader (Ed.), *Manual of psychiatric therapeutics.* Boston: Little, Brown.

12. Spitzer, R. L., Endicott, J., Woodruff, R. A., et al. (1977). Classification of mood disorders. In G. Usdin (Ed.), *Depression: Clinical, biological, and psychological perspectives.* New York: Brunner/Mazel.

13. Akiskal, H. S., & Mallya, G. (1987). Criteria for the "soft" bipolar spectrum: Treatment implications. *Psychopharmacology Bulletin, 23,* 68.

14. Akiskal, H. S. (1989). Validating affective personality types. In L. Robins & J. Barrett (Eds.), *The validity of psychiatric diagnosis.* New York: Raven.

15. American Psychiatric Association. (1994). *Diagnostic and statistical manual* (4th ed.). Washington D.C.: A.P.A.

16. Dubovsky, S. L. (1990). Understanding and treating depression in anxious patients. *Journal of Clinical Psychiary, 51*(Suppl. 10), 3.

17. Roth, M., Gurney, C., Garside, R. F., et al. (1972). Studies in the classification of affective disorders: The relationship between anxiety states and depressive illnesses. *British Journal of Psychiatry, 121,* 147.

18. Schapira, K., Roth, M., Kerr, T. A., et al. (1972). The prognosis of affective disorders: The differentiation of anxiety states from depressive illnesses. *British Journal of Psychiatry, 121,* 175.

19. Grinker, R. R., Miller, J., Sabshin, M., et al. (1961). *The phenomena of depression.* New York: Hoeber.

20. Overall, J. E., Hollister, L. E., Johnson, M., et al. (1966). Nosology of depression and differential response to drugs. *Journal of the American Medical Association*, 195, 946.

21. Paykel, E. S. (1972). Correlates of a depressive typology. *Archives of General Psychiatry*, 27, 203.

22. Zajecka, J. M., & Ross, J. S. (1995). Management of comorbid anxiety and depression. *Journal of Clinical Psychiatry*, 56(Suppl. 2), 10.

23. Clayton, P. J. (1990). The comorbidity factor: Establishing the primary diagnosis in patients with mixed symptoms of anxiety and depression. *Journal of Clinical Psychiatry*, 51(Suppl. 11), 35.

24. Liebowitz, M. R. (1993). Depression with anxiety and atypical depression. *Journal of Clinical Psychiatry*, 54(Suppl. 2), 10.

25. West, E. D., & Dally, P. J. (1959). Effect of iproniazid in depressive syndromes. *British Medical Journal*, 1, 1491.

26. Stewart, J. W., McGrath, P. J., Rabkin, J. G., et al. (1993). Atypical depression: A valid clinical entity? *Psychiatric Clinics of North America*, 16(3), 479.

27. Schatzberg, A. F. (1995). Fluoxetine in the treatment of comorbid anxiety and depression. *Journal of Clinical Psychiatry*, 13(2), 2.

28. Goldberg, R. J. (1995). Diagnostic dilemmas presented by patients with anxiety and depression.*American Journal of Medicine*, 98, 278.

29. Liebowitz, M. R. (1993). Mixed anxiety and depression: Should it be included in *DSM-IV*? *Journal of Clinical Psychiatry*, 54(Suppl. 5), 4.

30. Katon, W., & Roy-Byrne, P. P. (1991). Mixed anxiety and depression. *Journal of Abnormal Psychology*, 100(3), 337.

31. Kasanin, J. (1933). The acute schizoaffective psychoses. *American Journal of Psychiatry*, 13, 97.

32. American Psychiatric Association. (1980). *Diagnostic and statistical manual* (3rd ed.). Washington D.C.: A. P. A.

33. American Psychiatric Association. (1987). *Diagnostic and statistical manual* (3rd ed., revised). Washington D.C.: A. P. A.

34. Kendler, K. S., McGuire, M., Gruenberg, A. M., et al. (1995). Examining the validity of *DSM-III-R* schizoaffective disorder and its putative subtypes in the Roscommon Family Study. *American Journal of Psychiatry*, 152(5), 755.

35. Bertelsen, A., & Gottesman, I. I. (1995). Schizoaffective psychoses: Genetical clues to classification. *American Journal of Medicine and Genetics*, 60, 7.

36. Coryell, W., Pfohl, B., & Zimmerman, M. (1984). The clinical and neuroendocrine features of psychotic depression. *Journal of Nervous and Mental Disease*, 172, 521.

37. Schatzberg, A. F., & Rothschild, A. J. (1992). Psychotic (delusional) major depression: Should it be included as a distinct syndrome in *DSM-IV*? *American Journal of Psychiatry*, 149(6), 733.

38. Akiskal, H. S., Walker, P., Puzantian, V. R., et al. (1983). Bipolar outcome in the course of depressive illness: Phenomenologic, familial and pharmacologic predictors. *Journal of Affective Disorders, 5,* 115.

39. Charney, D. S., & Nelson, J. C. (1981). Delusional and nondelusional unipolar depression: Further evidence for distinct subtypes. *American Journal of Psychiatry, 138,* 328.

Chapter 6

Epidemiology
Who Becomes Depressed?

The epidemiology of depression seeks to identify persons at risk by focusing on issues like age, gender, race, social class, and climate. It also tabulates the frequency of depression, as measured by hospitalizations and outpatient visits. Cross-national studies document real increases in the rates of major depression, especially for those born since World War II.[1] The accuracy of such data is affected by the degree of adherence to diagnostic criteria by the clinicians whose reporting gives rise to the statistics. In addition, as hospitalization becomes a less frequent occurrence in depression's treatment, its value as an indicator of prevalence diminishes.

Depression does not respect chronological age, appearing in every age group—children, adolescents, adults, and the elderly. In general, depression is more frequently observed in women than in men, although there is variability related to its form (e.g., unipolar, bipolar, dysthymia). The research focus, once exclusively on samples of men, has begun to shift. The senselessness of studying only males in a predominantly female disorder has finally struck home. Interest has been particularly directed at the stages of the menstrual cycle and its cessation (menopause), as well as at pregnancy and its immediate aftermath (the postpartum period).

In a society becoming "older," the myths about depression and aging, the presentation of depression in the elderly, and management issues in the older patient have all gained primacy. In a society becoming increasingly multicultural, research on depression in people of color still is invisible. Social class has not been studied as a variable that defines vulnerability to depression, yet all seem vulnerable, within their own circumstances.

While climate is generally considered to be relevant to mood, research now posits a clear relationship between light and depression for some individuals. The diagnostic term *seasonal affective disorder* has become popularly accepted, although perhaps less so clinically, and treatment in the form of light therapy is now generally available.

In this chapter, we will focus on prevalence rates, depression in women and in the elderly, and seasonal depression.

PREVALENCE

Epidemiology studies the distribution and determinants of disorders. It seeks to identify risk factors that may lead to the uncovering of causal factors. The application of this knowledge leads to the development of strategies for prevention and control. In this pursuit, definitive outcome measures are crucial; therefore, the publication of *DSM-III* in 1980 paved the way for meaningful epidemiological contributions in depression. Conversely, the ongoing nosologic controversies pose a continuing problem for epidemiologists.

The NIMH Epidemiologic Catchment Area (ECA) survey sampled 20,000 persons, age 18 or older, from five research sites across America in the period 1980–84.[2] It then used the 1990 census figures to calculate estimates of adults with mental disorders. The prevalence of affective disorders was calculated to be 9.5%—or 17.4 million people. For bipolar disorders, corresponding rates were 1.2% (2.2 million people); for major depression, 5.0% (9.1 million people); and for dysthymia, 5.4% (9.9 million people). Comparable figures for schizophrenia (1.1%), alcohol abuse (7.4%), and drug abuse (3.1%) are all lower than the prevalence rates of affective disorders. Only the estimate for anxiety disorders (12.6%) was higher.[3]

Mental health services were sought by only 45.7% of those with affective disorders, with an average of 18 outpatient visits per person, per year. The highest utilization of services was for those with bipolar disorder (60.9%).[4]

Affective disorders were found at higher rates in women (6.6%) than in men (3.5%). These disorders were concentrated among 25- to 44-year-olds and were significantly less common in the age group over 65 years old. In the sociodemographically defined groups, the highest rate was among those separated or divorced (11.1%), with the next highest rate among the widowed (5.6%).[5]

DEPRESSION IN WOMEN

There have been a multiplicity of explanations offered to account for the higher incidence of major depression in women: more willingness to seek treatment, greater likelihood to be prescribed medication, "permission" to cry when depressed. None of these begin to account for the 2:1 female-to-male ratio generally found.[6]

Do physiological changes associated with female reproductive function make up the difference? Having a menstrual period is not a unique risk for major depression in women, even though it may be a risk factor for sadness that is unique to women.[6]

With the mean age of onset of major depression coinciding with child-bearing years in women, it is astonishing that so little attention has been directed to depression in women in the past. Research samples were limited to males, with findings generalized to females. As the focus shifted, there followed a concentration on times of hormonal change, then the realization that statistics did not support vulnerability at these times for all women, and finally an attempt to identify those women who are at risk.

Pajer summarized the three approaches taken to understanding female pre-ponderance in depression as: the artifact hypothesis, the biological hypothesis, and the psychosocial hypothesis.[7] The artifact hypothesis targets methodological error, patterns of utilization of clinical services favoring women, and cultural biases that account for a tendency to diagnose depression more readily in women than in men. The biological hypothesis asserts that the characteristic shifts in gonadal hormone levels might serve to provoke depression in genetically vulnerable women who are under psychosocial stress. The psychosocial hypothesis emphasizes dependency and the culturally supported tendency of women to internalize stress, along with a societal devaluation of women's traditional roles and corresponding powerlessness as a precursor to depression in circumstances of stress.

If the generalization that women derive their self-worth more often from external factors (and men from internal factors) is believed, that could predict more vulnerability to depression among women, because their external focus could lead to dependency, self-blame, and internalizing stress (for fear of alienating significant others). When a society specifies a female role as caretaker and nurturer, and then assigns lower status to that role, this too predisposes to a depressive reaction to stress. Finally, Pajer notes that in a society in which women are more likely than men to be victimized, learned helplessness (discussed in chapter 7) could be another pathway to depression.[7]

Premenstrual Dysphoria

The problem of distinguishing depressive pathology from normal reaction is nowhere more clearly met than in premenstrual dysphoria. Most menstruating women have experienced a change in the premenstrual week involving mood or physical discomfort. A group of women, however, complain of changes of such severity that normal functioning is disrupted. While a subsample also experience affective disorder with premenstrual worsening, there remains a group of women with depressive symptoms solely related to this part of the menstrual cycle. Studies focused on documenting psychological as opposed to biological impairment in this group have been inconclusive.[8]

Diagnostic criteria consist of the repeated occurrence of either anxious, sad, or labile mood, and decreased interest in activities during the luteal phase of the menstrual cycle, remitting in a few days after the onset of menses.[9] Associated symptoms include abdominal bloating, breast tenderness, headache, fatigue, oversensitivity, crying spells, withdrawal, difficulty concentrating.[8]

Study findings have been consistent with the subsyndromal designation given to the syndrome by *DSM-IV*.[10] There are no convincing biological studies to date that support an etiology for PMS.

Treatment with TCAs has not been successful. Progesterone blockers have not brought relief. Fluoxetine (Prozac) has been used successfully when prescribed daily throughout the menstrual cycle and, to a lesser degree, when given only over the second half of the cycle.[11] It has been cited that 60–70% of women with severe PMS will experience relief with serotonergic antidepressants.[12] Research with SSRIs is still in an early stage. Alprazolam (Xanax), a benzodiazepine, has been successfully used as well, calling attention to the interaction of progesterone and the GABA receptor.[8] The study dose of Xanax was 0.25 mg three times a day from cycle day 20 to the second day of menstruation, with gradual dose reduction thereafter.[13]

Depression during Pregnancy

Data are not yet available to answer the question of whether pregnancy is a time of vulnerability or one of respite for the risk of major depression.[14] The prevalence of all depression in pregnancy has been estimated at 10%. Rates do not appear particularly different for pregnant women than for age-matched controls. Rather, a past history of depression is the best predictor of depression occurring in pregnancy.

The decision to treat major depression in pregnancy with antidepressant drugs pits the perils of untreated symptoms against the risk of fetal harm by the drug. All psychotropic drugs cross the placenta. With tricyclic drugs, there is no evidence for teratogenicity even with first trimester exposure.[15] With MAOIs the data are inadequate to make a determination. For SSRIs, there are data only for fluoxetine (Prozac), which provides no evidence for an increase in major malformations.[15] Lithium carbonate has been associated with an elevated risk of Ebstein's anomaly of the heart. A careful review of the literature found a risk of about 1 in 2,000 with first-trimester lithium use.[16] Neural tube defects occurred about 1% of the time with carbamazepine (Tegretol) and 3–5% of the time with valproic acid (Depakote).[15] ECT is generally thought to be a safe alternative.[17]

Cohen has offered guidelines for the use of psychotropic drugs in pregnancy:[15]

- The goal remains nonexposure.
- Identify subgroups of patients who require continuation of treatment.
- Identify subgroups of patients who can tolerate discontinuation.
- Try to avoid exposure during the first trimester.

For all but severe bipolar illness, he recommends discontinuation of lithium, with reintroduction only as needed. When the risk of relapse into severe bipolar disorder is high, he suggests continuation of lithium prophylaxis in pregnancy.

Postpartum Depression

The blues, major depression, and postpartum psychosis have all been reported to occur in the period immediately after childbirth. The blues are common (50–80%), major depression is significant (10%), and postpartum psychosis is rare (1–2 per 1,000).[18] In DSM-IV, the modifier "with postpartum onset" requires the onset of symptoms within four weeks after delivery for this diagnosis, but clinical experience suggests that the onset may be later.[18]

While pregnancy is associated with a decreased risk of hospitalization for a bipolar episode, the postpartum period is a time of increased risk.[14] The risk of depression at this time seems to correlate with past experience. With no prior disorder, it is 10%. However, with a past history of depression, it leaps to 25%, and with the specific past experience of postpartum depression, the risk is 50%.[14] Alerters to the risk of postpartum depression include: family history, personal history, affective symptoms during pregnancy, the presence of premenstrual syndrome, previous severe blues, as well as previous postpartum illness.[18] If antidepressants are prescribed within a day of delivery, the expected rate in this group may be decreased significantly.

The symptoms in postpartum bipolar depression may differ from typical presentations at other times. Confusion, delerium, and psychosis may dominate the picture.[14] The sensitization phenomenon noted for bipolar episodes in chapter 3 may be seen in postpartum depression as well. Once an episode occurs in one postpartum period, subsequent episodes increase in likelihood.

Postpartum blues usually begins in the first week after delivery. Symptoms include insomnia, poor appetite, fatigue, headache, sad mood, irritability, anxiety, poor concentration, and confusion. Its effect on functioning is minimal. It is usually over within two weeks. It would fit the definition of a subsyndromal depression. However, up to 20% of women with so-called "maternity blues" go on to develop major depression in the first postnatal year.[19] Rates for postpartum blues may be higher in adolescent mothers.

Miller has reconceptualized maternity blues to emphasize its relationship to attachment.[20] She sees the common syndrome as a normal state of physiological reactivity that facilitates attachment and prepares the mother for nurturing behavior. She targets the cingulate gyrus, a neuroanatomical structure that may have a central role in the interface between attention and emotion. This could account for the mood lability and intense reactivity observed in postpartum blues. Further, she implicates the hormone oxytocin (levels of which increase with childbirth) and estrogen as triggers for parenting behavior. It remains for future research to elucidate the mechanisms by which the cingulate gyrus, oxytocin, estrogen and other hormones, and neurotransmitters may lay the groundwork for attachment behavior between mother and newborn. if this approach is borne out, then someday postpartum blues may be seen as a natural phenomenon of adaptation, rather than as a variant of depression.

Postpartum depression (PPD) may begin anytime within six months after delivery, and may last for up to fourteen months. Typically, the affected mother has real difficulty caring for her newborn infant, usually exhibiting excessive anxiety. Bearing preterm infants[21] or twins[22] has been associated with a higher incidence of PPD. The symptom picture features a labile mood, with fewer prominent vegetative symptoms than in nonpuerperal major depression. Diagnosis may be complicated by the attribution of any physical complaints to "normal sequellae of childbirth."[19] Treatment for this full-syndrome depression is no different than treatment for nonpuerperal depression. When

considering postpartum depression, it is important to rule out hypothyroidism, which can present a similar clinical picture.

Postpartum psychosis has its onset typically two days to three weeks after
delivery. Its format may be mania, depression, or schizophrenia. Treatment is
directed at the specific type, and is similar to that for nonpuerperal illness.

Depression during Menopause

Historically, the period of menopause in a woman's life has been identified
as a time of particular risk for affective disorder. Changes in the reproductive
cycle and changes in role definition have been the principal areas of focus for
those seeking an association between menopause and depression. The term
"involutional melancholia" was proposed with this period in mind; however,
the consensus of the field is that involutional melancholia as a distinct entity does not exist. The remaining questions are:

- Does menopause confer an increased risk for affective disorder?
- Does the depression seen in this period fit the classical description—i.e.,
  a patient with an obsessive-compulsive personality but no previous history of depression or mania, who is agitated and hypochondriacal, with
  somatic delusions?

Schmidt and Rubinow reviewed the literature on menopausal depression
and concluded that:[23]

- There is no distinct symptom pattern.
- There is no distinct pattern of previous episodes.
- There is no increased risk of suicide or hospitalization.

Further, the mean age at menopause (50–51 years) is less relevant than the
age range (41–59 years). And symptoms of depression (without the full syndrome) are not uncommon. Therefore, isolating a sample to be studied has
not been easy.

It would seem that hormone levels might provide a better definition of
menopause. The ability of the ovaries to produce estradiol decreases, with a
corresponding increase in follicle-stimulating hormone (FSH). However,
even hormone levels cannot provide a precise definition of menopause,
despite documented improvement in some women who receive hormone
replacement therapy.

Psychosocial factors implicated as causes of life stress during this period include: role changes, changes in support system, aging and the onset of physical ailments, and interpersonal loss and separation.

Schmidt and Rubinow recommend attending to hormone replacement first when symptoms of depression occur during menopause.[23] When past history of depression or positive family history is present, however, the use of antidepressant therapy may be indicated.

To understand this period in a woman's life, physiologically marked by the decline in sex hormone activity, it is necessary to understand the sex steroidal hormones. Research studies of rat brain have identified estrogen receptors in areas that modulate mood.[12] It is thought that estrogen affects the serotonergic amine system by increasing the rate of degradation of the enzyme MAO, resulting in increased serotonin levels. Also, tryptophan (serotonin's amino acid precursor) is displaced from its binding sites to albumin by estrogen, making more free tryptophan available, further increasing serotonin levels. Studies in nondepressed women support the role of estrogen enhancing mood;[12] however, they fail to support a therapeutic effect for estrogen in postmenopausal women with major depression. One series of studies by Prange suggests that estrogen may have a role as a potentiator of imipramine (speeding the response) in women with major depression.[24]

Hormone replacement therapy (HRT) typically combines estrogen and progesterone preparations. Some women receiving HRT complain of depressive symptoms. Progesterone, interestingly, increases the concentration of MAO in the brain, effectively lowering brain serotonin. It has been suggested by Sherwin that HRT employ the lowest possible dose of progesterone.[12]

DEPRESSION IN THE ELDERLY

As the population ages, one of the problems we face increasingly in the clinic is the recognition and treatment of emotional disorders in the older person. The most common psychiatric disorders in later life, with the exception of dementia, are depression and anxiety.[25]

Cultural Myths

Cultural myths of old age have led to under-recognition and undertreatment of the older person. Some of these myths are:[26]

- Old age should be a time of leisure, without stress.
- Old age ushers in a life of inevitable suffering.

- Depression and anxiety are normal accompaniments of aging.
- Drug treatment is dangerous in the elderly.
- The elderly are too inflexible to benefit from psychotherapy.

Let's examine each one in turn. As the body parts age and wear, there is the potential for breakdown, leading to distress and disability. Psychologically, as friends age and some die, there may be frequent periods of grieving. The changes that accompany aging require periodic adaptations that some make easily, but that frustrate and overwhelm others. As such, old age is rarely a blissful time of leisure without stress. However, debilitating physical changes are by no means inevitable, and some people deal quite well with the psychological stressors. So, neither suffering nor leisure is "inevitable." Neither clinical depression nor clinical anxiety typically accompanies aging. The presence of either must alert the clinician to seek treatable causes, just as it would in a younger patient.

Metabolism of medications may change in the older patient. If the clinician minds the maxim, "Start drugs low, and go slow," gratifying results often are obtained in the treatment of depression in the elderly. Drug treatment is by no means dangerous, as long as the clinician is guided by common sense.

Inflexibility is not a function of aging, but rather one of personality organization. As such, some older individuals are inflexible (and they may have been similarly rigid in their youth!), while others are quite capable of learning new approaches to problems. Psychotherapy can be a gratifying venture with a motivated older individual.

Perhaps in part due to these societal myths, the clinician often carries a *lower functional expectation* of his or her older patient than is realistic. This may deprive the elderly of both pharmacotherapy and psychotherapy, each of which may relieve distress in appropriate cases.

Clinical Presentations

The presentation of depression in the elderly may differ from the same syndrome observed in a younger person. Sad mood may be less prominent and physical complaints may dominate the picture.[26] Misattribution of physical symptoms to aging is one problem; misattribution of depressive symptoms to a concurrent medical condition is another. In fact, depression can be *precipitated* by a wide variety of medical conditions (see Table 6.1). In addition, a wide variety of medications commonly prescribed to older patients can cause depression (see Table 6.2). Finally, psychosocial stressors and economic pressures inherent to aging in today's society may also precipitate depression (see Table 6.3).

Pseudodementia is a syndrome marked by memory impairment and cognitive inefficiency. As its name suggests, it mimics dementia. It occurs in people with no organic illness and may be a manifestation of clinical depression. Because depression is its actual cause, which it is usually treatable, it is important to differentiate pseudodementia from dementia.

Primary sleep disorders (like sleep apnea) may disrupt sleep and be confused with depression in the elderly. *Character disorders*, often evident throughout the patient's life, may be confused late in life with depression, particularly when the clinician meets the elderly patient for the first time and has no referent for his or her personality style.

Two forms of subsyndromic depression are commonly encountered in the elderly: dysthymia and secondary depression (secondary to another psychiatric or medical condition). They must each be differentiated from major depression. Comorbidity, often present in the younger adult population, is an even bigger problem in the elderly.

Table 6.1 **MEDICAL CONDITIONS THAT CAN PRECIPITATE DEPRESSION**
Cardiovascular disease • Neurological disease • Osteoarthritis
Metabolic diseases • Neoplasms • Infectious diseases
Sensory loss • Dementia
Adapted from Fernandez et al., 1995[26]

Table 6.2 **MEDICATIONS THAT CAN PRECIPITATE DEPRESSSION**
CNS depressants • Antihypertensives
Corticosteroids • Anticonvulsants
Cancer chemotherapy agents
Adapted from Fernandez et al., 1995[26]

Table 6.3
PSYCHOSOCIAL PRECIPITANTS OF DEPRESSION
Retirement (inactivity; status loss) • Home relocation
Financial changes • Social isolation • Bereavement
Chronic medical illness • Loss of autonomy
Adapted from Fernandez et al., 1995[26]

Epidemiology

How prevalent is depression in the elderly? In the community, symptoms of depression are found in 15% of residents over age 65; major depression occurs in less than 3%.[27] Rates for "minor depression" vary from 5% in the clinic to 15–20% in nursing homes.

Recurrence is significant, as it is in younger populations. Up to 40% continue to experience depression over time.[27] Of the approximately 800,000 persons who are widowed each year (most of whom are elderly), 33% meet criteria for major depression in the first month of grieving.[27] Significantly, half of these remain clinically depressed one year later.

The rate of completed suicides is typically higher as people age. For example, in 1988 the suicide rate in the general population was 12.4 per 100,000.[27] In the 80- to 84-year-old age group, it was 26.5 per 100,000. Typically, the person had been clinically depressed prior to death. Often the diagnosis had been missed, and the depression went untreated.

Elderly depressed patients utilize health care services at a significant rate. They are admittedly more difficult to diagnose, their treatment compliance is also often poor, and hospitalizations for treatment are likely to be longer than for their younger counterparts.[27]

While pseudodementia is a vital clinical concept, it is also important to acknowledge that depression may complicate the course of dementia in Alzheimer's disease. In one recent study, Migliorelli et al. reported that of 103 persons with probable Alzheimer's disease, 23% were diagnosed with concurrent major depression and 28% with concurrent dysthymia.[28]

Duffy and Coffey note that typical vegetative symptoms of depression (e.g., withdrawal, lost libido, insomnia) are commonly seen in the natural course of Alzheimer's disease.[29] They identify the following changes as more reliable indicators of depression in this group: irritability, demandingness, increased dependency or complaining, and somatic preoccupation.

SEASONAL AFFECTIVE DISORDER

The associations between seasons, light, geography, and affective disorder can be traced back to Hippocrates (400 B.C.). More specifically, Cook, in 1894, accompanying explorer Robert Peary to the Arctic, described a syndrome in both Eskimos and observers that resembled clinical depression.[30] However, it remained for Norman Rosenthal and his colleagues at NIMH to systematically describe, research, and establish treatment guidelines for depressions with clear seasonal variation.[31]

Rosenthal focused on individuals who are especially vulnerable to changes in daylight that varies with the seasons. He defined seasonal affective disorder (SAD) as: "a condition of depressions that occur regularly during a particular season, alternating with non-depressed periods at other times of the year." [32] *DSM-IV* acknowledges Rosenthal's work by denoting "with seasonal pattern" as a specifier. Added diagnostic criteria are:[9]

- Full remissions occur also at a characteristic time of the year.
- Two major depressive episodes must have occurred with no intervening nonseasonal episodes over a two-year period.
- Seasonal episodes must substantially outnumber nonseasonal ones over the individual's lifetime.

While original reports focused on "winter SAD," more recent work acknowledges "summer SAD" as well. While original work demanded "full syndromes" of depression, recent work acknowledges the occurrence of subsyndromal (sub-SAD) depression.

Hypotheses about causes of SAD vary, but include abnormal secretion of melatonin and abnormal timing of circadian rhythms, in addition to disturbed brain serotonin pathways.[32]

Typical symptoms of SAD are: decreased energy and activity, hypersomnia, overeating, carbohydrate craving, weight gain, social withdrawal.[32] (Note the resemblance to atypical depression, which was discussed in chapter 5.) A minority of SAD patients report more typical features of depression (insomnia, anorexia, and weight loss).

Epidemiological studies find the prevalence of SAD to vary from 1% to 10%, and sub-SAD to occur at about twice that rate.[32] About 30% of SAD patients report at least one first-degree relative with the condition.

The hypothesis that deprivation of sunlight was a key ingredient in the seasonal variation led to the suggested treatment of light therapy. Controlled trials have identified artificial light intensities between 2,500 and 10,000 lux as effective antidepressant treatment.[32] Treatment is administered by a light box (fluorescent tubes behind a plastic diffusing screen) for thirty minutes to two hours, once to twice daily. Results are frequently found in two to four days, but may require up to several weeks in some patients. Side effects include headache, eye strain, fatigue, and overactivation.[32] They usually respond to the patient's sitting further from the light source or decreasing the duration of exposure.

Notes

1. Cross National Collaborative Group. (1992). The changing rate of major depression: Cross-national comparisons. *Journal of the American Medical Association*, 268(21), 3098.

2. Regier, D. A., & Kaelber, C. T. (1995). The Epidemiologic Catchment Area (ECA) program: Studying the prevalence and incidence of psychopathology. In M.T. Tsuang, M. Tohen, & B. Zahner (Eds.), *Textbook in psychiatric epidemiology*. New York: Wiley-Liss.

3. Regier, D. A., Narrow, W. E., Rae, D. S., et al. (1993). The de facto U.S. mental and addictive disorders service system. *Archives of General Psychiatry, 50*.

4. Bourdon, K. H., Rae, M. A., Narrow, W. E., et al. (1994). National prevalence and treatment of mental and addictive disorders. In R. W. Manderscheid & M. A. Sonnenschein (Eds.), *Mental health, United States, 1994*. Washington D.C.: U.S. Government Printing Office.

5. Regier, D. A., Farmer, M. E., Rae, D. S., et al. (1993). One month prevalence of mental disorders in the United States and sociodemographic characteristics: The Epidemiologic Catchment Area study. *Acta Psychiatrica Scandinavica, 88*, 35.

6. Kaelber, C. T., Moul, D. E., & Farmer, M. E. (1995). Epidemiology of depression. In E. Becker & W. Leber (Eds.), *Handbook of depression*. New York: Guilford.

7. Pajer, K. (1995). New strategies in the treatment of depression in women. *Journal of Clinical Psychiatry, 56*(Suppl. 2), 30.

8. Mortola, J. F. (1996). Recent developments in premenstrual syndrome. In *The proceedings of mood and hormonal changes across the life cycle in women, Third international conference on refractory depression*. Ohio: Current Therapeutics.

9. American Psychiatric Association (1994). *Diagnostic and statistical manual of mental disorders* (4th ed.). Washington D.C.: American Psychiatric Association.

10. Mortola, J. F., Girton, L., Beck, L., et al. (1989). Depressive episodes in premenstrual syndrome. *American Journal of Obstetrics and Gynecology, 161*, 1682.

11. Wood, S. H., Mortola, J. F., Chan, A. F., et al. (1992). Treatment of premenstrual syndrome with fluoxetine: A double-blind, placebo-controlled crossover study. *Obstetrics and Gynecology, 80*, 339.

12. Sherwin, B. B. (1996). Mood disturbances and sex hormone changes in post-menopausal women. In *The proceedings of mood and hormonal changes across the life cycle in women, Third international conference on refractory depression*. Ohio: Current Therapeutics.

13. Smith, S., Rinehart, J. S., Ruddock, V. E., et al. (1987). Treatment of premenstrual syndrome with alprazolam: Results of a double-blind, placebo-controlled, randomized crossover clinical trial. *Obstetrics and Gynecology, 70*, 37.

14. Altshuler, L. L. (May 5, 1996). *Mood and anxiety disorders in pregnancy*. Mood and Anxiety Disorders in the Childbearing Years, A.P.A. Annual Meeting, New York, New York.

15. Cohen, L. S. (May 5, 1996). *Treatment of psychiatric illness during pregnancy*. Mood and Anxiety Disorders in the Childbearing Years, A.P.A. Annual Meeting, New York, New York.

16. Cohen, L. S., Friedman, J. M., Jefferson, J. W., et al. (1994). A re-evaluation of risk of in utero exposure to lithium. *Journal of the American Medical Association, 271*(2), 146.

17. Miller, L. J. (1994). Use of electroconvulsive therapy during pregnancy. *Hospital and Community Psychiatry, 45*, 444.

18. Sichel, D. (May 5, 1996). *Postpartum mood and anxiety disorders: Diagnosis and treatment*. Mood and Anxiety Disorders in the Childbearing Years, A.P.A. Annual Meeting, New York, New York.

19. Winn, S. S., Stowe, Z. N., & Nemeroff, C. B. (1996). Diagnosis and treatment of postpartum depression. *Clinical Advances in the Treatment of Psychiatric Disorders, 10*(1), 1.

20. Miller, L. J. (1996). Beyond the blues: Postpartum reactivity and the biology of attachment. *Primary Psychiatry, 35*.

21. Kumar, R., & Robson, K. M. (1984). A prospective study of emotional disorders in childbearing women. *British Journal of Psychiatry, 144*, 35.

22. Thorpe, K., Golding, J., MacGillivray, I., et al. (1991). Comparison of prevalence of depression in mothers of twins and mothers of singletons. *British Medical Journal, 302*, 875.

23. Schmidt, P. J., & Rubinow, D. R. (1995). Menopause-related affective disorders: A justification for further study. *American Journal of Psychiatry, 148*(7), 844.

24. Prange, A. J. (1972). Estrogen may well affect response to anti-depressants. *Journal of the American Medical Association, 219*, 143.

25. Myers, J. K., Weissman, M. M., Tischsler, G. L., et al. (1984). Six month prevalence of psychiatric disorders in three communities, 1980–82. *Archives of General Psychiatry, 41*, 959.

26. Fernandez, F., Levy, J. K., Lachar, B. L., et al. (1995). The management of depression and anxiety in the elderly. *Journal of Clinical Psychiatry, 56*(Suppl. 2), 20.

27. NIH Consensus Development Panel on Depression in Late Life. (1992). Diagnosis and treatment of depression in late life. *Journal of the American Medical Association, 268*(8), 1018.

28. Migliorelli, R., Teson, A., Sabe, L., et al. (1995). Prevalence and correlates of dysthymia and major depression among patients with Alzheimer's disease. *American Journal of Psychiatry, 152,* 37.

29. Duffy, J. D., & Coffey, C. E. (1996). Depression in Alzheimer's disease. *Psychiatric Annals, 26*(5), 269.

30. Oren, D. A., & Rosenthal, N. E. (1992). Seasonal affective disorders. In E. S. Paykel (Ed.), *Handbook of affective disorders* (2nd ed.). London: Churchill Livingstone.

31. Rosenthal, N. E., Sack, D. A., Gillin, J. C., et al. (1984). Seasonal affective disorder: A description of the syndrome and preliminary findings with light therapy. *Archives of General Psychiatry, 41,* 72.

32. Rosenthal, N. E. (November 18, 1995). *SAD: Biology and treatment.* Presented at the Eighth U.S. Psychiatric and Mental Health Congress, New York, New York.

Chapter 7

Understanding Depression
Five Models

The challenge of understanding depression and providing relief to the afflicted population has brought together a diverse group of investigators with varied backgrounds and differing primary focuses. Approaches to conceptualizing depression have taken the form of biological investigations, genetic studies, psychoanalytic theories, and animal models, as well as cognitive and behavioral formulations. Often the approach has evolved from consideration of a particular form of depression, or from one or two of its discrete characteristics, or occasionally from serendipitous findings. This chapter will review the various ways that have been offered to think about depression.

BIOLOGICAL MODELS

There are numerous clues to suggest the likelihood that biological factors play a significant role in at least some forms of depression:

- Depression coincides with periods of known hormonal change: premenstrual, postpartum, involutional.
- Depression may occur in apparently well-adjusted personalities.
- Depressive symptoms have remained constant among people differing in age, gender, race, culture, and era.
- Medications and electroshock therapy are effective interventions for some depressions.
- Depression may be precipitated by drugs taken for another purpose.
- Abnormalities have been demonstrated in a variety of physiological systems in depressed persons.

Not surprisingly, biological research has targeted the more severe depressive disorders. These syndromes are typically "primary" (occur earliest in the patient's course), "melancholic" (feature loss of pleasure, unreactiveness, early morning wakening, psychomotor changes, and anorexia or weight loss symptoms), "major" (full syndrome), and may be either unipolar or bipolar. Typically, they are acute rather than chronic. They may or may not have psychotic features.

The first half of the twentieth century produced literally hundreds of studies examining "every accessible cell, tissue and fluid by every technique available."[1] By 1940, there had been no clear-cut positive findings or useful leads. Over the following 25 years, researchers bemoaned the lack of a generally accepted framework for depression.

In the 1950s, reserpine, a drug used to treat hypertension, was associated with a clinical state resembling depression. The main signs were sedation and psychomotor retardation. The best predictor for this side reaction (which is not the drug's main effect) was a past history of depression.[2] It was thought that the syndrome produced was a result of the depletion of a class of brain amine called catecholamines.

Also in the 1950s, the drug iproniazid was used to treat tuberculosis and was noted to produce elated mood and overactive behavior in some patients. It was found to be an inhibitor of the enzyme monoamine oxidase (MAO). This enzyme was known to play a role in the inactivation of brain amines.

In the late 1950s, the tricyclic (TCA) drugs were found to be effective treatments for depression. Among other effects, these drugs prevented the reuptake of brain amines norepinephrine and serotonin in the synapse between nerve cells, raising their concentration in that space.

Methodological Problems

The generation of useful biological data in humans has posed significant problems for biological researchers studying the affective disorders. Reasons are many and varied: (1) The accessibility of the brain to research in human subjects is limited. (Biopsy, for example, is not feasible for the brain as it is for liver, kidney, and lung.) (2) While identification of the metabolites of brain chemicals in blood or urine is feasible, most substances released by the brain are released by other organs as well, so that measurement of these chemicals peripherally (in blood or urine) may not be representative of brain activity. (3) A closer approach to the brain may be made by the examination of cerebrospinal fluid (CSF). This substance courses through parts of the brain and along the spinal column. The fluid can be obtained by inserting a needle into the spinal canal between two vertebrae in the lower back. This "spinal tap" is an important diagnostic procedure in the identification of various medical illnesses, ranging from brain hemorrhage or infection to some systemic, metabolic, and endocrine disorders. The collection of spinal fluid from "normal controls" (for research comparison purposes) poses consent problems that are usually not encountered with urine or blood samples. (4) Additional factors may cloud the picture: *gender* (e.g., 5-HIAA, a metabolic end product of serotonin, a brain amine, is predictably lower in the CSF of men than it is in women), *diet* (which has been found to affect MHPG, a metabolic end product of norepinephrine, another brain amine, when it is measured in urine of depressed persons), *activity level* (MHPG excretion in urine is increased with exercise in depressed patients), *stress, sleep, body size, circadian rhythms* (the time of day when the sample was collected can affect the result), *phase of depressive illness* (readings may differ in the same patient when manic, depressed, or when severity of illness changes), and *complicating medical conditions.* Even the patient's psychological reaction to being hospitalized may distort the relevance of data gathered to brain activity. (5) The body's drive to maintain homeostasis may lead to a host of compensatory mechanisms, obscuring the desired finding. Finally, (6) for decades, the lack of standard diagnostic criteria for depression has hampered research efforts.

The Amine Hypotheses

The limbic system of the brain has been found to be implicated in the regulation of sleep, appetite, arousal, and sexual function, as well as fear and rage. Many of these functions are disturbed in depression. Before examining the limbic system's abnormal functioning during depression, let's first turn to its *normal* functioning.

Neurons (nerve cells) carry information in the form of electrical currents. Information transfer between cells occurs utilizing chemical signals. These chemicals are called neurotransmitters. Neurotransmitters facilitate the movement of nerve impulses from one nerve cell to another. In different parts of the brain, this transmission requires different chemical facilitators. Neurotransmitters come in three general types: amino acids (e.g, gamma aminobutyric acid or GABA), biogenic amines (e.g., norepinephrine, serotonin, dopamine), and peptides (e.g., cholecystokinen).[3]

Neurotransmitters are synthesized and stored in nerve terminals and cell bodies. When the nerve cell is activated, transmitter substance is released and binds to specific receptor sites, affecting the firing rate of the neuron.

Neurotransmitters are called "first messengers," because they initiate the process that second and third messengers inside the nerve cells complete. Ion channels in the cell open or close to regulate the effects of neurotransmitter substance. Integration of this input to the cell takes place at the level of G proteins.[4] Some have suggested that the G protein is the cell structure upon which lithium carbonate (a mood stabilizer) exerts its effect.

Receptors (specific recognition sites) for the binding of neurotransmitter substance provide the selectivity by which a tissue responds to a specific biological signal.[5] Once a neurotransmitter binds to its receptor, a series of intracellular events occurs, resulting in a physiological change. Substances that can act on a receptor and cause this change are called *agonists*. Substances that bind to a receptor and block this change are called *antagonists*. Presynaptic receptors (those located on the nerve cell before the synapse) regulate the release of neurotransmitters. Postsynaptic (on the nerve cell after the synapse) receptor sensitivity may adapt to the level of presynaptic neurotransmitter output.

Of the 75 (now) known neurotransmitters, the principal agents in the limbic area are the biogenic amines. Cannon first called attention to the importance of these amines in 1915 when he postulated that epinephrine (adrenalin) is secreted when an animal responds to rage- or fear-inducing stimuli. While the monoamines are not generally involved in life-threatening situations, they seem to serve instead to modulate more subtle and complex emotional responses.

Biogenic amines can be divided into two groups by their chemical structure: the *catecholamines* (epinephrine, norepinephrine, dopamine) and the *indoleamines* (serotonin, histamine). Schildkraut's catecholamine hypothesis concentrates on one catecholamine, norepinephrine. It states that "some, if not all, depressions are associated with a *deficiency* of catecholamines (particularly norepinephrine) at important receptor sites in the brain. Conversely, elation may be associated with an excess of such amines."[6]

Norepinephrine (NE) is synthesized from the amino acid tyrosine (see Figure 7.1) in body tissues where catecholamines are found (including the liver, kidney, gastrointestinal tract, and brain, among others). The conversion of tyrosine to NE is a three-stage process involving three different enzymes (Figure 7.1). Once the amino acid enters the nerve cell (Figure 7.2,

Figure 7.1
THE SYNTHESIS AND BREAKDOWN OF NOREPINEPHRINE

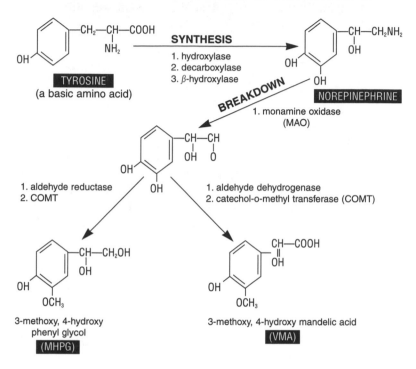

Modified from Frazier and Stinnett [66]

arrow 1), the production of NE begins. The synthesized NE is taken up and stored within granules of the nerve cell (Figure 7.2, arrow 2). The stable form remains stored and is released only when supply is insufficient. The labile form of NE is directly involved in nerve impulse transmission (Figure 7.2, arrow 3). A nerve impulse can stimulate release of NE (Figure 7.2, arrow 4) into the space between two nerve cells (synaptic cleft). The released NE can then act on the receptor site of a second nerve cell (Figure 7.2, arrow 5) to facilitate transmission of the nerve impulse to that cell. The transmitter agent, having done its job, is then inactivated in a variety of ways:

- predominantly by a process of reuptake with storage in the original nerve cell (Figure 7.2, arrow 6);

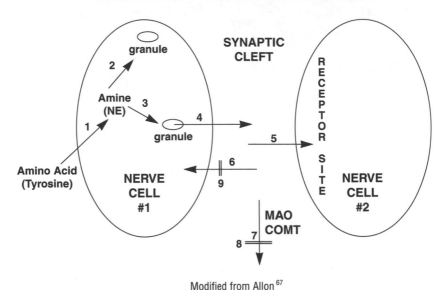

Modified from Allon[67]

- secondarily, by breakdown (Figure 7.2, arrow 7), catalyzed by the enzymes monoamine oxidase (MAO) and catechol-o-methyl transferase (COMT);
- or by diffusion into the bloodstream.

In tissues other than brain, the end product of NE metabolism (see Figure 7.1) is 3-methoxy, 4-hydroxy mandelic acid (VMA). The end product of NE metabolism in the brain (see Figure 7.1) is 3-methoxy, 4-hydroxy phenyl glycol (MHPG).

To take one example, a decrease in presynaptic NE would lead to an adaptive increase in the number of postsynaptic receptors (hypersensitivity). Later on, if presynaptic NE output were to increase, the higher level of NE would interact with a now supersensitive receptor complex, perhaps resulting in an exaggerated clinical response, like mania.[5] Depression might then occur when excess NE down-regulated (decreased the sensitivity of) the postsynaptic receptor.

Two groups of antidepressant drugs have demonstrated effects on this catecholamine system. The monoamine oxidase inhibitors (MAOIs) block the action of the enzyme MAO (Figure 7.2, double-line 8), increasing the level of NE (and other biogenic amines) in the brain. The tricyclic antidepressants (TCAs) block the reuptake of NE (Figure 7.2, double line 9), interfering with inactivation and increasing the availability of NE to postsynaptic receptors.

It must be borne in mind that these drugs have effects other than those described above. Their purported mechanism of action in depression does not constitute proof of the catecholamine theory.

While American research of the 1960s and onward has concentrated on the catecholamines, research in Great Britain has focused on the indoleamine serotonin. This neurotransmitter has been "the rage" of the '80s and '90s; its association with depression has been broadened to encompass obsessive-compulsive disorder as well. Catecholamine and indoleamine pathways are widely distributed throughout the brain. Drugs that increase the functional output of these systems are *stimulants* and can precipitate mania or act as antidepressants. Drugs that decrease the functional output of these amines act as *sedatives* or antimanics.

Phenothiazines (e.g., Thorazine) are useful in treating acute mania. This class of drugs primarily blocks dopamine receptors. They exert their effect on the hyperactivity-arousal component of mania, as well as decreasing psychotic disorganization. The major amine effect of lithium carbonate (an antimanic drug and a bipolar preventative) is to decrease functional noradrenergic (NE) output. Its clinical effect is slower than the phenothiazines, and focuses more on decreasing the elation-grandiosity component of mania. It avoids the sedative properties of neuroleptics like the phenothiazines. Clearly, several neurotransmitters are at work in mania, where dopamine seems to play a larger role than it does in depression. The biology of mania, in fact, may relate more to neurotransmitter imbalance than to neurotransmitter excess.

The biochemical lens focused first on the neurotransmitter. Investigators then turned their interest toward receptors. Most recently, the quest to understand the process of neuronal communication has led researchers to trace the path of the electrical signal inside the cell. At this point, the pathway forks into two avenues: ion channels and intracellular second messengers. However, the receptor itself does not appear to communicate directly with a second messenger.[7] Instead, information is transferred to a "coupling protein." These G proteins couple to a variety of second messengers and may regulate transit through ion channels as well. The G proteins may be targets for hormonal regulation. Manji et al. believe that G proteins may form the basis of an information processing network that integrates the many signals that a cell receives.[7]

What follows is a series of events that can go so far as to entirely modify the function of a nerve cell. It is thought, therefore, that understanding the complex mechanisms surrounding G proteins may hold the key to solving the mystery of the complex functioning of the nervous system and what goes awry in the affective disorders. Since a number of medications (like lithium carbonate) may exert clinically relevant effects at the site of G proteins, understanding these effects could lead to the development of site-specific treatments for clinical illnesses.

Norepinephrine

Nuclei containing NE are concentrated in the upper brain stem (e.g., locus coeruleus), but also are organized into ganglia in the peripheral sympathetic nervous system. One function of noradrenergic neurons is to increase the sensitivity of brain regions to external stimuli. This may play a significant role in the stress response.[5] Many antidepressants have marked effects on these NE systems. Some drugs that mainly inhibit serotonin uptake (like imipramine) have metabolites that inhibit norepinephrine (like desipramine). Some drugs may not affect NE in vitro, but may do so in vivo.

Compensatory mechanisms will down-regulate postsynaptic receptors when the level of NE rises in the synapse. Lithium may act here by stabilizing the receptor, thus exerting a preventive effect in both mania and depression.[5]

Serotonin

Many serotonin-containing cell bodies are located in the raphe nucleus, which has widespread connections throughout the brain. Serotonin (5-hydroxytryptamine) appears to play a critical modulating role in the central nervous system (CNS), dampening a range of neurotransmitter systems and their functions.

There are at least seventeen varieties of serotonin receptors.[8] More than fifty years ago, it was found that serotonin affected blood pressure, gastrointestinal activity, and uterine contraction. With its multiplicity of receptor types, serotonin is thought to play a major role in signaling the central nervous system. Antidepressants, both old and new, have a wide range of effects on these serotonin receptors.

The permissive hypothesis proposed by Kety suggests that both the manic and depressive phases of bipolar illness may be characterized by low central amounts of 5-HT functioning, permitting the excesses of depression and mania by failing to modulate other amine systems.[9] The role of lithium in the 5-HT system (as with NE) may be to stabilize the system.

Dopamine

Centrally, dopamine (DA) is most concentrated in the nigrostriatal region, which is thought to mediate movement (and is implicated, for example, in Parkinsonism). Its connections to the limbic system (which mediates emotion) are thought to play a role in reward-motivated behavior.[5] Neuroleptic drugs (like pimozide) that selectively block DA receptors are effective antimanic drugs. It has been suggested that DA abnormalities are involved in the hyperactivity and psychosis components of mania, while NE abnormalities are involved in the euphoria and grandiosity components.[10]

Phenothiazines (like Thorazine) block mainly DA receptors. These drugs exert their effect on hyperactivity-arousal as well as on decreasing psychotic disorganization.

It seems that each of the drugs that has a rapid and definite effect on hyperactivity-arousal and psychosis in mania also decreases the functional output of DA systems. Therefore, the biological model of mania seems more related to neurotransmitter imbalance and interaction than it does to simple neurotransmitter excess.

Amine Research

Research based upon the amine hypotheses has focused on examining amine metabolites in urine and cerebrospinal fluid (CSF). The assumption is that these findings will reflect CNS events. Major metabolites are: 5-hydroxy-indoleacetic acid (5HIAA), homovanillic acid (HVA), and 3-methoxy, 4-hydroxyphenylglycol (MHPG), for brain serotonin, dopamine, and norepinephrine. L-tryptophan and L-dopa (precursors of serotonin and dopamine, respectively) each increase accumulation of their metabolite. There is, however, a large peripheral contribution to 5HIAA, so this measure in urine may not well reflect brain activity. This may be true, as well, for HVA. In Parkinsonism, for example, there is central DA deficiency, but levels of urinary HVA are no less than that seen in controls.

Some studies have found low levels of 5HIAA in the CSF of depressed patients; however, others show no significant difference. Some investigators have noted a bimodal (high and low) distribution. The matter is unresolved. Similarly, there is no consistent agreement about levels of MHPG in CSF. In urine samples, however, MHPG seems to decrease reliably in depression, with bipolar depressed patients showing the lowest levels.

The Two-Amine Theory

In the ideal world, there would be depressions based upon functional serotonin deficiency, and other depressions based upon functional norepinephrine deficiency. Antidepressant drugs include compounds that predominantly or selectively affect one amine or the other, and some that affect the two amines equally. For example, of the heterocyclic agents, clomipramine (Anafranil), amitriptyline (Elavil), and trazodone (Desyrel) exert their reuptake blocking effects primarily on serotonin. The newer SSRIs (selective serotonin reuptake inhibitors) include fluoxetine (Prozac), sertraline (Zoloft), and paroxetine (Paxil). While generally causing fewer side effects than the TCAs, these drugs concentrate, too, on serotonin blocking.

Conversely, desipramine (Norpramin), maprotiline (Ludiomil), and nortriptyline (Pamelor) are primarily NE uptake blockers. Since desipramine is a metabolite of imipramine, prescription of the parent drug provides some of each blocking effect. A newer drug, venlafaxine (Effexor), blocks reuptake of both amines. An older drug, bupropion (Wellbutrin), has little effect on either NE or 5HT; its major target is dopamine. Each is a successful antidepressant treatment for some depressed persons some of the time.

The two-amine theory remains unproven, but continues to be a rough clinical guideline for the prescription of antidepressant drugs. That there are meaningful biochemical subtypes of depression awaits the findings of future research.

In summary, simple notions of "too much" or "too little" neurotransmitter in depression or mania have not been substantiated. Furthermore, alterations in one amine system may induce changes in complementary or opposed systems. Additionally, presynaptic effects on synthesis or release and postsynaptic changes in receptor sensitivity are likely to be involved. Within the complex interactions of one neurotransmitter system with another, and within the domain of the G proteins that may amplify, integrate, and relay information, may lie the final pathway needed to understand the effect of depression on the nervous system.

Endocrine Studies

Cortisol is a steroid hormone produced in the adrenal glands, two small glands situated above the kidneys; it is secreted directly into the bloodstream. Its production is regulated by the pituitary gland via a hormone called ACTH (adrenocorticotropic hormone). The production of ACTH is, in turn, regulated by the hypothalamus, which secretes corticotropin-releasing factor (CRF). This hypothalamic-pituitary-adrenal (HPA) axis is thought to play a significant role in the physiology of the affective disorders.

Steroid hormone release is increased in response to general stress. Depression has been observed in patients with Cushing's disease (a disease charcterized by excess production of adrenocortical hormones). Treatment with exogenous steroids has produced both depression and mania in some patients. About half of patients with major depression have been found in studies to have increased cortisol levels, an abnormality that remits with recovery.[11] Similarly, hypersecretion of CRF has been demonstrated in depressed patients; so has a blunted ACTH response to CRF.[12] It is hypothesized that the HPA axis defect in depression lies in the hypothalamic regulation of ACTH secretion.

Cortisol secretion is suppressed in nondepressed individuals by the synthetic hormone dexamethasone. Carroll et al. showed that, in some depressed patients, cortisol suppression did not occur with dexamethasone challenge,[13] and Carroll proposed the dexamethasone suppression test (DST) as a diagnostic aid in depression.[14] In this test the corticosteroid is given orally and, by affecting feedback receptors in the brain, normally turns off endogenous secretion of ACTH and cortisol in nondepressed individuals. Lack of suppression, in theory, indicates depression.

Unfortunately, the DST had many false positives and some false negatives, so it did not become a usable standard for identifying depression in the clinic. Like elevated cortisol levels, dexamethasone suppression normalizes with recovery from depression. If cortisol nonsuppression persists in a clinically recovered depressed patient, relapse is thought to be more likely.[5]

The relationship of the thyroid gland to depression has long been a focus of research interest. Thyroid hormones may alter the course of some cyclic depressions, potentiate the action of antidepressants in some patients, and precipitate mania in bipolar disorder.[5] The release of thyroid hormone is regulated by the pituitary hormone TSH (thyrotropin-stimulating hormone). In turn, the release of TSH is controlled by the hypothalamic hormone TRH (thyrotropin-releasing hormone). The end products of the HPT (hypothalamic-pituitary-thyroid) axis are produced when the thyroid synthesizes and releases T3 and T4.

There are multiple connections between the thyroid gland and the affective disorders:

- Patients with hypothyroidism typically manifest symptoms of depression.
- As Prange noted about twenty-five years ago, the response of the pituitary to TRH is blunted in depressed patients.[15]
- Thyroid hormone potentiates the clinical response to antidepressants in some depressed women.[16]
- Research has associated female gender, hyperthyroidism, and rapid cycling in bipolar disorder.[5]
- It is known that lithium carbonate, prescribed over time, can induce hypothyroidism.

The clinical symptoms observed in depression suggest hypothalamic dysfunction (affecting mood, sex drive, sleep, appetite, and autonomic activity). The neurotransmitters that regulate the relationship between the hypothalamus and the pituitary are the same group that has been associated with depression (e.g., norepinephrine, serotonin, acetylcholine). The somatic manifestations of this hypothalamic dysfunction that are best understood today involve the adrenal and thyroid glands.

GENETIC MODELS

It is thought that major depression (and especially bipolar disorder) runs in families. However, inheritance is complex, and a single gene cannot account for all cases. Furthermore, inheritance may not be "pure" in that there is an aggregation of unipolar depression and schizoaffective disorder in the families of bipolar patients.[17] Relatives of bipolar disorder patients are more likely to develop bipolar illness but also about as likely to develop unipolar illness as are relatives of unipolar depressed patients. There seems, therefore, to be an overlap in the inherited susceptibility to bipolar and unipolar illness.

There are four criteria that must be fulfilled to indicate a genetic factor as causative in an illness.[18] They are:

- higher prevalence in relatives of the index case (proband) than in the general population,

- an increased frequency of defects in the functional system under study among relatives,
- a greater tendency for a twin to develop the illness if his or her twin is identical, as opposed to fraternal,
- and onset at a characteristic age without a precipitating event.

History

As early as 1921, Kraepelin reviewed a number of studies identifying hereditary transmission in 70–90% of patients studied with manic-depressive psychosis.[19] Slater, in 1936, noted the occurrence of manic-depression in successive generations, and hypothesized the existence of a *single* (as opposed to multiple), *dominant* (as opposed to recessive), *autosomal* (as opposed to being located on a sex chromosome) gene with low *penetrance* (i.e., the trait is not manifested in most of those with a genetic predisposition for it).[20]

In 1938, Slater published in German the first familial investigation that included a clear definition of the illness being studied: "episodes of both mania and depression, or at least three separate episodes of mania or depression." [21] He found the risk of developing manic-depressive psychosis to be 11.5% among parents of probands and 22.2% among their children.

Hopkinson, in 1964, divided his sample of depressed patients into early and late onset groups, using age 50 as his dividing line.[22] Depression in relatives was twice as common for the early onset group.

In 1966, Perris completed the first study utilizing a definition of depression (at least three episodes of psychotic depression) that is applicable today.[23] He sampled 138 bipolar and 139 unipolar patients. His findings were significant. There was a greater risk for bipolar illness among relatives of a bipolar proband, and for unipolar illness among relatives of a unipolar proband. There was an equal sex distribution for relatives of probands with bipolar psychosis, but a clear female preponderance for relatives of probands with unipolar psychosis. This work laid the basis for the unipolar-bipolar distinction in depression that we utilize today.

Winokur, in 1970, investigated families with a two-generation history of affective disorder and families with no affective illness in any relative.[24] He found that more probands with a family history were suffering from mania upon hospital admission. Winokur hypothesized that a *dominant, X-linked gene* was necessary for the occurrence of a primary affective disorder, and that a second gene was required for the occurrence of mania. The hypothesis derived from his finding that when a father (who has one X chromosome) was the affected parent, there were thirteen daughters with disorders, but no sons! However, when a mother (who has two X chromosomes) was the affected parent, both male and female children were affected equally.

Winokur's group in 1972 went on to suggest a division of unipolar depressives by family history into three groups: depressive spectrum disease, pure depressive disease, and sporadic depressive disease.[25] In each group, the proband is depressed. In the first group, there is a higher incidence of *alcoholism* or *sociopathy* among first-degree relatives. In the second group, there is a higher incidence only of *unipolar depression* among first-degree relatives (hence "pure"). In the third group, there is *no* higher than normal incidence of depression, alcoholism, or sociopathy among first-degree relatives (hence "sporadic"). While this approach has helped direct genetic inquiry, it has not appeared in the classification manuals for affective disorders.

Genetic Research Strategies

There have been four approaches in the quest to define hereditary vulnerability to depression. In *twin studies*, investigators compare monozygotic (identical) twin pairs with dizygotic (fraternal) twins. Identical twins share all genes, while fraternal twins are genetically similar—but not identical. When twins have been reared together, they are assumed to share a similar environment. Therefore, when identical twins have a trait in common at a far higher rate than fraternal pairs, genetic factors are expected to be involved. Twin studies have consistently shown identical twins to be more concordant for affective disorder than fraternal twins.

In *adoption studies*, the biological relatives who have been raised separately from probands are examined. If the trait follows the biological kinship rather than the environmental difference, genetic factors are supported. While less impressive for biological relatives than for identical twins, concordance (sharing a trait) is more commonly related to "nature" than to "nurture."[26]

In *family studies*, a trait is suspected to be genetic if it is concentrated in a relatively limited number of families. Kallmann, in 1952, found a risk of 23.5% for parents' developing manic-depressive illness if the proband was manic-depressive, and a risk of 23% for siblings.[27] A family study by Winokur's group, in 1969, excited the field by suggesting X-chromosome, single-locus transmission of bipolar illness.[28] Later analyses by Gershon and others did not support the finding.[17] This has been a common pattern for single-gene studies.

The final approach involves *linkage studies*. Two genes on two separate chromosomes are inherited together 50% of the time. When two genes are a considerable distance apart, but still on the same chromosome, inheritance is also roughly 50%, based upon recombination frequency. *Recombination* is the crossover of a gene from one to another chromosome. Genes close together on the same chromosome survive recombination more than half the time and are said to be "linked." Recombination frequency (how often genes are inherited together) can, therefore, be a way of locating (*mapping*) a trait. The gene with the known location is called a *marker* for the unknown gene. Linkage studies in affective disorder, therefore, attempt to identify families with both a mood disorder and the marker trait.

For example, Mendlewicz reported linkage of a type of colorblindness (protan and deutan) and a type of blood group (XgA) to bipolar pedigrees.[29] The large genetic distance on the X chromosome between these two markers made the two findings inconsistent. Later work did not support the findings.[17] A second X chromosome study examined the locus for a blood clotting factor with reported linkage to bipolar illness. Again, there was no consistent replication.[17]

At present, there is no widely accepted and consistently replicated linkage found for affective disorder. Researchers maintain their optimism that a genetic approach will bear fruit.

PSYCHOANALYTIC MODELS

Psychoanalytic insights into the problem of depression began not with Freud but with Abraham in 1911.[30] He contrasted melancholia and grief in terms of the presence of anger ("unconscious hostility") demonstrated in the ambivalence of the melancholic. The border of normalcy (the grief reaction) is crossed, according to Abraham, once the mourner's reaction to the lost person is marked by anger as well as love.

Freud's landmark paper, "Mourning and Melancholia," was the next major contribution to the evolving psychoanalytic model of depression.[31] Freud, too, began with a consideration of the similiarities between grief and depression. For him, the distinction lay in the presence of a "consciously perceived, realistically lost object" in grief, and an "unconsciously perceived, imagined loss of an object" in depression. Freud defined melancholia in terms of lowered self-esteem, self-accusation, and a delusional need for self-punishment. His conceptualization was based upon his energy model of libido flow. Within this framework, he saw first a real or imagined loss of a love object, followed by the withdrawal of one's investment (libido) in the object. There followed unconscious rage at the object for leaving, an introjection (incorporation) of the object by the "ego," and a subsequent identification with the now intro-jected object. With libido reattached to the introjected object, the rage orig-inally felt toward the lost object was now directed against the self. Freud attributed the self-destructive and punitive behavior he saw in the depressed patient to an attempt to punish the abandoning love figure.

Abraham, in 1927, elaborated on this model when he introduced the notions of *infantile disappointment* (narcissistic injury, primal depression, loss of love) and an *oral predisposition* (dependent characteristics with defects in self-esteem).[32] These factors helped him determine who would react to loss with depression. Rado, in 1928, expanded the notion of predisposition to include those who had an intense need to be loved and approved.[33] He used Freud's notion of "superego" to account for the self-abusive behavior of the depressive. He attributed the inability of the depressive to reverse this mode of thinking to a sense of guilt related to his original response of rage to the loss. Self-punishment served, therefore, to cleanse the bereaved of his guilt.

The late 1940s and early 1950s brought revisions of Freudian theory. Abandoned were concepts of energy flow, introjection, and narcissism. Neuroses were now seen as overreactions. The focus on loss was broadened to include fail-ure and rejection. Fenichel, in 1945, emphasized loss of self-esteem.[34] Bibring, in 1953, wrote about helplessness and powerlessness.[35] These ideas were an impor-tant jumping-off point for cognitive theorists (see the next section). Klein, in 1945, postulated a normal stage of development (the depressive position) through which everyone must pass (at the age of six months to one year) and to which a person may regress when depression occurs in adulthood.[36] Finally, in 1971, Jacobsen examined the vulnerability of some people to depression and emphasized a defective mother-child relationship.[37]

From a somewhat different perspective, the work of Spitz[38] and Bowlby[39] considered the circumstance of separation as a model for depression. Spitz's "anaclitic depression" paved the way for significant animal behavioral research, which may be relevant to the human condition.

Psychoanalytic models of depression consider its development, define some common underlying issues, and offer a treatment approach aimed at resolving underlying conflicts. These models seem largely applicable to the milder forms of depression, although they have been applied equally to severe and psychotic forms.

COGNITIVE MODELS

The prevailing assumption about the development of depression has assigned primacy to the emotional changes evident in the depressed patient. It was further assumed that the behavioral and cognitive (thinking) symptoms and signs were a consequence of these emotional changes. A group of investigators, beginning from a psychoanalytic perspective, have challenged these assumptions.

Beck's Model

Beck described the transition in his thinking from a psychoanalytic model to the identification of the cognitive changes that he saw as the "core problem in depression." [40] His initial aim was to test the notion that depression was characterized by "anger turned inward." Toward this end, Beck measured hostility in the manifest content of the dreams of a group of depressed patients. Rather than symbols of anger, however, he found a consistent self-representation of the dreamer as a "loser." Consistent with a psychoanalytic framework, he assumed that these dreams represented the dreamer's "need to suffer," and he called them "masochistic dreams." [41]

Subsequent studies, however, failed to confirm that his depressed sample really wanted to suffer. A more parsimonious explanation for Beck's finding was that the patient who dreamed of himself as a loser actually pictured himself that way in real life.

Turning next to a collection of the free associations of depressed patients in psychotherapy, Beck noted a predominance of certain themes. These themes were idiosyncratic to patients with depression and atypical of patients without depression. They were:

- A negative view of the self (low self-esteem)
- A negative view of the world
- Negative expectations for the future (pessimism).

Beck labeled this "negative cognitive set" the cognitive triad of depressed symptoms. [40] The depressed person construes his or her experiences as presenting insuperable obstacles or making exorbitant demands, and interprets

interactions with others as resulting in defeat, deprivation, and disparage-
ment. The self-view is one of being deficient, inadequate, or unworthy,
because of defects of a physical, mental, or moral nature. The depressed
patient expects the difficulties to continue indefinitely. Beck proposed that
the predominance of this belief system was the primary change in depression.

In 1963, Beck classified the cognitive distortions he had observed in his
depressed patients as "paralogical, stylistic and semantic." [42] He later defined
each systematic error in detail; Beck's 1967 textbook on depression named
five qualities that defined the changes he had observed in the thinking of his
depressed patients. [43] (See Table 7.1.)

There are four components to the cognitive model for depression: a set of
basic principles, the concept of the automatic thought, the definition of a
series of cognitive errors, and the elaboration of cognitive schemas. [44] The
cognitive model describes the individual as an information-processing organ-
ism, who takes in data and generates appraisals.

When a depressed person assigns meanings to situations and events, he or
she exercises a negative bias informed by a distorted view of self, world, and
future. These appraisals are accessible to the individual (not unconscious)
and can be identified and examined. Beck named these cognitions *automatic
thoughts*. [45] He characterized them as specific and discrete, shorthand, and seen
as plausible by the patient—in short, a "stream of self-talk." [45]

Within this self-talk, the thinking of the depressed patient typically illustrated a series of systematic cognitive errors: polarization, personalization, and
overgeneralization. *Polarization* refers to black/white, categorical (as opposed to
dimensional) thinking. *Personalization* is an orientation overly focused on the
self, excluding consideration of others. *Overgeneralization* is the tendency to
draw conclusions that go beyond the data available to support them.

Schemas are the rules that govern the thinking of an individual. [46] In
depression, the distortions in these basic elements of thought give rise to the
automatic thoughts noted above.

Beck saw the depressed patient as his own worst enemy, processing distorted feedback to worsen the disorder. As the depressed person becomes
aware of his own sadness, withdrawal, and physiological disruption, he feeds
back these observations, reinforcing his negative expectations and further
lowering his self-esteem.

Beck's model gives rise to a psychotherapeutic treatment approach to
many forms of depression—cognitive therapy (discussed in chapter 10).

Table 7.1
QUALITIES OF DEPRESSIVE THINKING
Global • Moralistic • Irreversible
Personalistic • Dichotomous
From Beck, 1967[43]

Learned Helplessness

Bibring,[35] Adamson and Schmale,[47] and Engel[48] all emphasized *helplessness* as a central feature of depression. Later Seligman elaborated a model of depression in animals based upon the phenomenon of *learned helplessness*.

Seligman found helplessness in the dog to be characterized by passivity in the face of trauma and difficulty in learning that responding produces relief. A naive dog (one who has never been in the situation before) given escape-avoidance training in the shuttlebox (see Figure 7.3) soon learns to jump a barrier on cue to avoid the forthcoming mild electric shock to the grid on one side of the box. However, a naive dog pretreated with inescapable shock responds to escape-avoidance training by sitting down and passively taking the shock.[49] The dog fails to learn that jumping over the barrier produces termination of the shock (relief). A similar phenomenon has been demonstrated with rats, cats, fish, and mice.[50]

Figure 7.3
ESCAPE-AVOIDANCE TRAINING

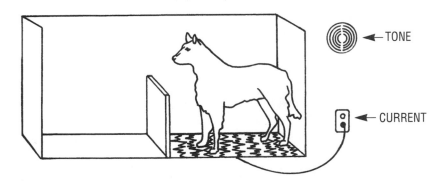

TONE

CURRENT

Seligman found that *immunization*—that is, giving the naive dog an experience of avoidable shock prior to inescapable shock—successfully prevented the development of the helplessness reaction. Once learned helplessness is present, however, the only "cure" was a forcible demonstration (physically carrying the dog from one compartment to the other) that responding produced relief.[51]

The model was extended and applied to human situations. When the human subject perceived that he was helpless, cognitive theory suggested that he would seek to "attribute" (assign a meaning to) his situation. Depending upon the nature of this attribution, helplessness might be acute or long-lasting, generalize to other situations or remain specific, lower self-esteem or not. Abramson, Seligman, and Teasdale elaborated categories of attribution: stable-unstable, global-specific, and internal-external.[52] For example, if the person's attribution were stable (unchanging), global (widely applicable), and internal (irreversible), it would be expected to lower self-worth.

From helplessness, Seligman's attention turned to the importance of optimism,[53] and later to the implications of helplessness for child-rearing.[54] Those who follow the development of Seligman's thinking in this cognitive area will be rewarded with a broadly applicable rendering of cognitive theory.

BEHAVIORAL MODELS

Behavioral models, by and large, reject the topographic catalogue of symptoms other models employ to define depression. Rather, their framework is a *functional analysis of behavior*, specifying the antecedent and consequent conditions that control the behaviors in question. This model confines its focus to observable events. In conceptualizing depression, the primary observable characteristic is defined as a "reduced frequency of many normal activities . . . speaking, walking, carrying out routine tasks."[55] The depressed person's complaints or requests for help are seen as a prominent behavior. Many of his or her behaviors can be functionally defined as directed toward avoidance and escape. (Suicide may be the ultimate example of this.) The depressed person's behavioral repertoire is dominated by passivity. The behavioral model suggests that the central antecedent feature for depression is *insufficient response-contingent positive reinforcement*.[56]

The behavioral model has been modified and expanded by Lazarus[57] and tested extensively by Lewinsohn.[58] Lewinsohn has noted three important aspects of the diminution of positive reinforcement seen in depression:

- The number of potentially reinforcing factors is seen as diminished.
- These factors are less available to the individual.

• His or her skill at eliciting the available reinforcers is low.

In 1972, Lewinsohn and Libet found a significant correlation between self-reports of mood and reports of pleasant activities.[59]

The concept of *social skill* and its relationship to depression was studied by Libet and Lewinsohn.[60] They defined social skill as the ability to emit behaviors that are positively reinforced by others and not to emit behaviors that are punished by others. In this interpersonal sense, a group of depressed patients were shown to be less skillful than nondepressed controls. This approach, emphasizing clinical observation, led naturally to a consideration of the depressed patient's home environment. Home visits followed.[61] (The 1971 pioneering report by Lewinsohn and Shaffer makes fascinating reading, especially for the office-bound clinician.)

Traditionally, behavioral models do not begin with humans. First animal behavior is observed, hypotheses are generated and tested, and contingencies are manipulated. Then the findings' applicability to humans is explored. Animal models of depression have evolved from Spitz's work and particularly his concept of anaclitic depression.[38] Harlow's group performed a variety of experiments involving the separation of infant monkeys from their mothers at birth to produce a depression-like state.[62] Kaufman and co-workers have demonstrated intraspecies differences in the response of monkeys to separation.[63] McKinney and Bunney summarized the animal separation literature and described a three phase reaction commonly observed: agitation (24–36 hours), decreased activity (five to six days), and spontaneous recovery in stages, alternating with depression.[64] A more comprehensive report on the impact of animal models was accomplished by McKinney in 1988.[65]

Today, pure behavior therapy is less commonly encountered in the clinic; the cognitive and behavioral schools have made a marriage of convenience, producing cognitive-behavior therapy. This approach to depression combines the structure and emphasis on habits contributed by the behaviorists with the focus on distorted thinking contributed by the cognitive school.

Notes

1. Cleghorn, R. A., & Curtis, G. C. (1959). Psychosomatic accompaniments of latent and manifest depressive affects. *Canadian Psychiatric Association Journal, 4* (Suppl.), 513.
2. Winokur, G. (1982). *Depression: The facts.* New York: Oxford University Press.
3. Hedaya, R. (1996). *Understanding biological psychiatry.* New York: Norton.

4. Manji, H. K., Guang, C., Shimon, H., et al. (1995). Guanine nucleotide binding proteins in bipolar affective disorder. *Archives of General Psychiatry, 52*, 135.

5. Goodwin, F. K., & Jamison, K. R. (1990). *Manic-depressive illness*. New York: Oxford University Press.

6. Schildkraut, J. J. (1965). The catecholamine hypothesis of the affective disorders: A review of supporting evidence. *American Journal of Psychiatry, 122*, 509.

7. Manji, H. K. (1992). G proteins: Implications for psychiatry. *American Journal of Psychiatry, 149*(6), 746.

8. Shelton, R. C. (May, 1996). Serotonin receptors: Subtypes and clinical significance. *Brainwaves, 1*.

9. Kety, S. (1971). Brain amines and affective disorders: An overview. In B. T. Ho & W. M. McIsaac (Eds.), *Brain chemistry and mental disease*. New York: Plenum.

10. Goodwin, F. K., & Sack, R. L. (1974). Central dopamine function in affective illness: Evidence from precursors, enzyme inhibitors, and studies of central dopamine turnover. In E. Usdin (Ed.), *The neuropsychopharmacology of monoamines and their regulatory enzymes*. New York: Raven Press.

11. Board, F., Persky, H., & Hamburg, D. A. (1956). Psychological stress and endocrine functions: Blood levels of adrenocortical and thyroid hormones in acutely disturbed patients. *Psychosomatic Medicine, 18*, 324.

12. Nemeroff, C. B. (1988). The role of corticotropin-releasing factor in the pathogenesis of major depression. *Pharmacopsychiatry, 21*, 76.

13. Carroll, B. J., Martin, F. I., & Davies, B. (1968). Resistance to suppression by dexamethasone of plasma 11-OH.C.S. levels in severe depressive illness. *British Medical Journal, 3*, 285.

14. Carroll, B. J. (1982). The dexamethasone suppression test for melancholia. *British Medical Journal, 140*, 292.

15. Prange, A. J., Lara, P. P., Wilson, C. C., et al. (1972). Effect of thyrotropin-releasing hormone in depression. *Lancet, 2*, 999.

16. Prange, A. J., Wilson, I. C., Rabon, A. M., et al. (1969). Enhancement of imipramine antidepressant activity by thyroid hormone. *American Journal of Psychiatry, 126*, 457.

17. Gershon, E. S. (1995). Recent developments in genetics of bipolar illness. In G. L. Gessa, W. Fratta, L. Pani et al. (Eds.), *Proceedings of the eighth Sardinian conference on neuroscience*. New York: Raven Press.

18. Hanna, B.L. (1965). Genetic studies of family units. In J. O. Neel, M. W. Shaw, & W. J. Schull (Eds.), *Genetics and the epidemiology of chronic diseases*. Washington D.C.: U.S. Government Printing Office.

19. Kraepelin, E. (1921). *Manic depressive insanity and paranoia*. Edinburgh: Livingstone.

20. Slater, E. (1936). The inheritance of manic-depressive insanity. *Proceedings of the Royal Medical Society, 29*, 39.

21. Slater, E. (1938). Zur Erbpathologie des manisch-depressiven Irreseins: Die Eltern und Kinder von Manisch-Depressiven. *Zeitschrift Ges. Neurologie und Psychiatrie, 163,*1.

22. Hopkinson, G. (1964). A genetic study of affective illness in patients over fifty. *British Journal of Psychiatry, 110,* 244.

23. Perris, C. (1966). A study of bipolar (manic-depressive) and unipolar recurrent depressive psychoses. *Acta Psychiatrica Scandinavica, 42* (Suppl.), 1.

24. Winokur, G. (1970). Genetic findings and methodological considerations in manic-depressive disease. *British Journal of Psychiatry, 117,* 267.

25. Marten, S. A., Cadoret, R. J., Winokur, G., et al. (1972). Unipolar depression: A family history study. *Biological Psychiatry, 4,* 205.

26. Nurnberger, J. I., Galdin, L. R., & Gershon, E. S. (1994). Genetics of psychiatric disorders. In G. Winokur & P.J. Clayton (Eds.), *The medical basis of psychiatry.* Philadelphia: Saunders.

27. Kallmann, F. (1952). Genetic aspects of psychosis. In Millbank Memorial Fund, *Biology of mental health and disease.* New York: Hoeber.

28. Reich, T. Clayton, P., & Winokur, G. (1969). Family history studies: V. The genetics of mania. *American Journal of Psychiatry, 125,* 1358.

29. Mendlewicz, J., & Fleiss, J. L. (1974). Linkage studies with X-chromosome markers in bipolar (manic-depressive) illness. *Biological Psychiatry, 9,* 261.

30. Abraham, K. (1911/1968). Notes on the psychoanalytical investigation and treatment of manic-depressive insanity and allied conditions. In W. Gaylin (Ed.), *The meaning of despair.* New York: Science House.

31. Freud, S. (1917). Mourning and melancholia. In J. Strachey (Ed. and Trans.), *The complete psychological works of Sigmund Freud* (Vol. 14, pp. 237–258). New York: Norton.

32. Abraham, K. (1927). A short study of the development of the libido. In *Selected Papers of Karl Abraham.* London: Hogarth.

33. Rado, S. (1928/1968). Psychodynamics of depression from the etiological point of view. In W. Gaylin (Ed.), *The meaning of despair.* New York: Science House.

34. Fenichel, O. (1945/1968). Depression and mania. In W. Gaylin (Ed.), *The meaning of despair.* New York: Science House.

35. Bibring, E. (1953). The mechanism of depression. In P. Greenacre (Ed.), *Affective disorders.* New York: International Universities Press.

36. Klein, M. (1945/1968). A contribution to the psychogenesis of manic-depressive states. In W. Gaylin (Ed.), *The meaning of despair.* New York: Science House.

37. Jacobsen, E. (1971). *Depression: Comparative studies of normal, neurotic, and psychotic conditions.* New York: International Universities Press.

38. Spitz, R. (1946). Anaclitic depression. *Psychoanalytic Study of the Child, 2,* 313.

39. Bowlby, J. (1973). *Separation.* New York: Basic Books.

40. Beck, A. T. (1970). The core problem in depression: The cognitive triad. *Science and Psychoanalysis, 17,* 47.

41. Beck, A. T., & Ward, C. H. (1961). Dreams of depressed patients: Characteristic themes in manifest content. *Archives of General Psychiatry, 5,* 462.

42. Beck, A. T. (1963). Thinking and depression: I. Idiosyncratic content and cognitive distortions. *Archives of General Psychiatry, 9,* 324.

43. Beck, A. T. (1967). *Depression: Clinical, experimental and theoretical aspects.* New York: Harper and Row.

44. Schuyler, D. (1991). *A practical guide to cognitive therapy.* New York: Norton.

45. Beck, A. T. (1976). *Cognitive therapy and the emotional disorders.* New York: International Universities Press.

46. Beck, A. T. (1964). Thinking and depression. II. Theory and therapy. *Archives of General Psychiatry, 10,* 561.

47. Adamson, J. D., & Schmale, A. H. (1965). Object loss, giving up and the onset of psychiatric disease. *Psychosomatic Medicine, 227,* 557.

48. Engel, G. L. (1968). A life setting conducive to illness: The giving-up-given-up complex. *Bulletin of the Menninger Clinic, 32,* 355.

49. Seligman, M. E. P., & Maier, S. (1967). Failure to escape traumatic shock. *Journal of Experimental Psychology, 74,* 1.

50. Seligman, M. E. P. (1972). Learned helplessness. *Annual Review of Medicine, 23,* 207.

51. Seligman, M. E. P. (1975). *Helplessness: On depression, development and death.* San Francisco: Freeman.

52. Abramson, L. Y., Seligman, M. E. P., & Teasdale, J. D. (1978). Learned helplessness in humans: Critique and reformulation. *Journal of Abnormal Psychology, 87(1),* 49.

53. Seligman, M. E. P. (1991). *Learned optimism.* New York: Knopf.

54. Seligman, M. E. P. (1995). *The optimistic child.* New York: Knopf.

55. Ferster, C. B. (1974). Behavioral approaches to depression. In R. Friedman & M. M. Katz (Eds.), *The psychology of depression.* Washington D.C.: Winston.

56. Moss, G. R., & Boren, J. H. (1972). Depression as a model for behavioral analysis. *Comprehensive Psychiatry, 13,* 581.

57. Lazarus, A. (1968). Learning theory and the treatment of depression. *Behavioral Research and Therapy, 6,* 83.

58. Lewinsohn, P. M. (1974). A behavioral approach to depression. In R. J. Friedman & M. M. Katz (Eds.), *The psychology of depression.* Washington D.C.: Winston.

59. Lewinsohn, P. M., & Libet, J. (1972). Pleasant events, activity schedules and depression. *Journal of Abnormal Psychology, 79,* 291.

60. Libet, J., & Lewinsohn, P. M. (1973). Concept of social skill with special reference to the behavior of depressed persons. *Journal of Consulting and Clinical Psychology, 40,* 304.

61. Lewinsohn, P. M., & Shaffer, M. (1971). The use of home observations as an integral part of the treatment of depression: Preliminary report and case studies. *Journal of Consulting and Clinical Psychology, 37,* 87.

62. Seay, B., Hanson, E., & Harlow, H. F. (1962). Mother-infant separation in monkeys. *Journal of Child Psychology and Psychiatry, 3,* 123.

63. Rosenblum, L. A., & Kaufman, I. C. (1968). Variations in infant development and response to maternal loss in monkeys. *American Journal of Orthopsychiatry, 83,* 418.

64. McKinney, W. T., & Bunney, W. E. (1969). Animal model of depression. I. Review of evidence: Implications for research. *Archives of General Psychiatry, 21,* 240.

65. McKinney, W. T. (1988). *Models of mental disorders: A new comparative psychiatry.* New York: Plenum.

66. Frazier, A., & Stinnett, J. L. (1973). Distribution and metabolism of norepinephrine and serotonin in the central nervous system. In J. Mendels (Ed.), *Biological psychiatry.* New York: Wiley.

67. Allon, A. G. (1972). Biochemistry of depression: A review of the literature. *Behavioral Neuropsychiatry, 3*(2).

Chapter 8

Depression's Fatal Consequence
Suicide

The riddle of suicide has not yet been solved. Is there a chemical event that transforms a clinical depression into a life-threatening illness? Are there cognitive clues that hide within the thinking changes in depression that predict a suicidal outcome? Although there is no defined "suicidal personality," are there personality traits that make self-destructive behavior more likely in the midst of depression?

The ethical issues raised for those charged with the responsibility to intervene and influence the suicidal individual toward life are nowhere more clearly drawn. Szasz, among others, has contended that an individual has the right to take his or her life, regardless of his or her emotional state.[1] Beck and others have written that clinical depression alters a person's thinking so as to make it unrepresentative of his or her usual state of mind prior to the onset of depression.[2] It is this principle that supports involuntary confinement of the suicidal individual for the period of time ("suicide crisis") during which the wish to die is intense. What is the ethical response—intervention or nonintervention? When a physician is asked to assist a terminally ill person in ending his or her life, is this permissible and advisable?

The clinician working with suicidal individuals has usually confronted these ethical issues and resolved them for him- or herself. However, the suicidal person may have reached a different resolution.

All who are depressed cannot fairly be assumed to be suicidal. And all who are suicidal have not necessarily suffered from depression. However, clinical depression appears to be a precursor in the vast majority of suicidal deaths and it is clear that successful treatment of depression usually quiets suicidal ideas. How do we identify those people at greatest risk? And what can the clinician do to alter the course?

The emotional illnesses can be disabling, but only rarely are they fatal: the catatonic schizophrenic and the anorectic who refuse nourishment; the hallucinating psychotic "commanded" to perform a self-destructive act; the drug addict who accidentally or purposefully overdoses. The most significant mortality associated with emotional illness is found in depression. That mode of death is suicide.

This chapter will discuss the magnitude of the problem of suicide, the achievement of a standard nomenclature, the elusive notion of suicidal motivation, risk factors for suicidal behavior, management strategies for the clinician treating a suicidal patient, and the special problems facing significant others of suicide victims.

MAGNITUDE OF THE PROBLEM

Somewhere between 50,000 and 75,000 people will probably die by suicide this year in the United States, but official statistics will record only about 30,000 suicidal deaths. The National Center for Health Statistics, in 1993, tabulated 31,102 suicidal deaths.[3] This was 1.4% of the total number of deaths recorded and made suicide the ninth leading cause of death in the U.S. that year. The age-adjusted suicide rate for men was 19.9 per 100,000, while for women it was 4.6 per 100,000, a better than 4:1 ratio. For purposes of comparison, in 1993 heart disease accounted for 288.4 per 100,000 deaths, and was the leading cause of death.

Statistics on suicide are derived from mortality data. There are no worldwide standardized criteria. In the U.S., data come from death certificates. Criteria for these determinations had always varied from state to state. In the late 1980s, operational criteria for classifying a death as suicide were established for the first time in the U.S.[4] Credentials for reporting officials vary as well. This provides one powerful reason for the belief that statistics have underreported likely suicidal deaths. A second reason relates to the persistent stigma attached to suicide. The stigma that society attaches to suicidal behavior persists and often is applied uncritically to the victim's survivors. The power of the suicidal act as a "last word in a quarrel" confers a legacy of emotional turmoil on the survivors. When wealth or power can lead to a suicidal death's being certified as "natural" (the official is influenced), and poverty or obscurity can have the same end result (the death escapes notice), it is difficult to accept the statistics as anything but an underestimate.

The spectrum of suicidal death is thought to be much broader than con-sideration of overt suicidal behavior would suggest. Many one-car accidents on clear roads may be suicide. The medically ill who discontinue life-main-taining medication and those who "flirt with death" in high-risk occupations or avocations or by adopting habits with known lethal consequences (heavy smoking, drinking or drug abuse)—these, too, may be located somewhere on the spectrum of suicide. In some cultures in which murder is defined as active and masculine, and suicide is seen as passive and feminine, "victim-precipi-tated homicide"—that is, one male adolescent provoking another to kill him—is a form of suicide.[5]

There is no comparable system to account for suicide attempts. One major problem is the measurement of suicide intent. One potential solution is to employ medical lethality as one indicator of seriousness of intent. (For a dis-cussion of the concepts of suicide intent and medical lethality, see the section on Suicidal Motivation.)

Suicide rates are typically highest in the western United States.[6] Worldwide, the lowest suicide rates (as of 1993) are in Greece, Mexico, and the Netherlands. The highest rates are in Hungary and Finland.

In general, suicide rates increase with increasing age.[6] Among 15- to 24-year-olds, suicide is the third leading cause of death. For men, there is a peak at mid-life and again at 80 years of age. For women, after a peak in mid-life, the rate declines.

Among American ethnic groups, Native Americans and Alaskan natives have the highest rates. In African-Americans, suicide rates peak in young adult life for both men and women.

Firearms are the most commonly employed method of suicide for Americans, with hanging a distant second.[6] Seasonally, suicide rates peak in the spring (May) and again in the fall (October). As noted earlier, men are four times as likely as women to commit suicide. However, the majority of sui-cide attempts are by women. If a suicide attempt is a person's chosen method of expressing distress, the clinician must take into account the meaning of choosing such an extreme behavior. All suicide attempts (regardless of med-ical lethality) merit inquiry. The most common method of attempted suicide is drug overdose.

It seems evident now that completed suicides and attempted suicides rep-resent two overlapping, but not identical, populations.[7] Approximately 1 in 100 of those who have previously attempted suicide will kill themselves each year, and 10–20 of 100 attempters will eventually die of suicide.[8]

NOMENCLATURE

In the study of suicidal behaviors, it seems that a confusing terminology once again has affected progress toward understanding. *Suicide* has been defined as "any act of deliberate self-damage in which the person committing the act could not be sure to survive."[9] A *suicide attempt* indicates the occurrence of self-destructive behavior, with any of several possible motivations. The term *suicide gesture* has been employed to indicate self-destructive behavior, with minimal intent to die and maximal instrumental purpose (to influence someone else's behavior). Some investigators have opted for a behavioral definition of suicide that avoids the thorny issue of motivation. For instance, Kessel proposed "self-poisoning" to refer to suicide attempts related to drug ingestion.[10] This term would include accidental as well as willful poisoning.

The probability that suicidal behavior will occur in the future has generally been called *suicidal risk*. A group of investigators in Los Angeles, however, instead adopted the term *lethality* to mean the probability of suicide.[11] Another group in Philadelphia employed the term *lethality* to refer to the medical damage incurred in the suicidal act.[12] Unhappy with the the notion of a "suicide attempt" because of the implication about low intent, Kreitman et al. proposed the term *parasuicide* to supplant it.[13] Terminology for suicidal motivation abounds. Beck's *suicide intent*[14] and Shneidman's *intentioned, subintentioned, unintentioned, contraintentioned*[15] are only two of the many attempts to translate motivation into operational forms.

Finally, in 1970, a task force of 50 leaders in the field of suicide study was convened by the National Institute of Mental Health. They established a standard nomenclature for suicidal behavior (see Table 8.1). Their system considers three categories: completed suicide, suicide attempts, and suicidal ideas. It requires the evaluation of *medical lethality* (physiological damage incurred in a suicidal act), *psychological intent* (motivation), *mitigating circumstances*, and *method* proposed or carried out. The ensuing 26 years have added little of consequence to the nomenclature of suicide.

One last term remains to be discussed. When a person commits suicide, the essential source necessary to understand this behavior within a life's framework is removed. Suicide research is, of necessity, retrospective. It often involves a *psychological autopsy*—that is, a retrospective recreation of the psychological events and relationships impinging on the deceased prior to death.[16] This inquiry depends upon the recollection of relatives of the

Table 8.1 STANDARD NOMENCLATURE FOR SUICIDAL BEHAVIOR		
I. COMPLETED SUICIDE	II. SUICIDE ATTEMPT	III. SUICIDAL IDEAS
A. Certainty of rater	A. Certainty of rater	
B. Lethality	B. Lethality	
C. Intent	C. Intent	
D. Mitigating circumstances	D. Mitigating circumstances	
E. Method	E. Method	
Adapted from Resnik and Hathorne[35]		

deceased. Often, such remembrances are contaminated by the passage of time, insensitivity to clues, and psychological denial (a defensive reaction to the anxiety evoked by the death). The general state of grief that follows the death of a loved one may hopelessly compromise the value of the recollections of significant persons for the worker attempting a psychological autopsy.

SUICIDAL MOTIVATION

One of the trickiest areas to define in an operational way has been the "intent" of the suicidal person. The assumption that everyone who engages in suicidal behavior is motivated to die was central to the definition of a suicide attempt as a "failure." The motivation for suicidal behavior seems, rather, to be complex and varied.[17] For some individuals, the intent of suicidal behavior is indeed to die. Death may provide for escape (surcease) from an intolerable external situation or an equally intolerable internal (intrapsychic) one. For these individuals, the consequences of their demise upon others are either not considered or not felt to be a sufficient deterrent. Other suicide attempters wish to "escape by sleep"—if they could only "stop the world" for a while and then come back, all might work out. Sleeping pills, therefore, may sometimes be taken in excess with no conscious intent to die. German philosophers have referred to this wish for "cessation but not death" as *parasuicide*. Stengel, among others, believed that suicidal motivation is almost always ambivalent, that the suicidal individual wishes both to live and to die.[18]

If one wishes to survive, why engage in potentially self-destructive behavior? Seiden noted the poverty of resources that must be present in individuals who choose this mode of communication to appeal to others for help.[19] The fact remains, however, that the motivation for some is to influence the behavior of a significant other. When this appeal goes unheeded, however, suicidal behavior with intent to die may follow. There are individuals, sometimes suffering a psychotic illness, who wish to influence another by their death. Motives include revenge, rejoining a dead loved one, or having the "final word" in a quarrel.

I place escape and instrumental action at opposite ends of a spectrum of suicidal motivation[20] (see Figure 8.1). At times, there are elements of both in the intent of the suicidal person. Once a suicide attempt has occurred, a retrospective evaluation of intent may provide prospective clues to the likelihood of future suicidal behavior. Yet, obtaining this information accurately has proven fraught with problems. In the ideal situation, one might interview the attempter as he or she undertakes the suicidal act. Practically, one interviews the individual several hours (or days) later. In some cases, the intervening period may have been marked by a comatose state. In most cases, the level of arousal during this period makes retrospective inquiry difficult to achieve with accuracy.

Figure 8.1
SUICIDAL MOTIVATION: A CONTINUUM

| ESCAPE (surcease) | SLEEP (cessation) | INSTRUMENTAL (via intended death) | INSTRUMENTAL (with intended survival) |

Some people may not have formed an intent prior to a suicidal act (e.g., "I didn't think about the outcome one way or the other"). Others may not recall their state of mind during the act. Still others may choose to falsify their report to serve some immediate purpose (e.g., discharge from an emergency room). The standard approach to the measurement of motivation is dependent upon the answer to the question: "Were you trying to kill yourself?" Clearly, this alone is inadequate.

Another approach has been to infer intent from an assessment of medical lethality. Thus, someone who took a sublethal dose of medication has made a "gesture," while someone who is brought to the hospital unconscious must have made a "serious" attempt. In some situations, medical lethality is indeed a reasonable indicator of psychological intent. A few anecdotes, however, will serve to point out the unreliability of this approach. A woman, wishing to encourage her husband to be more attentive to her needs, swallowed the contents of a bottle of sleeping pills at 5 p.m., anticipating her husband's arrival at 5:30 p.m., as usual. He arrived two hours later to find her dead. An elderly person appeared in a busy emergency room and told the doctor on call about her suicide attempt with three aspirin tablets. The harrassed doctor responded: "You'd need many more aspirins than that to kill yourself," and sent her home. She swallowed the remainder of the bottle's contents and was brought back to the ER, dead on arrival. She was educated by the doctor about medical lethality, but ignored regarding suicide intent.

In considering lethality and intent, there are four possible interactions meriting attention (see Figure 8.2). In the first and fourth situations shown, the degree of medical damage is an accurate indicator of psychological intent. However, in the second and third situations, it can be fatally misleading.

Figure 8.2
THE RELATIONSHIP BETWEEN INTENT AND LETHALITY

	High lethality	Low Lethality
High Intent	1	2
Low Intent	3	4

To assist and quantify clinical judgment, objective criteria have been formulated to evaluate suicide intent after a suicidal act. The approach defined circumstantial and inferential criteria for measuring intent. These factors have been elaborated by Beck et al. to create a Suicide Intent Scale[21] (see Table 8.2). The clinical usefulness of these criteria rests on their capacity to guide a clinician's evaluation of the patient after a suicide attempt has been made. Weisman and Worden approached motivation with a similar emphasis on circumstantial factors.[22] They operationally defined the implementation of the suicidal act on the basis of five "risk" variables and five "rescue" variables (see Table 8.3). They provided a table to enable computation of a risk-rescue rating that quantifies suicidal motivation. How one's motivation relates to predicting suicidal risk has not yet been determined. We will consider the prediction problem next.

Table 8.2
SUICIDE INTENT FACTORS

CIRCUMSTANTIAL DATA:

• Degree of isolation

• Timing

• Precautions against intervention

• Action to gain help

• Final acts on anticipation of death

• Degree of planning

• Suicide note

• Communication of intent before act

INTROSPECTIVE DATA:

• Concept of the method's lethality

• Degree of premeditation

• Self-report of intent

• Concept of reversibility of behavior

Modified from Beck, Schuyler, and Herman [21]

Table 8.3
RISK-RESCUE RATING

RISK FACTORS:

• Agent used

• Degree of impaired consciousness

• Lesions/toxicity

• Reversibility

• Treatment required

RESCUE FACTORS:

• Location

• Person initiating rescue

• Probability of discovery

• Accessibility to rescue

• Delay until discovery

Modified from Weisman and Worden [22]

SUICIDE RISK

Predicting suicidal behavior has bedeviled researchers for many reasons. The task of predicting a "rare event" necessitates lengthy follow-up observation. Predictors, derived from a population of suicides and applied to a sample of suicide attempters, may be of little validity. Conversely, predicting risk of suicidal death from data gathered on a sample of attempters may also be of little use. There is a need to specify:

- What is being predicted: suicidal behavior or suicidal death?
- For how long after data are gathered is the prediction valid (days, weeks, months, years)?
- Are the predictors strong enough to retain their power despite the intervention of drug therapy (e.g., for depression or schizophrenia) or a new significant relationship or experience?

A suicide spectrum can be defined (see Table 8.4). Mental disorders and addictive behaviors are major risk factors for suicidal behavior; psychological autopsy findings suggest that more than 90% of suicidal deaths are associated with mental or addictive disorders.[8] Of the mental disorders, *affective disorder* is the condition most commonly associated with suicide (60–80% of cases), but comorbid diagnoses are common. A widely quoted figure is that 15% of samples of either bipolar or unipolar depressed patients will eventually die by suicide.[23] While suicide in a manic state is rare, suicidal behavior is a serious concern in mixed states, and may be even more common in bipolar II disorders than in bipolar I disorders.[24] Patients with psychotic depression have a five times greater suicide risk than their nonpsychotic depressed counterparts.[8]

Table 8.4 A SUICIDE SPECTRUM
1. Ideation, without a plan
2. Ideation, with a plan
3. Suicidal behavior, with low intent to die and low lethality
4. Suicidal behavior, with low intent to die and high lethality
5. Suicidal behavior, with high intent and low lethality
6. Suicidal behavior, with high intent and high lethality
7. Completed suicide

Substance abuse plays a major role in suicidal behavior. Intoxication at the time of death is a highly significant correlate of suicide (25–50% of cases are alcohol-related).[25] The lifetime risk for suicide in alcoholics is about 15%.[26]

Previous suicide attempts, as noted earlier, are an important risk factor for suicidal behavior. Beck has identified *hopelessness* as a strong indicator of suicide potential.[27]

The association of personality disorder and suicide has received much research attention. Frances has noted that persons with antisocial and borderline personality disorders are particularly suicide-prone.[28] When these individuals manifest impulsivity and aggression, the risk rises.[29]

Situational factors may precipitate suicidal behavior in a predisposed individual. Recent bereavement, early parental loss, separation or divorce, and decreased social support have each been identified as risk factors.[30] In addition, the availability of firearms in the home, any profound loss or rejection, loss of a job, being confronted with a prison term, or a diagnosis of AIDS—all may be situational risk factors for suicide.[6]

A family history of death by suicide may affect an individual psychologically (by identification with, or imitation of, a family member) and/or genetically. Either way, a history of suicide in the family does not auger well for the suicidal person. (J. D. Salinger wrote: "Sons of suicide ne'er do well.") What is transmitted genetically is not known, but Kety has speculated that the factor may relate to impulsivity.[31]

Biologically, we are in an era of "serotonergic dominance." Not unexpectedly, therefore, studies have found evidence of serotonin dysregulation in suicidal persons, both before[32] and after[33] death.

A useful clinical clue is that disrupted sleep often seems to be an antecedent of a suicidal act. In their classic work, *Manic-Depressive Illness*, Goodwin and Jamison have accumulated a helpful group of suicide risk factors (see Table 8.5) that are universal across all categories and can alert the clinician to consider suicide risk in his or her patient.

MANAGEMENT OF THE SUICIDAL PATIENT

It is sad, but true, that records show that most of those who commit suicide were seen by a physician not long before their deaths. Often, both diagnosis and management were inadequately done. Following are some guidelines to formulating an appropriate response to suicidal patients and providing quality care.

Table 8.5
GENERAL SUICIDE RISK FACTORS

- Stated plans
- Delusions or hallucinations
- Mixed or transitional affective states
- Family history of suicide
- Six- to twelve-month period after hospital discharge
- Previous suicide attempt

- Poor medication response
- Noncompliance
- Substance abuse
- History of violence or impulsivity
- Communication of suicide intent to others

Adapted from Goodwin and Jamison, 1990[24]

Locate your patient on the suicide hierarchy. Logic dictates that thoughts precede action and, in fact, surveys find that *suicidal thoughts*, the bottom step in the hierarchy, occur at a high frequency in nondepressed, low-suicide-risk populations. When the thoughts, however, occupy more and more space in the patient's awareness, steps may be taken by the patient to translate thinking into behavior.

An intermediary step often involves *communication*. It has been long known clinically that people preoccupied with suicide usually tell someone directly (or indirectly) about their thinking. Direct communication may take the form of a threat. Indirect communication may manifest in giving away possessions, making other provisions for death, or revealing one does not plan to be present at an upcoming event or activity.

The next stage on this suicide hierarchy involves formulating a *suicide plan*, e.g., shooting, hanging, overdosing, drowning. An intermediate next step is *obtaining the lethal resources* needed to carry out the plan. It is here that a gun, a collection of pills from a variety of doctors, a drive to the beach, or renting a hotel room alone may take on special significance.

The thoughts formulated into a plan result in potentially *self-destructive behavior*. If carefully planned to minimize the probability of interruption, only a chance occurrence may save the patient's life. It is here that the concepts of intent and lethality are of major importance. What is the patient's motivation to die? And, if suicide has already been attempted, what degree of medical damage resulted from the suicidal act?

Once you have determined the seriousness of a suicidal person's situation, it is prudent to ask about *potential consequences* of his or her death. How would it affect significant others? What would he or she gain by dying? This is often a major issue to be considered in the psychotherapy of the suicidal patient.

After you have inquired about the patient's view of the effect of his or her behavior on survivors, tell the patient about the consequences of his or her act on you. After all, the therapist is a significant survivor, too.

Make yourself available, especially to the suicidal patient being treated as an outpatient. Give the patient your home phone number, and encourage him or her to call your beeper at any time of day or night that a crisis arises or self-control slips. Schedule sessions with increased frequency. Schedule phone calls that you, the therapist, initiate between sessions. Stress your availability.

If you have doubt about how to proceed, consult with a colleague experienced in handling suicidal crises. Prescribe a measured amount of medication, even if it means more frequent trips to the pharmacy for the patient. Seek to involve significant others (especially family members, where appropriate) and increase their involvement with the patient.

Conceptualize the suicidal period as a "crisis," meaning that it has an escalating phase to a peak, followed by a decelerating phase leading to some resolution. It is not forever. Discourage the patient from making major life decisions during the crisis period. As is true in depression, the suicidal patient's thinking is not likely to be representative of his or her usual thinking; therefore, major commitments should not be decided at this time.

Alcohol plays a significant role in influencing the behavior of many people who are suicidal, whether "unplanned" (the alcoholic carries a suicidal risk by means of his or her addiction alone) or incorporated deliberately into a suicidal plan ("I'll drink until I'm drunk, and then there will be less internal opposition to my suicidal plan"). The suicidal person must be discouraged from drinking. Even more basically, alcohol interferes with sleep, and inadequate sleep enhances suicide risk; alcohol worsens depression, and adding to the severity of depression enhances suicide risk; and finally, alcohol may interfere with response to antidepressant medication. That medication, for some depressed and suicidal persons, may be life-saving.

Symptoms of depression that the clinician may usually wait for antidepressant medication to treat over time must be attended to directly when suicide risk is present. This means that insomnia may require special attention, delusions may be treated directly, and severe anxiety may need supplementary pharmacotherapy.

While drug therapy may be the first line of treatment for usually drug-responsive depressions, ECT will often work faster. When speed of response is an urgent need in the suicidal patient, ECT should be considered. In some instances it may be a life-saving treatment; in addition, ECT generally has less effect on cyclicity than antidepressant drugs.

Finally, although the patient's expectations for treatment are always a necessary clinical concern, the ante is increased in a situation of suicide risk. Discuss your concept of recovery from depression with your patient. Emphasize that the course of recovery is typically "saw-toothed," with improvement and regression experienced for periods of time *even during the same day*. Note how some depressed patients in recovery infer arbitrarily that regression indicates that they are not getting better and, further, that their condition is probably irreversible. Reassure your patient that this is not the case. Rather, the up-and-down course is a phase that precedes full recovery for a majority of depressed people. Goodwin and Jamison provide guidelines for the clinician managing a suicidal patient.[24] Table 8.6 adapts these for this discussion.

In treating suicidal patients it is necessary to adopt an active therapeutic style and relate to the patient in "real time." Often the clinician will need to initiate more—to be less passive. On some issues, a direct response or even command may be useful.

The usual requirement for empathy is redoubled in work with the suicidal patient. Try to look at the patient's life through his or her cognitive lens, and

---

Table 8.6
MANAGEMENT OF THE SUICIDAL PATIENT

• Increase contact	• Encourage postponement of major decisions
• Stress availability	
• Consult specialist	• Encourage avoidance of alcohol
• Prescribe limited amounts of medication	• Treat depressive symptoms vigorously
• Involve family members	• Consider ECT
• Consider hospitalization	• Educate the patient about recovery's course

Adapted from Goodwin and Jamison, 1990[24]

experience for a moment the feelings that this evokes. This will augment your understanding of the seriousness of the situation, especially if its concrete elements seem unrealistic to you. Be more reassuring than usual. Try to constantly offer hope of relief from constant pain.

Because a suicide threat endangers the life of your patient, the usual confidentiality that is the hallmark of psychotherapy is suspended at this time. Make sure your patient is aware that you will not be bound by confidentiality if that jeopardizes your efforts to act toward preserving life.

Table 8.7 summarizes these issues for the psychotherapist, once again adapting material presented by Goodwin and Jamison.[24]

Table 8.7 PSYCHOTHERAPY WITH THE SUICIDAL PATIENT	
• Relate actively	• Empathize with patient's feelings
• Take more initiative	• Offer reassurance where appropriate
• Be more direct	• Emphasize hope
• Identify patient's thinking	• Explain limitation on confidentiality

Adapted from Goodwin and Jamison, 1990 [24]

SUICIDE SURVIVORS

Consideration must be given to suicide survivors, those who had a close association with suicide victims. They often suffer emotional distress for no cause of their own making. If we take a conservative estimate of 50,000 to 75,000 suicidal deaths annually in the United States, that assigns 250,000 people to the group of suicide survivors (at the estimate of five persons seriously affected by each suicide). This is a number that merits clinical attention.

I have been consulted by a number of suicide survivors and have evolved a loose protocol for their evaluation and clinical care.[34] Their psychological needs differ from those of patients with more usual bereavement due to the deliberate nature of their loved one's departure. Furthermore, society's generally warm and accepting response to mourners is often denied to suicide survivors because of the stigma still associated with death by suicide.

The mourning ritual is complicated in this group by investigations conducted by police, coroners, and insurance agents. Religious ceremony and

burial of the suicide victim may be denied to the victim's family. The sud-
denness of the loss deprives the bereaved of any benefit gained from antici-
patory grieving.

The clinical picture is dominated by *guilt*, usually in the service of finding
an explanation for the deceased's choice of mode of death. Another common
affect is *anger* at the deceased for his or her willful desertion. The death ushers in a period dominated by the *search for meaning*. Candidates for *scapegoat*
include the treating clinician (if present) or hospital, drugs or alcohol (if
involved in the suicide), and a significant other (if present). There may be a
period of *identification* with the deceased, in some cases leading to suicidal
behavior among survivors. The process of grieving may be so overwhelming
as to lead to *clinical depression*. A common consequence of the grief process in
this group is *social isolation*.

In treatment, a good first step is the evaluation of each member of the family to determine who among the survivors would profit from what kind of
clinical intervention. Psychotherapy should serve the individual's need for
catharsis and support, and at the same time be oriented to the patient's need
to find acceptable meaning, return to usual patterns of conduct and relationships, and move on with life.

Particular difficulty with places, songs, news reports, and books that evoke
memories of the deceased should be expected and understood by the therapist. As the patient progresses in his or her grief work, expect the preoccupation seen at the outset to diminish. The special problems entailed in dealing
with society's agents (police, etc.) should be anticipated as well. The therapist should help the patient cope with these added burdens during the time
of grieving.[34]

Notes

1. Szasz, T. S. (1974). The ethics of suicide. *Bulletin of Suicidology, 9.*
2. Beck, A. T. (1963). Thinking and depression. I. Idiosyncratic content and cognitive distortions. *Archives of General Psychiatry, 9,* 324.
3. Gardner, P., & Hudson, B. L. (1966). Advance report of final mortality statistics,
   1993. *Monthly Vital Statistics Report, 44*(Suppl. 7).
4. Rosenberg, M. L., Davidson, L. E., Smith, J. C., et al. (1988). Operational criteria for the determination of suicide. *Journal of Forensic Science, 33,* 1445.
5. Wolfgang, M. E. (1968). Suicide by means of victim-precipitated homicide. In H.
   L. Resnik (Ed.), *Suicidal behavior.* Boston: Little, Brown.

6. Moscicki, E. K. (1995). Epidemiology of suicidal behavior. *Suicide and Life-Threatening Behavior, 25*(1), 22.

7. Linehan, M. M. (1986). Suicidal people: One population or two? *Annals of the New York Academy of Science, 487*, 16.

8. Blumenthal, S. J. (1988). Suicide: A guide to risk factors, assessment and treatment of suicidal patients. *Medical Clinics of North America, 72*(4), 937.

9. Stengel, E. (1969). *Suicide and attempted suicide*. Harmondsworth: Penguin.

10. Kessel, N. (1965). Self-poisoning. *British Medical Journal, 2*, 1265.

11. Shneidman, E. S. (1969). *On the nature of suicide*. San Francisco, CA: Jossey-Bass.

12. Beck, A. T. (1973). Classification and nomenclature. In H. L. Resnik & B. C. Hathorne (Eds.), *Suicide prevention in the '70s*. Washington, D.C.: U.S. Government Printing Office.

13. Kreitman, N., Philip, A. E., Greer, S., et al. (1970). Parasuicide. *British Journal of Psychiatry, 116*, 460.

14. Beck, A. T. (1973). *The diagnosis and management of depression*. Philadelphia, PA: University of Pennsylvania Press.

15. Shneidman, E. S. (1968). Orientations toward death. In H. L. Resnik (Ed.), *Suicidal behaviors*. Boston, MA: Little, Brown.

16. Shneidman, E. S. (1969). Suicide, lethality and the psychological autopsy. *International Psychiatric Clinics, 6*, 225.

17. Stengel, E. (1960). The complexity of motivations to suicide attempts. *Journal of Mental Science, 106*, 388.

18. Stengel, E. (1968). Attempted suicide. In H. L. Resnik (Ed.), *Suicidal behavior*. Boston, MA: Little, Brown.

19. Seiden, R. H. (1969). *Suicide among youth*. Washington D.C.: U.S. Government Printing Office.

20. Schuyler, D. (1972). Suicidal motivation: Measurement and meaning. *St. Bartholomew's Hospital Journal, 76*, 23.

21. Beck, A. T., Schuyler, D., & Herman, I. (1974). Development of suicide intent scales. In A. T. Beck, H. L. Resnik, & D. J. Lettieri (Eds.), *The prediction of suicide*. Bowie, MD: Charles Press.

22. Weisman, A. D., & Worden, J. W. (1972). Risk-rescue rating in suicide assessment. *Archives of General Psychiatry, 26*, 553.

23. Guze, S. B., & Robins, E. (1970). Suicide and primary affective disorder. *British Journal of Psychiatry, 117*, 437.

24. Goodwin, F. K., & Jamison, K. R. (1990). *Manic-depressive illness*. New York: Oxford University Press.

25. Barraclough, B., Bunch, J., Nelson, B., et al. (1974). A hundred cases of suicide: Clinical aspects. *British Journal of Psychiatry, 125*, 355.

26. Frances, R., Franklin, J., & Flavin, D. (1986). Suicide and alcoholism. *Annals of the New York Academy of Science, 487*, 316.

27. Beck, A. T. (1986). Hopelessness as a predictor of eventual suicide. *Annals of the New York Academy of Science, 487,* 90.

28. Frances, A. (1986). Personality and suicide. *Annals of the New York Academy of Science, 487,* 281.

29. Brown, G., Ebert, M., Goyen, P., et al. (1982). Aggression, suicide and serotonin: Relationship to spinal fluid metabolites. *American Journal of Psychiatry, 139,* 741.

30. Blumenthal, S. J., & Kupfer, D.J. (1986). Generalizable treatment strategies for suicidal behavior. *Annals of the New York Academy of Science, 487,* 327.

31. Kety, S. (1986). Genetic factors in suicide. In A. Roy (Ed.), *Suicide.* Baltimore, MD: Williams and Wilkins.

32. Brown, G. L., & Goodwin, F. K. (1986). Cerebrospinal fluid correlates of suicide attempts and aggression. *Annals of the New York Academy of Science, 487,* 175.

33. Mann, J. J ., Stanley, M., McBride, P. A., et al. (1986). Increased serotonin, and beta-adrenergic receptor binding in the frontal cortices of suicide victims. *Archives of General Psychiatry, 43,* 954.

34. Schuyler, D. (1973). Counseling suicide survivors: Issues and answers. *Omega,* 4(4), 313.

35. Resnick, H. L., & Hathorne, B. C. (eds.). (1973). Suicide prevention in the '70s. Washington D.C.: U. S. Government Printing Office.

Chapter 9

Depression's Other Spectrum
Syndromes that May or May Not Be Depression

For a time, my family doctor was a cardiologist who had himself suffered a significant cardiac illness. He took a detailed history, seemingly questioning closely those aspects that raised a suspicion of heart disease. He did an extremely competent physical exam, spending substantial amounts of time listening to heart sounds. And it seemed that, whatever my complaint might be, he always did an electrocardiogram. I believe he came by his "cardiosensitivity" honestly and I was mostly grateful to him for it.

I have been interested in clinical depression for more than 25 years. While I see my share of patients with anxiety disorders and personality problems, my antennae will normally raise at even a hint of depression.

It is with this mindset that I approached four different types of patients who have consulted me over the years. The first complained of exhaustion, the second of generalized pain and tenderness, the third of a physical deformity, and the fourth of a bodily odor. None presented the classical symptoms and signs of major depression, yet each seemed to me, in his or her own way, clinically depressed.

Were these problems forms of depression? Or was depression a comorbid feature? Had the depression been a reaction to the impact of the presenting problem? Would these patients respond to usual psychotherapeutic and chemotherapeutic approaches to depression?

This chapter will consider four clinical problems that reside on "depression's other spectrum." Someday, they may be understood as manifestations of a depressive disorder. It is equally likely, however, that they may be seen as aspects of some other emotional disorder. Or, perhaps, they may be deemed worthy of consideration as independent entities.

One is familiar to the practice and casual reading of most clinicians: *chronic fatigue syndrome*. The second has probably presented to most mental health workers, either by name or in disguise: *fibromyalgia*. The remaining two may be less common in the U.S., but appear often elsewhere in the world: *body dysmorphic disorder* and *olfactory reference syndrome*.

CHRONIC FATIGUE SYNDROME

I was consulted by Rita, a 35-year-old woman, divorced for seven years, with two daughters (aged 8 and 10) who lived with her. Her presenting complaint was: "I have been continuously depressed since I had 'mono' seventeen years ago." Three different family members on her father's side had suffered from depression, one of whom committed suicide. She had three older brothers. None had ever been depressed.

Since her divorce, this bright and attractive college graduate was doing office work, until she quit her job four weeks before consulting me. She was "too tired" to continue working. She felt that the fatigue was constant and incapacitating. She was always sleepy, lethargic, procrastinating, and found concentration difficult. Her relationship with her ex-husband had deteriorated badly, complicating decisions about the girls. She felt frustrated about her illness, because nothing she had done seemed to help. She had previously been treated by three different clinicians, with multiple trials of antidepressant drugs, and three different psychotherapeutic approaches, all to no avail.

Rita's self-view had become fixed: she saw herself as a "damaged person." She felt powerless as a parent. She suffered from "bouts of loneliness." She had little self-confidence.

My working diagnosis was the equivalent of today's dysthymic disorder. Five additional antidepressant drug trials were of little use. Over time, Rita told me about constant aching in her muscles and joints. Her nighttime sleep was constantly disrupted. No matter what we discussed, she returned to an emphasis on how tired she always seemed to be.

After ten sessions, I began to consider the diagnosis of chronic fatigue syndrome, comorbid to her chronic depression. We had found that phenelzine (Nardil) relieved her depression, but had no effect on fatigue. She refused an offer of psychotherapy, maintaining that the cause of her problem was biological and that the solution needed to be a medical one.

She called me periodically over a five-year time span, reporting life events and increases or decreases in phenelzine. I called her recently to ascertain her course since our visits ended.

A sleep study had been done, but there was no definitive treatment offered for a wide range of problems discussed with her. She was prescribed dexedrine, long after the phenelzine was discontinued. It helped her to concentrate and she was able to return to work part-time. But it had no effect on her paralyzing fatigue.

Two years earlier, her muscle aches were accompanied by generalized pain "everywhere," and she consulted a rheumatologist. His diagnosis was fibromyalgia! She had multiple tender points now, which hurt when pressure was applied. She was given a course of low-dose amitriptyline (Elavil), without benefit. She was then treated with paroxetine (Paxil), then venlafaxine (Effexor), each of which diminished her depression, and relieved some of her muscle aching, but left her fatigue unaffected.

In summary, her symptom picture met the criteria for dysthymic disorder, chronic fatigue syndrome, and, later, for fibromyalgia. Despite multiple treatment approaches over a lengthy time span, her fatigue remained the dominant, unresponsive condition.

Symptoms and Epidemiology

Typically, chronic fatigue syndrome (CFS) presents with incapacitating fatigue or exhaustion and a marked reduction in activity level. Objective signs include fever, pharyngitis (sore throat), and palpable lymph nodes (swollen glands). Subjective signs range from headaches, myalgia (muscle pain), arthralgia (joint pain), and prolonged fatigue after exercise, to muscle weakness, sleep disturbance, and neuropsychiatric symptoms.

There may be an abrupt onset of fatigue. The syndrome may or may not follow a recent viral infection. Holmes et al. have contributed the research definition the Center for Disease Control has offered to encourage study of the syndrome: six months of severe, debilitating fatigue, in the absence of any identifiable etiology.[1]

Since many of the criteria are subjective and are themselves part of a variety of conditions (e.g., depression), there is controversy over whether CFS is a discrete entity. Is it a heterogeneous collection of soft signs and symptoms? Is it merely an explanatory label for a group of functional somatic symptoms?[2]

It is clear that CFS may be extremely debilitating. Its sufferers are usually unable to continue their jobs, and many receive disability payments. Often there are impaired interpersonal relationships in its wake. Its course may be continuous, with only gradual improvement, or there may be recurrent relapses, with periods of improved function.[2]

CFS occurs with a prevalence of about 0.3%, and more often in women than in men. It has been considered a "fad disease" and "camouflage" used by patients and their doctors to avoid a diagnosis of psychiatric illness. However, it may instead be triggered by exposure to a viral disease outbreak, or to incomplete recovery from an infection, like lyme disease[3]—or it may be one of a number of syndromes defined by its era in terms relevant to the concerns of the time.[2]

Etiology

In 1869, Beard described thirty cases of a syndrome quite similar to CFS. These cases were characterized by exhaustion, pains, alterations in sensation, morbid fears, impaired cognitive functioning and alterations in mood.[2] The syndrome was called *neurasthenia*; its literal Greek meaning was a "lack of nerve strength." At one time it boasted 75 different symptoms. Today, some of them would be seen as part of phobia, panic, affective, or psychotic disorders. The typical picture, however, resembles nothing else as much as it does CFS.

Neurasthenia was an "upper-class affliction," disproportionately affecting women and "hard-working professionals" in the nineteenth century.[4] When stress depleted the body's store of nervous energy, the results were thought to be seen in the brain, the digestive tract, and the reproductive system. Beard attributed this depletion to the advent of modern technological changes: steam power, the telegraph, and other scientific advances. (Remember, we are talking about the nineteenth, not the twentieth, century!) By the time World War I began, neurasthenia had mostly disappeared.

In the 1940s, disabling fatigue was associated with the period following an acute infection with brucellosis (a disease of cattle caused by a micro-organism that could cause undulant fever in humans). Hypoglycemia, total allergy syndrome, fibrositis, and chronic candidiasis were subsequent candidates for the etiology of this overwhelming fatigue state.[5]

Cluster outbreaks of fatigue-type illnesses were recorded in 1934 (L.A. County Hospital), in 1956 (Punta Gorda, Florida), and then in 1985 (Lake Tahoe).[5] These "epidemics" shared common features of low-grade fever, headaches, sore throat, myalgia, and malaise. Fatigue and sleep disturbance persisted for months to years after the initial acute syndrome was over. Most of the patients were young to middle-aged and highly educated. About 80% were female. It was unclear whether these outbreaks represented transmission of a viral agent or hysteria.[6]

In 1979, a patient was referred to Dr. Stephen Straus at the National Institutes of Health Hospital in Bethesda, Maryland. He complained of severe, persistent fatigue, one year after suffering acute mononucleosis. He had high titers of antibodies to the Epstein-Barr virus. The link produced a viable hypothesis of cause: perhaps the EB virus caused CFS.[7] However, later research showed that there was no correlation between EBV antibody titers and clinical states. In addition, antibodies to EBV persisted for two to four years in healthy individuals (with no fatigue) after acute infection.[8]

Undaunted, researchers throughout the world pursued a viral etiology for CFS. In England, the relationship between an enterovirus and CFS was examined.[9] Others studied human herpes virus-6 in CFS patients.[10] No specific viral etiology has ever been established.

The association of fatiguability and muscle pain suggested that CFS might be a primary muscle disorder. Physiologic research found this hypothesis to be false.[11]

The next etiologic focus for CFS was the immune system. Perhaps sustained immunologic activation once the acute infection was resolved was responsible for the symptoms of CFS.[12] It was undeniable that many patients with CFS had evidence of abnormalities in immune response. There were, however, difficult methodological obstacles to overcome: few findings could be consistently replicated; the specificity of these findings could not be established; and comorbid medical problems or depression could account for some of the changes observed.[3]

Persistent, severe fatigue has been noted in a wide variety of medical disorders, presenting the clinician and his CFS patient with a substantial diagnostic problem. Possible diagnoses include: lyme disease, multiple sclerosis, SLE, primary sleep disorders, hypothyroidism, and Parkinson's disease.[3] The observation that fatigue in CFS was characteristically worse after exertion that was easily tolerated in the past led researchers at Johns Hopkins Hospital to explore another medical link to chronic fatigue, *neurally mediated hypertension* (NMH)—a disorder of autonomic, cardiovascular regulation. After a period of orthostatic stress (e.g., standing for a long period of time), these patients develop severe lightheadedness or syncope (fainting). Patients with neurally mediated syncope develop prolonged fatigue. In adolescents, this syndrome of NMH has been observed to lead to debilitating fatigue, even without a history of syncope. Successful treatment has been shown to lead to improvement in chronic fatigue, cognitive disturbance, and lightheadedness.[13] The investigators suggest that a subgroup of patients with CFS may actually have NMH.

There is a diagnostic test for NMH (the upright tilt table test), which was positive in 96% of 23 patients (vs. 29% of 14 controls).[13] Nine patients reported nearly complete resolution of CFS symptoms with treatment, and an additional seven patients improved. NMH can be exacerbated by low salt intake, diuretics, vasodilator medications, and tricyclic antidepressants. The mechanism of action of NMH is thought to be a paradoxical reflex in susceptible individuals that is initiated when blood flow to the heart is reduced by venous pooling. Treatment consists of increasing dietary salt intake and prescribing fludrocortisone or a beta-blocker to increase blood volume.

CFS and Depression

The psychiatric link to CFS may be a significant one, with real treatment implications. During the 1957 influenza outbreak, Imboden et al. did a prospective study of 600 people susceptible to flu.[14] Twenty-six of the 600 subjects did contract flu. They were further subdivided into rapid and slow recovery groups. The delayed recovery group was noted to have higher scores on psychological inventories, suggesting a predisposition to psychopathology.[14]

Many of the minor symptoms of CFS (see Table 9.1) overlap symptoms of primary psychiatric disorders, especially depression. In a study by Kruesi et al., 21 of 28 CFS patients had identifiable psychiatric diagnoses.[15] Major depression was most common (13 of 21), with anxiety disorder, somatization, and dysthymia less frequent. For the majority, depression was concurrent to or fol-

---

Table 9.1
CDC CRITERIA FOR A DIAGNOSIS OF CHRONIC FATIGUE SYNDROME

1. New onset of severe and debilitating fatigue, present for at least six months

2. No identifiable etiology

3. Objective signs: fever, sore throat, painful palpable lymph nodes

4. Minor symptoms: headache, myalgia, arthralgia, muscle weakness, prolonged fatigue after exercise, neuropsychiatric symptoms, sleep disturbance, abrupt onset of fatigue

Diagnosis requires that the patient meet criteria 1 and 2, plus eight minor symptoms or two objective signs plus six minor symptoms.

Adapted from Holmes et al., 1988[1]

lowed the onset of CFS. In support, Hickie et al. found 45% of his CFS sample had comorbid depression.[16] Be advised, however, that in 25–35% of CFS patients studied, there was *no evident psychiatric condition*. So CFS could not be wholly attributed to psychological factors.[3]

Since the research effort in depression and CFS is still meager, important contributions come from clinicians' letters to the editor, following reports of a study or case report in the literature. Lane et al.[17] note that when structured psychiatric interviews are employed, a high comorbidity rate of major depression can be demonstrated in CFS.[16] They go on to observe that CFS patients generally do not volunteer sad mood or anhedonia unless asked and often reject the diagnosis of depression if it is offered as an explanation for CFS. Lane et al. strongly urge treatment for depression, however, when it is present.

Treatment

Chronic fatigue may be a symptom of depression, it may be comorbid to depression, or depression may be a reaction to the consequences of CFS. In any case, the patient's plight may be eased substantially by treating depression. Treatment should begin by a competent evaluation that rules out other medical causes of fatigue, like hypothyroidism, collagen vascular disease, and neurological disease. Next, the presence of major depression, somatization, phobia, or dysthymia should be considered.

A wide range of medications have been offered for the treatment of CFS. The antidepressant drugs have been tested in CFS, but far more extensively in fibromyalgia.[18] Doses tend to be lower than those employed for major depression. Response may take longer than the typical four to six weeks seen in depression. Responses may be less complete than those seen in depression. Serotonergic drugs may have more anti-pain effect and, paradoxically, less antidepressant effect in these patients than do adrenergic drugs.[18] The studies with TCAs report very few patient trials. The studies with the MAOI phenelzine (15–30 mg) show that 80% of 21 patients had a good response. There are positive case reports involving treatment with fluoxetine, sertraline, bupropion, and venlafaxine, but clearly controlled studies of significant samples have not yet been done. Consistent with theories emphasizing viral and immune etiologies, antiviral and immune-supporting agents have been tried in CFS. None was consistently superior to placebo.[3]

With no pharmacologic treatment having proven efficacy, the door has remained ajar for psychotherapy. Cognitive therapy leaped into the breech. Its basic rationale in CFS was stated recently by Sharpe et al.: "People with CFS exhibit inaccurate and unhelpful beliefs, ineffective coping behaviors, negative mood states, social problems and pathophysiological processes, all of which interact to perpetuate the illness." [19] The focus of the treatment is to help the CFS patient reevaluate his or her understanding of the illness and adopt more effective coping behavior. More patients who received cognitive-behavior therapy (CBT) than "medical care only" controls achieved scores of normal functioning on a rating scale used in one study. More improved their work status (63% vs. 20% for controls). More reported significant subjective improvement (60% vs. 23% for controls) than did the control group. The authors have published a guide to their cognitive therapy approach to CFS. [20] Their caution applies equally to drug therapies and to advocates of NMH: "Although the overall treatment effect was substantial, few patients reported complete resolution of symptoms, and not all improved."

FIBROMYALGIA

Rhoda, a 30-year-old, single accountant, consulted me several years ago. She had suffered medically from high blood pressure, irritable bowel syndrome, and TMJ (tempero-mandibular joint tightness). Her presenting complaint was a lack of self-confidence and low self-worth. She went on to describe a very restrictive upbringing in the American South, family membership in a church that preached avoidance of outside contact, and (perhaps as a result) a lack of self-identity. She saw herself as "subordinate and dependent, intent on pleasing others, and reluctant to express (or often to have) an opinion."

Although there were some schizoid and avoidant personality traits, my working diagnosis was what would now be called dysthymic disorder. She became engaged surprisingly readily in a useful cognitive therapy. Her depressive symptoms responded as well to the prescription of an SSRI antidepressant drug. She learned to view her parents and their community more objectively, to take responsibility for herself, and to combat a tendency toward perfectionism.

Over a two-year period of psychotherapy, Rhoda fleshed out an identity that felt increasingly comfortable to her. She had problems with intimacy, but gradually became able to open herself up to others. More and more she saw herself as a responsible adult of reasonable worth.

At this point, Rhoda consulted her family doctor with concern about increasing fatigue, morning stiffness, a rash, and photosensitivity. A provisional diagnosis of systemic lupus erythematosis (SLE) was made.

Within a month, this connective tissue disorder was no longer a major consideration, because she developed widespread aching and pain throughout her body. Consultation with a rheumatologist led to the finding of multiple points tender to palpation and pressure. Her diagnosis for my patient was fibromyalgia.

By now, Rhoda was sleeping extremely poorly. Overexertion led to work absence and time spent in bed. There were new anxiety symptoms. She had numbness and tingling in her hands and feet. She felt the joints swell at her elbows, wrists and fingers, knees and ankles, but there was no objective swelling. She reported that her hands would get "discolored" from cold temperatures. At times, she lost her balance. More disturbing, she couldn't retain numbers easily at work, had difficulty concentrating, and would grope, unsuccessfully at times, for words.

With treatment, Rhoda's symptoms abated, but did not disappear. She learned ways to cope with the distress that remained. She began daily exercise, took ibuprofen for pain, and was placed on a regimen of low-dose amitriptyline. The SSRI I had prescribed earlier for depression was discontinued. She maintained her characterological gains made in psychotherapy. She had periodic depressive symptoms, but, on the whole, was much less troubled with depression than she had been when we met.

Symptoms and Epidemiology

Fibromyalgia is a chronic condition that features generalized pain, with no systemic etiology. Its defining sign is the appearance of multiple *tender points* at characteristic anatomic locations. Tender points are anatomic sites where pain is elicited by applying pressure.[21] Accessory symptoms (which may or may not all be present) include disturbed sleep, chronic fatigue, and stiffness.[22] Additional complaints are subjective swelling or numbness, headaches, irritable bowel symptoms, paresthesias, and anxiety. Fibromyalgia causes chronic pain and fatigue, but it is not degenerative or deforming, and it has no known mortality.

There are no characteristic pathological changes. There are no characteristic lab or x-ray abnormalities. Some researchers have suggested, therefore, that the syndrome may be psychogenic in nature.[23] Others believe that fibromyalgia may not be a discrete syndrome at all, but rather a nonspecific collection of signs and symptoms akin to chronic fatigue syndrome and multiple chemical sensitivities syndrome.[24]

Fibromyalgia is most commonly encountered in the ambulatory rheumatology practice, but may find its way to the office of a mental health worker as well. There is consensus that the prevalence of fibromyalgia in the general population is about 2% (a greater prevalence than that for rheumatoid arthritis!). There is at least a 6:1 female-male difference (prevalence rates of 3.4% in women and 0.5% in men). The age at onset is variable, but the highest rates occur in patients aged 50 and above.[25] Studies have noted high levels of psychological distress, with depression preceding, co-occurring with, or following diagnosed fibromyalgia. A second significant psychiatric association is fibromyalgia's link to somatization disorder.[25] Whether the two occur in tandem or fibromyalgia reflects a generalized hyperirritability is not known.

History

Tender points were reported to be associated with rheumatism as early as 1824. Musculoskeletal aches and pains, in the absence of arthritis, were called "muscular rheumatism" as early as the seventeenth century in Europe.[22] But it was not until 1904 that Sir William Gowers introduced the term "fibrositis" to describe muscular rheumatism of the back. He described persons at risk colorfully as: "Elderly ladies of blameless habits and elderly abstemious clergymen."[27] Additional names given to the problem were "myofacial pain" and "fibromyositis."

By 1968, fibrositis described a more narrowly defined syndrome of musculoskeletal aching, stiffness, fatigue, poor sleep, and tenderness at characteristic sites.[28] The term "fibrositis" became objectionable because there was no demonstrable inflammation and, in the decade between 1975 and 1985, the name *fibromyalgia* became established. The first detailed, controlled study was published in 1981.[29] In 1990, the American College of Rheumatology published formal criteria for a diagnosis of fibromyalgia: a history of widespread pain on both the right and left sides of the body, above and below the waist, and in the axial skeleton, as well as tenderness in 11 of 18 tender point sites on digital palpation[22] (see Figure 9.1).

Figure 9.1
TENDER POINTS IN PATIENTS WITH FIBROMYLAGIA

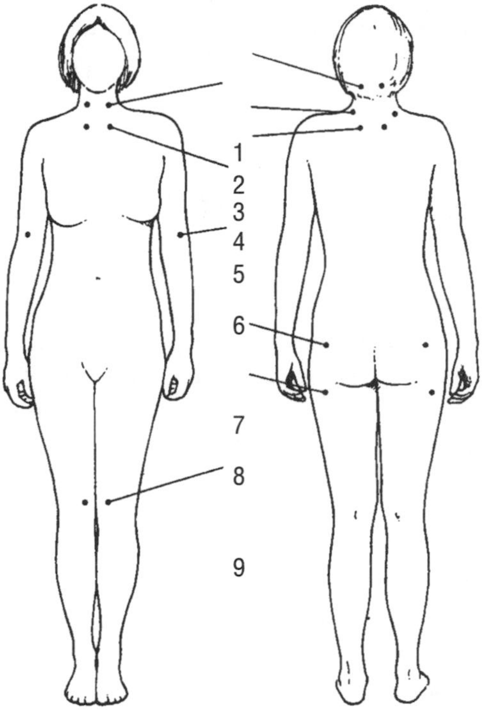

Diagnostic Clones

There are many medical conditions that overlap fibromyalgia (see Table 9.2). Some (e.g., hypothyroidism, hypokalemia, disordered calcium metabolism, primary sleep disorder) can be ruled out by careful history-taking, physical examination, and laboratory testing. Fibromyalgia may be indistinguishable from, or may accompany, chronic fatigue syndrome.

Often fibromyalgia is accompanied by serious sleep disruption; this is one point of confusion between fibromyalgia and primary sleep disorders or depression. The manifestation may be initial insomnia (trouble falling asleep), middle insomnia (trouble staying asleep), terminal insomnia (early morning wakening), or morning fatigue with stiffness.[30] The characteristic sleep EEG abnormality is an alteration of non-REM sleep during stages 3 and 4. Because serotonin has been associated with the regulation of non-REM

Table 9.2 DIFFERENTIAL DIAGNOSIS OF FIBROMYALGIA	
• Chronic fatigue syndrome	• Disordered calcium metabolism
• Malignant tumor	• Hypokalemia
• Polymyalgia rheumatica	• Inflammatory myopathy
• Multiple sclerosis	• Irritable bowel syndrome
• Depression	• Primary sleep disorder
Adapted from Wilke, 1996[30]	

sleep, pain threshold, and depression, it has been speculated that fibromyalgia may be a "serotonin-deficiency disease."[30] More simply, others have theorized that the symptoms of fibromyalgia may be due entirely to experiencing nonrestorative sleep.[31]

Fibromyalgia and Depression

Hudson et al. administered the Diagnostic Interview Schedule (DIS) to patients with fibromyalgia and a control group with rheumatoid arthritis.[32] There was an increased prevalence of depression in the fibromyalgia group, and it usually predated the onset of the fibromyalgia. Most patients with this syndrome have at least a mild associated depression.[25] Raised, but unresolved, are the questions:[24]

- Is fibromyalgia primarily a psychiatric condition, for example, either a form of depression or somatization disorder?
- Is depression a consequence of chronic pain or fatigue?
- Or is there a common neurotransmitter or hormonal imbalance involved in the fibromyalgia syndrome?

When depression and fibromyalgia co-occur, low-dose tricyclic antidepressants have proven efficacy.[33] They may also be useful in treating fibromyalgia alone.[33] However, there is as yet no formal approval for the use of TCAs in treating fibromyalgia that is not comorbid to depression; some of the study findings have been confusing. Given the speculation that low serotonin levels may be present in patients with fibromyalgia, a place for the SSRIs would be anticipated, but the early results here, too, are unclear.

Treatment

Pharmacologic treatment approaches feature the tricyclic antidepressant drugs in doses lower than those used to treat depression. Amitriptyline has been found effective.[33] Although the antidepressant effect of this compound requires three to six weeks, a sleep-modifying and analgesic effect may be noted in one to three weeks.[33] While regular sedative drugs are often counterproductive, low-dose TCAs improve the sleep of many fibromyalgia patients. Their analgesic effect may come from a potentiation of brain endorphins.[32] The recommended dose of amitriptyline is 10–50 mg at bedtime.[34]

A tricyclic compound (which is *not*, however, an antidepressant), cyclobenzaprine (Flexeril), at 10–40 mg has produced improvement in pain, sleep, and tender points.[35] Fluoxetine (Prozac) has been found to be ineffective in treating fibromyalgia in one study,[36] but effective in another.[37] It has been suggested that, for patients unresponsive to low-dose TCAs, supplementary perphenazine (Trilafon) at 2–4 mg at bedtime or alprazolam (Xanax) may be effective.[30] Nonsteroidal anti-inflammatory drugs (e.g., ibuprofen) are typically prescribed adjunctively.[33]

Aerobic exercise (30 minutes, three times a week) has been found to improve sleep, enhance endorphin release, and elevate mood.[30] Physical therapy emphasizing stretching, flexibility exercises, and massage has been useful. Psychotherapy—to help establish a rational understanding of the disorder, to reassure the patient about imagined consequences, and to encourage the patient to live within the restrictions imposed by the disorder—may be the most useful intervention of all.

A ten-year outcome study of patients with fibromyalgia documented its chronic nature.[38] Symptoms persisted, on average, for fifteen years; however, most patients experienced at least some improvement. Forty-one percent used low-dose antidepressant medication on a daily basis, as well as regular massage therapy. Most (69%) exercised regularly. Physician utilization decreased over time.

BODY DYSMORPHIC DISORDER

Richard, a 35-year-old man, was referred to me more than ten years ago with the chief complaint of "depression." He was an unmarried accountant who quit or been fired from a series of brief jobs. He was the youngest of three children in his family. His brother, whom he had always looked up to, was an accountant in a "Big Eight" firm. His sister was a successful attorney, married with three children.

Richard traced the onset of his depressive condition to the age of 15, when kids in school made fun of his appearance. In a collateral interview, his father (head of his own accounting firm) recalled that this was the period in which his son developed severe acne, which resulted in withdrawal and seeming loss of confidence. He related that his son was "unusually handsome" and became accustomed early in life to strangers' complimenting his appearance.

Once he became interested in girls, Richard had real difficulty (he recalled) asking for a date. Through his high school years, he thought daily about his "ugly face and features," even when, by age 17, his acne had completely cleared. He was persuaded by his parents to seek therapy, but he resisted it, feeling embarrassed to be seen sitting in a therapist's waiting room. His pattern was to attend four or five times, and then quit. Two doctors had prescribed antidepressant medications (Tofranil and Elavil), each of which Richard took briefly to no avail.

In his senior high school year, he became preoccupied with following his sister's footsteps to the University of Pennsylvania (where his father had gone as well). After a lengthy waiting list delay, he was accepted at Penn. In college, Richard continued to express dissatisfaction daily with his appearance, typically calling his mother three to four times each day. These calls stressed that he had no control over his appearance, could never marry, and he daily threatened suicide.

He took six years to graduate from Penn, failing several courses and having a few brief ungratifying relationships. In his early twenties, he focused his attention on "growing old too fast," in addition to the ugliness of his face. Soon thereafter, he added a concern with losing his hair. It was just another condition he had "no control over," and he felt he was destined for it because his father and brother had each become nearly bald by age 30. Toward the end of college, and through his early job opportunities, Richard visited the bathroom more than 30 times a day to "check his hairline." When he did so, it would bring on a powerful feeling of despair.

More recently, he had added a concern with a heavy beard—"darker and heavier than other men's"—to his continuing list of physical preoccupations. Richard now had few friends and was leading a rather isolated existence. He had just quit his latest job and was reevaluating his choice of career. He believed his parents didn't understand him and said that "neither did anyone else." His sleep was disturbed, he had little energy, and he had lost ten pounds over the past six months. He had passive suicidal wishes and often cried. There were no overt psychotic symptoms.

My diagnosis, in the terminology of today, was major depressive disorder in an obsessive-compulsive personality. I prescribed an antidepressant drug (imipramine, which he had taken before, but only briefly) and began an attempt to engage him in cognitive therapy. At a dose of 300 mg of imipramine, he was sleeping better, but there were no other changes. A second drug trial (Nomifensine, no longer available) went to 200 mg with a similar result. After ten visits (two and a half months), he abruptly quit treatment, reappearing about two and a half months later, with similar complaints. We began a third drug trial—a major tranquilizer (perphenazine) at a dose of 8 mg per day. One day, Richard's mother called me from home to say that her son had returned home to live for a while with his parents, and would not be continuing treatment. He was taking no medication.

A follow-up telephone call revealed several additional courses of treatment with other psychiatrists, including a reasonable trial of fluoxetine (Prozac) and, later, lithium carbonate, each with no improvement.

Symptoms and Etiology

Body dysmorphic disorder (BDD) is a preoccupation with an imagined or minimal defect in appearance, causing clinically significant distress, that is not better accounted for by another mental disorder.[39] It is classified in *DSM-IV* under *somatoform disorders*. In the *ICD-10*, BDD is considered a type of hypochondriasis. The clinician singularly responsible for educating doctors in the United States about BDD is psychiatrist Katharine Phillips of Butler Hospital in Providence, Rhode Island. Her work forms the backbone for the following description of what we know about BDD. It informed me, years later, of the true nature of what my patient suffered from in the case presented.

This problem has been called "imagined ugliness." It is often a secretive disorder; the sufferer will usually not reveal his or her concern unless asked directly. As such, it typically has gone undiagnosed and untreated. A significant proportion of patients seek nonpsychiatric treatment from surgeons and dermatologists for the alleged defect. Such treatment is often judged unsuccessful, and lawsuits may follow. Even when it is "successful," it rarely solves the underlying problem.

The most common location of the imagined defects are the skin, the hair, and the nose, but the focus can be anywhere. Ritualistic behaviors typically develop surrounding the defect. Patients constantly compare their appearance to others'. "Mirror-checking" is common, as are attempts to camouflage the alleged problem.[40]

The preoccupation often leads to avoidance of usual activities, impaired social relationships, and a disrupted job or school pattern. Some patients with BDD actually become housebound; some make serious suicide attempts; some require hospitalization.[40]

History

A century ago, a similar problem was described as "dysmorphophobia." It was thought to be a monosymptomatic, hypochondriacal psychosis. Other names included beauty hypochondria (circa 1930) and dermatologic hypochondria (circa 1950). The syndrome was once thought to represent a form of schizophrenia, later an atypical paranoid disorder, and more recently an atypical somatoform or delusional disorder.

Parameters and Diagnostics

Body dysmorphic disorder is associated with *obsessive-compulsive disorder* (OCD). Preoccupation with the defect may take the form of an obsession. The ideas may be intrusive, recurrent, and persistent.[41] Associated behaviors may be compulsive. The two disorders may merge and be difficult to tease apart.[42] BDD may occur in the course of OCD. Brawman-Mintzer et al. found the frequency of this co-occurrence to be 8%. In nearly 40% of patients studied with BDD, a diagnosis of OCD is made sometime over their lifetime.[41] There are some differences, however. In BDD, the preoccupations are more often associated with shame, rejection-sensitivity, and low self-esteem. In addition, ritualistic behaviors in BDD more often *increase* discomfort instead of decreasing it.[43]

That rejection-sensitivity is a common accompaniment of BDD is reminiscent of *atypical depression*. In one study of 80 cases of atypical depression, almost 14% met criteria for BDD, suggesting that the association is not rare.[44] Since relationships may be distorted in the process of BDD, and finally avoided entirely, there are real connections to *social phobia*. Embarrassment over the alleged defect leads to a high rate of work absence and job loss. Comorbid social phobia was found in 50% of patients with BDD in a study by Brawman-Mintzer.[41]

The disorder most commonly comorbid to BDD is, however, *major depression*. Fully 95% of BDD patients will have a depressive disorder in some form during their lifetime.[40] It was speculated that BDD may be a symptom of depression. However, BDD usually begins earlier in life than depression does. The gender ratio in BDD is generally equal, unlike the female preponderance observed in major depression. The course of BDD is typically chronic, only rarely episodic, while for major depression the reverse is true. Finally, the repetitive, ritualistic behaviors are not typical of major depression. It is therefore thought unlikely that BDD is a symptom of depression.

It seems clear that the focus in BDD may be a preoccupation or may be frankly delusional. When the focus of BDD becomes delusional, the question of its relationship to schizophrenia is often raised. It is infrequent, however, that the acute or the longitudinal picture is complicated by additional symptoms of schizophrenia. Fully 30% of one large sample, though, have been diagnosed as psychotic.[40]

Commonly, the BDD patient is single, due at least in part to the associated social isolation. The course is usually chronic, with at least a fifteen-year duration a typical finding. The onset is usually early, during the adolescent years.[44] The gender ratio is 1:1.[46] Over the course of the disorder, 80% of patients develop concerns about more than one body part.[47]

BDD and Depression

As will become clear later, some cases of BDD respond to antidepressant medication. This finding gains entry for BDD into a potentially important classification: the affective spectrum disorders (ASDs). Hudson and Pope suggested that these disorders, while not identical in etiology, may share a specific physiologic abnormality.[48] Family members include: major depression, bulimia, panic disorder, obsessive-compulsive disorder, attention-deficit disorder, cataplexy, migraine, and irritable bowel syndrome.

They noted that there is frequent comorbidity among ASDs and that there is some evidence for cross-inheritance (e.g., a high rate of major affective disorder in relatives of patients with bulimia, panic disorder, and attention-deficit disorder). Phillips et al. added generalized anxiety disorder, premenstrual dysphoric disorder, and social phobia to the ASD family tree. Then they raised the possibility that BDD is a long-lost relative![46]

Treatment

No controlled treatment studies of BDD have yet been completed.[47] There are research data available about Phillips' 100-case study,[46] Phillips' 30-case study,[45] and Hollander's 50-case study,[49] in addition to several case studies (e.g., Brady et al.[42]) in the literature. Most reports of treatment with tricyclic antidepressants and MAOIs have been negative.[47] Alprazolam (Xanax), diazepam (Valium), neuroleptics, and lithium carbonate have been equally ineffective.[47]

Serotonin reuptake inhibitors may be an effective choice. Often, a long duration of treatment (12–14 weeks) may be needed before results are seen, and higher doses than required to treat depression may be necessary.[47] Long-term treatment may be indicated, as relapses have been observed with discontinuation.[47] There are case reports of success[42,56] with clomipramine (Anafranil) and fluoxetine (Prozac). So, is BDD indeed a disorder of serotonin dysregulation?

Pimozide has been recommended for monosymptomatic hypochondriacal psychosis, leading to its prescription for BDD, with equivocal results. ECT is usually ineffective. For resistant cases, Phillips has had some success potentiating fluoxetine or clomipramine with 30–60 mg per day of buspirone (BuSpar).[47]

The delusional variant of BDD poses an interesting problem and a surprising finding. A major tranquilizer added to an SRI makes clinical sense, but a study by McElroy et al. demonstrated response of patients with BDD to an SRI alone, whether they were delusional or not![51] The finding raises the controversial possibility that psychotic BDD may be merely a subtype of BDD, rather than a different entity. This is reminiscent of a similar suggestion about "OCD with psychotic features" raised by Insel and Akiskal.[52]

A second surprise is found in investigating studies of psychotherapy's efficacy with BDD. While supportive and psychoanalytic psychotherapies have seemed ineffective, cognitive and behavioral therapies may be useful.[40]

Rosen et al. reviewed the psychotherapeutic treatment of 54 women with BDD.[53] Half received CBT and half had no treatment. They reported that for 22 of 27, their disorder was eliminated with psychotherapy alone (82%), with 77% maintaining gains at follow-up four and a half months later.[53] Their treatment manual is available.

OLFACTORY REFERENCE SYNDROME

Over ten years ago, Raquella, a 30-year-old, never-married Hispanic woman was referred to me by a former patient. Her presenting complaints were: "a bad odor I've noticed coming from my mouth" and "a lifelong problem with depression."

Raquella traced the onset of the mouth odor to early in adolescence. Born in South America, she came to the United States with her mother at the age of eighteen to attend college. Her father had died suddenly of a heart attack when she was only seven years old. Her mother remarried when Raquella was thirteen, and never spoke about her father's death. She remembers being close to her father, and being told that they looked alike. She feels that she never grieved his death. She recalls mother crying "every night for five years," and also her mother burning her father's clothing. Her stepfather was strict with her and emotionally distant.

As an undergraduate in a Washington-area university, Raquella learned English rapidly, but her identity remained firmly planted in her Latin American home of origin. Her mother, an attorney, raised her two daughters and son to believe that education held the key to their success. Raquella's sister and brother, both older, were each married, had children, and had successful careers.

Early in her teenage years, Raquella chewed gum or always had a breath mint to camouflage the odor in her mouth. She was an honors student in high school, and for the first two years she was popular and dated a lot. "People liked me," she said. Despite her achievements, she suffered from periodic "deep depression." When this happened, she would withdraw to her room, stop calling her friends, and cry often, but never miss any school.

After a period of adjustment, she did well in college, but her social life was limited. There was a constant concern that others were aware of, and reacting to, her mouth odor. She graduated and began to pursue a career in architecture. She obtained a job with a highly respected firm, but became concerned that she was in her late twenties with no prospect of marriage and children, both of which she dearly wanted.

Three years before we met, she became acutely depressed and was hospitalized and treated with an antidepressant drug. She recovered but had lost significant weight. Sleep was a continuing problem because her "mouth burned, her tongue hurt and she was aware of a bad odor." Despite her low body weight, she "felt fat" and had a "horrible self-image." As part of her outpatient treatment after being discharged from the hospital, she had a trial of Orap (pimozide). Her depressive symptoms worsened, and the mouth odor persisted.

Six months before she came to my office, she again became acutely depressed. Her mother was by now living in Chicago, and my patient was hospitalized there and treated with ECT. She was discharged on amitriptyline (Elavil) and alprazolam (Xanax). She had recently started smoking cigarettes "to camouflage the odor."

Prior to seeing me, she started a medical workup at the National Institutes of Health Hospital to pursue the source of her mouth odor. I received a copy of their report that opined that the odor problem was psychological, since it could not be detected by them or their instruments. She has diligently visited the dentist for oral prophylaxis care every six months.

My diagnostic impression was the equivalent of major depressive disorder. I saw her concern with halitosis as a symptom. I wondered whether she might have a borderline personality disorder. To start, I prescribed no medication and began a modified cognitive therapy approach with her.

For the first month, she talked mainly about feeling depressed and her preoccupation with the odor coming from her mouth and the social limitations that resulted. She felt "cheated" and guilty for not living up to mother's high expectations for her. She spent a weekend with her mother in Chicago, and we talked at length about her views of mother and herself, and pointed out distortions. Session ten was the first in which her mouth odor was not mentioned.

She asked many questions, illustrating her system of beliefs and superstitions about others as well as herself. We discussed issues of sexuality. After three months of weekly psychotherapy, we had redefined her main problem as her view of herself. She noted a return of her appetite and more interest in her work. She began a relationship with a man at work. In the fourth month of therapy she slipped, becoming noticeably more depressed, and her focus on halitosis returned. This lasted for four weeks and was followed by her decision to "accept who I am." She talked of more feeling of belonging to her family and to her adopted country. She had a "pregnancy scare" but maintained a calm, objective approach. She spoke of getting her confidence back and taking some social initiative with men for the first time. She associated her "mouth burning" now with situations producing anxiety.

Psychotherapy continued for one year. No antidepressant medication was prescribed. Although her beliefs about her mouth odor were addressed and disputed, this was not the therapy's focus. There appeared to be real changes in how she viewed herself. My diagnostic impression at termination was dysthymic disorder, with a history of two major depressive episodes. Periodic follow-up sessions occurred at her initiative over the subsequent seven years. There were no more major depressive episodes, and no further mention of mouth odor.

Symptoms and Epidemiology

As with body dysmorphic disorder, my knowledge about ORS owes a large debt to Dr. Katharine Phillips. ORS is a delusional belief that one emits a foul or offensive body odor. *DSM-IV* classifies the problem as a somatic delusion. To put ORS in perspective, let's systematically define its nosologic place. Delusional disorders require non-bizarre delusions of at least one month's duration (see Table 9.3). They differ from schizophrenia by the absence of delusions and hallucinations unrelated to the focal problem. Neither speech nor behavior is disorganized, and negative symptoms are absent. Globally, functioning is not markedly impaired, and mood episodes are either absent or not prominent.

There are five types of delusional disorders indicated in *DSM-IV* (see Table 9.4), of which somatic delusions form one category. Among the somatic delusions, three entities predominate: delusional body dysmorphic disorder, ORS, and parasitosis (infestation). The primary symptom of ORS may be a preoccupation with an offensive odor, referential thinking about it, or clear delusions of reference.[54]

ORS is more commonly seen in men than women. Its age of onset is usually in the early twenties. Among the signs of social impairment is the finding that about 70% never marry.[54]

Phillips has summarized the defining characteristics of the odor that comprise the patient's main complaint: [53]

- Intrinsic
- Preoccupying
- Shameful, thought to be offensive to others
- Source: skin, anus, mouth, feet, genitals, or axillae
- Possible olfactory hallucinations

Table 9.3
DELUSIONAL DISORDER
1. Non-bizarre delusions of at least one month's duration
2. Criterion A for Schizophrenia not met
3. Global functioning not markedly impaired
4. Mood episodes absent, or not prominent
From DSM-IV

Table 9.4
TYPES OF DELUSIONAL DISORDERS
1. Erotomania
2. Grandiose
3. Jealous
4. Persecutory
5. Somatic
From DSM-IV

Associated behaviors include:

• Camouflaging (e.g., washing, excess deodorant use, perfume use, smoking)
• Checking (e.g., smelling one's breath)
• Seeking reassurance

The seriousness of the syndrome is reflected not only in the social avoidance and occupational impairment but also in the reported frequency of hospitalization, suicide attempts, and housebound patients. Self-referral to ear, nose, and throat specialists, dentists, and surgeons is common. Since only a fraction of patients with ORS contact mental health workers, the literature may underestimate the frequency of its occurrence.

History

Hypochondriacal states have, in the past, been understood as related to depression, schizophrenia, and organic brain syndrome.[55] The delusional focus on one body part bears a resemblance, as well, to paranoia. Kraepelin's definition of paranoia lends credence to the association: "[Paranoia is] a permanent and unshakable delusional system resulting from internal causes, which is accompanied by perfect preservation of clear and orderly thinking, willing, and acting."[56] Hypochondriacal patients often have traits of the paranoid personality and exhibit behaviors of the social phobic. They consult nonpsychiatric physicians because they are convinced that their problem is a physical one. Rarely are they helped by these doctors.

Olfactory reference syndrome has also been also called *bromosis, bromidrosi-*

phobia, and *autodysosmophobia*. It fits the concept of a monosymptomatic hypochondriasis, and for years was described as such.[54] This disorder is characterized by a single, isolated delusion that has little effect on the personality but may have devastating impact on social and occupational functioning.[57]

The man who gave ORS its name, O. W. Pryse-Phillips, was studying olfactory hallucinations in the United Kingdom in the 1960s. He personally examined 99 cases and added case notes for an additional 38 patients to complete a sample size of 137.[58] Thirty-two patients met criteria for schizophrenia, 50 for one of the depressive illnesses, eleven had temporal lobe epilepsy, and eight were "unclassifiable." He concluded that the remaining 36 patients constituted a separate group, with a disorder he called olfactory reference syndrome.

He characterized the source of hallucination in his sample as intrinsic (coming from within the body) or extrinsic. He characterized the patient's reaction to the odor as minimal, reasonable, or contrite (ashamed, embarrassed). He characterized the odor's significance to the patient as subordinate, important, or dominant. For the ORS patient, the source was *intrinsic*, the symptom was *dominant*, and the reaction was *contrite*. "The typical case," he wrote, "resembled endogenous depression, but the mood symptoms were reactive to the dominant smell symptoms."[58] I believe this description fits my presented case well.

In 1982, Munro published a description of cases of delusional hypochondriasis that included a subset that could be described as ORS patients.[59,60] Nearly a decade later Osman, in Saudia Arabia, collected fifteen cases of ORS. He noted that each source area in his sample (genitals, mouth, armpits) "was expected to smell under certain conditions, and naturally emits a specific odor."[57] Further, the cultural meaning of a person's emitting a foul smell focused attention on poverty and poor personal hygiene and was stigmatizing.

The literature is unclear on the issues of whether the patient's dominant concern is typically overvalued or delusional, and whether it is typically secondary to an underlying (usually affective) illness or primary.[61] It is equally unclear whether its major relationship is to affective disorder, obsessive-compulsive disorder, social phobia, or paranoia.

Treatment

In earlier years, when ORS was strongly associated with paranoia, it was most often treated (usually abroad) with pimozide.[62] Data that might shed light on treatment outcome is scanty. Phillips has found antipsychotic drugs to be of little use, with the possible exception of pimozide.[54] She recommends an SRI or pimozide to start. Some have advocated psychotherapy,[63] and Phillips urges consideration of cognitive-behavior therapy. There are no controlled treatment trials as yet.

POSTSCRIPT

These four entities—chronic fatigue syndrome, fibromyalgia, body dysmorphic disorder, and olfactory reference syndrome—are at least frequently comorbid with clinical depression, at most forms or subforms of affective disorder. Someday, our thinking may be completely reformulated into an etiologically based nosology (e.g., disorders of serotonergic dysregulation). For now, it is important that clinicians recognize these syndromes and educate themselves and their patients about what is known about them, while providing a rational treatment approach.

Notes

1. Holmes, G. P., Kaplan, J. E., Gantz, N. M., et al. (1988). Chronic fatigue syndrome: A working case definition. *Annals of Internal Medicine, 108,* 387.

2. Abbey, S. E., & Garfinckel, P. E. (1991). Neurasthenia and chronic fatigue syndrome: The role of culture in the making of a diagnosis. *American Journal of Psychiatry, 148*(12), 1638.

3. Krupp, L. B., Mendelson, W. B., & Friedman, R. (1991). An overview of chronic fatigue syndrome. *Journal of Clinical Psychiatry, 52*(10), 403.

4. Kim, E. (1994). A brief history of chronic fatigue syndrome. *Journal of the American Medical Association, 272*(13), 1070.

5. Straus, S. E. (1988). The chronic mononucleosis syndrome. *Journal of Infectuous Diseases, 157*(3), 405.

6. Barnes, D. M. (1986). Mystery disease at Lake Tahoe challenges virologists and clinicians. *Science, 234,* 541.

7. Straus, S. E., Tosato, G., Armstrong, G., et al. (1985). Persisting illness and fatigue in adults with evidence of Epstein-Barr virus infection. *Annals of Internal Medicine, 102,* 7.

8. Horwitz, C. A., Henle, W., Henle, G., et al. (1985). Long-term serological follow-up of patients for Epstein-Barr virus after recovery from infectious mononucleosis. *Journal of Infectuous Diseases, 151,* 1150.

9. Yousef, G., Bell, E. J., Mann, G. F., et al. (1988). Chronic enterovirus infection in patients with post-viral fatigue syndrome. *Lancet, 1,* 146.

10. Josephs, S. F., Henry, B., Balachandran, N., et al. (1991). HHV-6 reaction in chronic fatigue syndrome. *Lancet, 337,* 1346.

11. Edwards, R. H. T., Gibson, H., Clague, J. E., et al. (1993). Muscle histopathology and physiology in chronic fatigue syndrome. In G. R. Bock & J. Whelan (Eds.), *Chronic fatigue syndrome* (CIBA Foundation Symposium #173). Chichester: Wiley.

12. Klimas, N. G., Salvato, F .R., Morgan, R., et al. (1990). Immunological abnormalities of chronic fatigue syndrome. *Journal of Clinical Microbiology, 28,* 1403.

13. Rowe, P. C., Bou-Holaigah, I., Kan, J. S., et al. (1995). Is neurally mediated hypotension an unrecognized cause of chronic fatigue? *Lancet, 345,* 623.

14. Imboden, J. B., Cantor, A., & Cluff, L. E. (1961). Convalescence from influenza. *Archives of Internal Medicine, 108,* 393.

15. Kruesi, M. J. P., Dale, J., & Straus, S. (1989). Psychiatric diagnoses in patients who have chronic fatigue syndrome. *Journal of Clinical Psychiatry, 50*(2), 53.

16. Hickie, I., Lloyd, A., Wakefield, D., et al. (1990). The psychiatric status of patients with chronic fatigue syndrome. *British Journal of Psychiatry, 156,* 534.

17. Lane, T. J., Nance, P., & Matthews, D. A. (1994). Reply to "Chronic fatigue syndrome (CFS) and psychiatric disorders" [letter to the editor]. *American Journal of Medicine, 94,* 485.

18. Goodnick, P. J., & Sandoval, R. (1993). Psychotropic treatment of chronic fatigue syndrome and related disorders. *Journal of Clinical Psychiatry, 54*(1), 13.

19. Sharpe, M., Hawton, K. Simken, S., et al. (1996). Cognitive behaviour therapy for the chronic fatigue syndrome: A randomized, clinical trial. *British Medical Journal, 312,* 22.

20. Sharpe, M. C., Peveler, R., & Mayou, R. (1992). The psychological treatment of patients with functional somatic symptoms: A practical guide. *Journal of Psychosomatic Research, 36,* 515.

21. Clauw, D. J. (1995). Fibromyalgia: More than just a musculoskeletal disease. *American Family Physician, 52*(3), 843.

22. Multicenter Criteria Committee. (1990). The American College of Rheumatology 1990 criteria for the classification of fibromyalgia. *Arthritis and Rheumatology, 33*(2), 160.

23. Goldenberg, D. L. (1987). Fibromyalgia syndrome: An emerging but controversial condition. *Journal of the American Medical Association, 257*(20), 2782.

24. Buchwald, D., & Garrity, D. (1994). Comparison of patients with chronic fatigue syndrome, fibromyalgia, and multiple chemical sensitivities. *Archives of Internal Medicine, 154,* 2049.

25. Wolfe, F., Ross, K., Anderson, J., et al. (1995). The prevalence and characteristics of fibromyalgia in the general population. *Arthritis and Rheumatology, 38*(1), 19.

26. Yunus, M. B. (1989). Fibromyalgia syndrome: New research on an old malady. *British Medical Journal, 298,* 474.

27. Gowers, W. (1904). Lumbago: Its lessons and analogues. *British Medical Journal, 1,* 117.

28. Traut, E. F. (1968). Fibrositis. *Journal of the American Geriatric Society, 16,* 531.

29. Yunus, B., Masi, A. T., Calabro, J. J., et al. (1981). Primary fibromyalgia (fibrositis): Clinical study of patients with matched normal controls. *Seminar in Arthritis and Rheumatology, 11,* 151.

30. Wilke, W. S. (1996). Fibromyalgia. *Postgraduate Medicine, 100*(1), 153.

31. Bennett, R. M. (1989). Beyond fibromyalgia: Ideas on etiology and treatment. *Journal of Rheumatology, 16*(Suppl. 19), 185.

32. Hudson, J. I., Hudson, M. S., Pliner, L. F., et al. (1985). Fibromyalgia and major affective disorder: A controlled phenomenology and family history study. *American Journal of Psychiatry, 142,* 441.

33. Godfrey, R. G. (1996). A guide to the understanding and use of tricyclic antidepressants in the overall management of fibromyalgia and other chronic pain syndromes. *Archives of Internal Medicine, 156,* 1047.

34. Carette, S., McCain, G. A., Bell, D. A., et al. (1986). Evaluation of amitriptyline in primary fibrositis. *Arthritis and Rheumatology, 29,* 655.

35. Campbell, S. M., Gatter, R. A., Clark, S., et al. (1985). A double-blind study of cyclobenzaprine in patients with primary fibrositis. *Arthritis and Rheumatology, 28,* 540.

36. Wolfe, F., Cathey, M. A., & Hawley, D. J. (1994). A double-blind, controlled trial of fluoxetine in fibromyalgia. *Scandanavian Journal of Rheumatology, 23,* 255.

37. Goldenberg, D. L., Mayskly, M., Mossey, C., et al. (1995). The independent and combined efficacy of fluoxetine and amitriptyline in the treatment of fibromyalgia [Abstract]. *Arthritis and Rheumatology, 38*(Suppl. 9), S 229.

38. Kennedy, M., & Felson, D. T. (1996). A prospective long-term study of fibromyalgia syndrome. *Arthritis and Rheumatology, 39*(4), 682.

39. American Psychiatric Association. (1994). *Diagnostic and statistical manual for mental disorders* (4th ed.). Washington D.C.: A. P. A.

40. Phillips, K. A. (June 14, 1996). Body dysmorphic disorder. *The Santa Fe Update: Dysthymia, Depression and Bipolar Disorder.*

41. Brawman-Mintzer, O., Lydiard, R. B., Phillips, K. A., et al. (1995). Body dysmorphic disorder in patients with anxiety disorders and major depression: A comorbidity study. *American Journal of Psychiatry, 152*(11), 1665.

42. Brady, K. T., Austin, L., & Lydiard, R. B. (1990). Body dysmorphic disorder: The relationship to obsessive-compulsive disorder. *Journal of Nervous and Mental Disease, 178*(8), 538.

43. Phillips, K. A., McElroy, S. L., Hudson, J. I., et al. (1995). Body dysmorphic disorder: A form of obsessive-compulsive spectrum disorder, a form of affective spectrum disorder, or both? *Journal of Clinical Psychiatry, 56*(Suppl. 4), 41.

44. Phillips, K. A., Nierenberg, A. A., Brendel, G., et al. (1996). Prevalence and clinical features of body dysmorphic disorder in atypical major depression. *Journal of Nervous and Mental Disease, 184*(2), 125.

45. Phillips, K. A., McElroy, S. L., Keck, P. E., et al. (1993). Body dysmorphic disorder: Thirty cases of imagined ugliness. *American Journal Psychiatry, 150*(2), 302.

46. Phillips, K. A., McElroy, S. L., Keck, P. E., et al. (1994). A comparison of delusional and non-delusional body dysmorphic disorder in 100 cases. *Psychopharmacology Bulletin, 30,* 179.

47. Phillips, K. A. (1995). Body dysmorphic disorder: Clinical features and drug treatment. *CNS Drugs, 3*(1), 30.

48. Hudson, J. I., & Pope, H. G. (1990). Affective spectrum disorder: Does antidepressant response identify a family of disorders with a common pathophysiology? *American Journal of Psychiatry, 147*(5), 552.

49. Hollander, E. H., Cohen, L. I.,& Simeon, D. (1993). Body dysmorphic disorder. *Psychiatric Annals, 23,* 359.

50. Hollander, E. H., Liebowitz, M. R., Winchel, R., et al. (1989). Treatment of body dysmorphic disorder with serotonin reuptake blockers. *American Journal of Psychiatry, 146*(6), 768.

51. McElroy, S. L., Phillips, K. A., & Keck, P. E. (1993). Body dysmorphic disorder: Does it have a psychotic subtype? *Journal of Clinical Psychiatry, 54*(10), 389.

52. Insel, T. R., & Akiskal, H. S. (1986). Obsessive-compulsive disorder with psychotic features: A phenomenologic analysis. *American Journal of Psychiatry, 143*.

53. Rosen, J. C., Reiter, J., & Orosan, P. (1995). Cognitive-behavioral body image therapy for body dysmorphic disorder. *Journal of Consulting and Clinical Psychology, 63*(2), 263.

54. Phillips, K. A. (June 14, 1996). Somatic delusional disorders: Olfactory reference syndrome. Clinical features of an unrecognized disorder. *The Santa Fe Update: Dysthymia, Depression and Bipolar Disorder.*

55. Bishop, E. R. (1980). An olfactory reference syndrome-monosymptomatic hypochodriasis. *Journal of Clinical Psychiatry, 41,* 57.

56. Kraepelin, E. (1976). *Manic-depressive insanity and paranoia.* New York: Arno Press.

57. Osman, A. A. (1991). Monosymptomatic hypochondriacal psychosis in developing countries. *British Journal of Psychiatry, 159,* 428.

58. Prysc-Phillips, W. (1971). An olfactory reference syndrome. *Acta Psychiatrica Scandinavica, 47,* 484.

59. Munro, A. (1982). *Delusional hypochondriasis: A description of monosymptomatic hypochondriacal psychosis* (Monograph Series No. 5). Toronto: Clark Institute of Psychiatry.

60. Munro, A. (1982). Paranoia revisited. *British Journal of Psychiatry, 141,* 344.

61. McKenna, P. J. (1984). Disorders with overvalued ideas. *British Journal of Psychiatry, 145,* 579.

62. Riding, J., & Munro, A. (1975). Pimozide in the treatment of monosymptomatic hypochondriacal psychosis. *Acta Psychiatrica Scandinavica, 52,* 23.

63. Nelki, J. (1988). Making sense of a delusion of smell: A psychotherapeutic approach. *British Journal of Medical Psychology, 61,* 267.

Chapter 10

Treatment Issues and a Menu of Choices

While scientific advances and conceptual progress have had a major impact on treatment in depression, movement toward a managed care system has contributed as well. There is an incentive to limit contact with your patient, to provide therapeutic services that work more rapidly, and to assign treatment responsibility to a changed (and changing) cadre of caregivers.

Drug therapy for acute, full-syndrome depression has become widely accepted practice in the United States over the last two decades. The original two classes of antidepressants, the tricyclics (TCAs) and the monoamineoxidase inhibitors (MAOIs), have been augmented by the selective serotonin reuptake inhibitors (SSRIs), and several even newer agents (see Table 10.1).

Electroconvulsive therapy (ECT) has been refined in ways that make it more available and less traumatic to the patient and his or her family. Unfortunately, while the stigma associated with acknowledging depression seems to have decreased, along with the stigma associated with accepting treatment, society's view of electroconvulsive therapy appears to be little changed. Although the media have helped destigmatize illness and treatment, they often continue to demonize ECT.

Table 10.1 CLASSES OF ANTIDEPRESSANT DRUGS			
Cyclic	**SSRIs**	**MAOIs**	**Newer Agents**
TCAs	Fluoxetine	Phenelzine	Venlafaxine
Trazodone	Sertraline	Tranylcypromine	Nefazodone
Bupropion	Paroxetine		

Psychotherapies for depression have evolved, too, into a range of short-term forms to complement long-term, traditional, psychodynamic psychotherapy. Market forces have strongly favored brief over extended treatments. While no one model has been proven consistently superior to another, once again there is an expansion of choices offered to treat depression. Manuals written to guide research have proven useful in the instruction of new clinicians.

Clinical guidelines have been offered by the American Psychiatric Association for the treatment of both major depression[1] and bipolar disorder.[2] They have provided terminology to organize and define the different phases of treatment: acute, continuation, and maintenance. *Acute* treatment is administered at the onset of an episode and concludes with remission. The *continuation* phase begins at remission and terminates when spontaneous remission would be expected to occur. *Maintenance* treatment starts when the episode would be expected to be over and may continue indefinitely. Its goal is to prevent or attenuate future episodes.

THE IMPACT OF MANAGING COST

In 1994, a great deal of national attention was directed to the delivery of health care services in America. An ambitious program to restructure health care was proposed by the President, debated, and then not enacted. Multiple issues were spotlighted. Cost was a primary concern. Health insurance coverage for some 30,000 uninsured Americans was another focus. It was predicted that, as the baby boom generation became eligible for Medicare, strain would bankrupt the program.

For the consumer, maintaining the right to choose one's doctor was stressed. In addition, the insurer's designation of "preexisting condition" seemingly had acted to deprive the consumer of access to health care in that area where it was most needed. Similarly, when an individual moved from one job to another, insurance regulations generally applied anew—often making health coverage unavailable at another critical point.

To hold down cost, it was thought that the provision of care would need to be regulated. Would that regulation come from the government? Would it be vested in private industry? Would the role of the insurance company be broadened to dictate what problems would and would not be covered?

By the fall of 1996, the U.S. Congress enacted legislation to protect the portability of a worker's health insurance. In these cases, insurance companies could not deny coverage for a preexisting condition. The more general principle of exempting from coverage a preexisting condition (often for one year) on a new policy, however, remained in force.

Throughout the national debate, mental health care advocates argued strongly for parity in the insurance coverage for the treatment of emotional illness. Typically, insurance companies had always provided a different (lower) class of coverage when the diagnosis was "mental" as opposed to "physical," both in terms of annual and lifetime benefits.

Although sweeping national health care reform was not enacted between 1994 and 1997, the effort stimulated major changes at a state and local level. The new format for these changes was called managed care. A number of corporations were established, forming networks that contracted with clinicians and regulated their provision of services.

Among clinicians, there was opposition to regulations concerning which doctor, with what background and training, could treat a patient's problem. A fundamental change in health care delivery had made the *third party payer* the central enabler of treatment. As it appeared to clinicians that (low) fees for service were more important for approval than either kind or quality of service, the designation "managed cost" seemed more accurate than "managed care."

The arrival of managed care had some specific consequences to mental health workers:

- Whenever applicable, drug therapy seems to be favored over psychotherapy for a given problem. It may not work better, or work on what the clinician sees as the relevant problem, but it is seen by the managed care company as working faster and therefore costing less.
- Short-term therapy is favored over long-term therapy (with especial regard to psychotherapy). Again the motivation is cost-cutting.
- The skill, expertise, and experience of the therapist providing psychotherapy take a back seat to the fee charged for the service. This has led to a redefinition of service provision in some regions, where psychiatrists now see patients for brief "med. checks" (medication management) and no longer do psychotherapy. The responsibility for providing psychotherapy is trickling down to those who charge least for it.
- The clinician's evaluation of what is needed to treat the patient, especially when it entails more cost, more sessions, or more procedures, is now insufficient to gain third party approval for payment. The decision-making team of doctor and patient has changed, with a company case manager now more often in the driver's seat.

- Legal questions of responsibility arise when the clinician recommends a course that is subsequently vetoed by the company. If a lesser course is followed or a potentially crucial diagnostic procedure is not done, who will be held liable for an unsatisfactory outcome? The problem is being adjudicated in the courts.

As a direct result of the changes in mental health service delivery and their consequences, some clinicians have experienced a decrease in caseload. Generalists are treating more patients, and specialists are receiving fewer referrals. Some managed care companies are offering disincentives to their "gatekeepers" (initial evaluators of the patient) for making referrals. In addition, most clinicians' paperwork has dramatically increased. There is a need for telephone time to coordinate care with the company. There are calls to defend treatment plans, ask for more sessions, and in general advocate the patient's coverage. In the past, the patient's insurance was his or her responsibility, with the clinician facilitating reimbursement. Now, it is a provider responsibility, with the patient often in the dark about the deliberations on his or her behalf. As computer use grows dramatically, there has been a push for electronic billing, changing the habits of many senior clinicians and bringing with it another layer of eyes to challenge confidentiality.

The impact of managed care has been felt in the arena of depression and its treatment. Inpatient care (generally more expensive) is strongly discouraged and closely regulated. This places the burden of managing a difficult patient (previously hospitalized, for example, during a suicidal crisis) solidly on the shoulders of the treating outpatient therapist. With a proliferation in the availability of antidepressant medications, drug treatment is often favored over psychotherapy. Even with chronic depression, short-term approaches are authorized over long-term ones.

Meanwhile, subscriptions to managed care plans are growing, albeit at different rates in different regions of the U.S. By the end of 1995, 58 million people had enrolled in HMOs (health maintenance organizations) and another mechanism for managing care, the PPO (preferred provider organization), had 91 million enrollees.[3] Both Medicare and Medicaid subscribers have been encouraged to join a managed plan. As a result of the proliferation of plans, about 67% of the United States population with health benefits have opted for some form of managed care.[3]

While 83% of all physicians have a managed care connection, the rate is only 68% for psychiatrists.[3] The debate among health care providers was in full swing by 1996. Would the psychiatric profession (for example) continue to practice as in the past, or would adaptations be made to accommodate the new realities? Would these adaptations follow the "union" model of self-protection (guarding the psychiatrist's standards of practice and income) or would psychiatrists willingly accept the role transition to that of (for example) educators of other providers?

One prediction foresees the future role of the psychiatrist as:[4]

- Combining with neurology to treat a broad range of brain diseases that might include Alzheimer's disease, parkinsonism, schizophrenia, and bipolar disorder.
- Educating (and thus enabling) primary care physicians to treat the bulk of anxiety and depressive disorders pharmacologically.
- Training psychotherapists to deliver the newer (e.g., cognitive and behavioral) therapies for problems amenable to psychosocial intervention.

A comprehensive (if somewhat chilling) account of one man's view of the impact of managed care on psychiatric treatment is that of attorney Alan Stone.[5]

Inevitably, there has been talk of managed care as merely a transitional format, to be replaced by contracts negotiated directly between employers and providers; with no further need for a "middle man," managed care would quietly "pass on." Past president of the American Psychiatric Association Harold Eist summarized the ongoing debate well by quoting former New York Yankee baseball manager Casey Stengel: "Predictions are hard to make," he said, "especially when they're about the future!"[6]

TREATING THE ACUTE DEPRESSIVE EPISODE

Research continues to support a response rate of 60–70% to antidepressant drugs for major depression. Full response usually takes four to six weeks, so patients must be advised not to expect more rapid changes. However, some patients claim much earlier indicators of response.

There are ten main areas of side effects associated with antidepressant drug treatment (see Table 10.2). The occurrence of these effects varies widely among the different drug classes. For the SSRIs and newer agents, side effects are generally less frequent, milder when they do occur, and somewhat different in character.

Monoamine-Oxidase Inhibitors (MAOIs)

In the United States of the 1950s, isoniazid was a drug prescribed to treat

| Table 10.2 |
| ANTIDEPRESSANT DRUGS' SIDE EFFECTS |

- Dizziness, sedation, fogginess
- Dry mouth, blurred vision, constipation, urinary hesitancy
- Weight gain • Sexual dysfunction
- Epileptogenic effects • Orthostatic hypotension
- Anti- (or Pro-) arrythmic influence • Conduction defect
- Insomnia • Anxiety

tuberculosis. When it was observed that tubercular patients treated with this drug were "stimulated" by it, serendipity had suggested the first antidepressant medication—iproniazid, a derivative of isoniazid. A decade later, the first report appeared in the literature of a fatality in a patient taking an MAOI; the patient had eaten cheese and experienced a sudden rise in blood pressure.[7] The MAOIs were withdrawn from the American market after a number of similar reports.

Research, meanwhile, elucidated the cause of the problem and confirmed the purported mechanism of action of these antidepressants. The enzyme monoamine-oxidase catalyzes the removal of norepinephrine and serotonin from the synaptic cleft. Inactivation of this enzyme results in an increase in the functional availability of these neurotransmitters, which, over time, reverses depression. The problem is that MAO exists elsewhere in the body besides the brain. Concentrations are highest, in fact, in the liver, but the enzyme is plentiful in the gastrointestinal tract, as well as elsewhere in the central nervous system. When an MAOI inactivates MAO in the G.I. tract, dietary tyramine is able to enter the circulation and act as a pressor, a compound that increases blood pressure.

To complicate matters further, two types of MAO have been identified: MAO-a and MAO-b. MAO-a is thought to be relatively specific for norepinephrine and serotonin. Inhibitors specific for MAO-b are not associated with tyramine-related hypertensive crises; however, there are also no data to support that they affect depression. The two most commonly prescribed MAOIs, phenelzine (Nardil) and tranylcypromine (Parnate), are each nonselective and affect both MAO-a and MAO-b. Hence the concern with the so-called "cheese reaction" (hypertensive crisis).

Unlike these drugs, the MAOI moclobemide is reversible, meaning that its binding to MAO can be displaced by tyramine, nullifying the hypertensive reaction. Work is in progress to better understand the reversible MAOIs. Currently available drugs irreversibly inactivate MAO, such that a two-week period must elapse after the last dose so that the body can resynthesize MAO and a person can safely ingest foods that contain tyramine.

When it became clear that dietary regulation (avoiding foods high in tyramine content) would protect against the cheese reaction, MAOIs were reintroduced. By this time, however, the tricyclic antidepressants (TCAs) had arrived and established themselves as first-line treatment agents for depression. MAOIs were little used. In the 1980s, a series of articles suggested the prescription of MAOIs for special populations of depressives.

When depression had a major anxiety component, phobic symptoms or panic attacks, the MAOIs seemed more effective than the TCAs.[8] Atypical depression (with reversed vegetative signs) became another indication for MAOIs.[9] Then bipolar depression, particularly severe depression in inpatients, and nonresponders to TCAs were added to the list.[10] There were good clinical reasons now for clinicians to rediscover the MAOIs.

Despite the lengthy existence of MAOIs, there was little guidance initially available for the practical management of the patient taking an MAOI. It is known that a fourteen-day washout period should follow the prescription of a TCA prior to initiating treatment with an MAOI. The usual dose of phenelzine is 45 mg per day in three divided doses, but over time, doses of 60 mg and 90 mg have been reported effective and safe for some patients. For tranylcypromine, the usual dose range is 20–40 mg per day in 10 mg divided doses.

Habits die hard, and apparently large numbers of clinicians forsook the MAOIs. In one survey done in the late 1980s, Clary et al. found that only 25% of psychiatrists responding reported "frequent use" of MAOIs.[11] The others found the dietary restriction of foods containing tyramine "too restrictive" and feared precipitating a hypertensive crisis in their patients. Furthermore, there were additional side effects associated with MAOIs: orthostatic hypotension, weight gain, insomnia, overstimulation (anxiety), and sexual dysfunction.[11]

By the mid-1990s, however, the MAOIs had made a significant comeback. The list of indications was too long to overlook. It had been learned that it takes, in general, large amounts of tyramine to produce a clinically significant rise in blood pressure. Furthermore, large amounts of tyramine more often result from aging or spoilage of food, so many foods were deemed safe when eaten fresh.[12] New food avoidance lists were offered, with the focus solidly on those with high tyramine content (see Table 10.3). There is a list of drug-drug interactions as well (see Table 10.4). The MAOIs are known to disturb sleep, so prescription is limited to morning and afternoon as much as possible. They also lower vascular tone, so hypotension is a common concern. Phenelzine has been associated with liver toxicity, so periodic liver function tests became part of the regimen of treatment.

That MAO activity can be measured in platelets led to further structure for management of the patient. Although platelets contain only MAO-B, it became established that 80% inhibition correlated well with clinical response, guiding dosage.

Finally, guidelines were disseminated for recognition of a hypertensive crisis, as well as for its treatment. The prodromal signs are: headache, stiff neck, sweating, nausea, and vomiting.[8] If these should occur, the patient is instruct-

Table 10.3 FOOD WITH HIGH TYRAMINE CONTENT	Table 10.4 DRUGS TO BE AVOIDED DURING MAOI TREATMENT
• Aged cheese (Cream and cottage cheese are okay.) • Fava or broad beans • Beer or red wine (A small amount of white wine, scotch, gin, vodka, or sherry is okay.) • Beef or chicken liver • Pickled or smoked fish, chicken, or meats (if not fresh) • Packaged soups • Yeast vitamin supplements • Meat extracts (e.g., Marmite, Bovril) • Dry summer sausage • Sauerkraut • Soy sauce, soy beans *Modified from Kaplan, Sadock, and Grebb, 1994*[8]	• Spinal or local anesthesis containing epinephrine (Lidocaine and procaine are okay.) • Anti-asthmatic drugs • Antihypertensive drugs • Narcotics, especially Demerol • Over-the-counter cold, hay fever, or sinus drugs, especially those containing dextromethorphan (Aspirin and acetaminophen are okay.) • Sympathomimetics (e.g., amphetamine, cocaine, methylphenidate, dopamine, isoproterenol) • SSRI antidepressants *Modified from Kaplan, Sadock, and Grebb, 1994*[8]

ed to go directly to an emergency room and inform the doctor that he or she is taking a prescribed MAOI. Treatment generally consists of nifedipine (Procardia), phentolamine (Regitine), or chlorpromazine (Thorazine) to return blood pressure to normal.

As a clear link was established between dietary compliance and MAOI safety, the comfort level of both doctor and patient rose, catalyzing a resurgence of interest and prescription of this important class of antidepressant drug.[12]

The Tricyclic Antidepressants (TCAs)

With the introduction of the SSRIs in the mid-1980s, it was thought that this original class of antidepressants might disappear from use. However, a decade later, instead of vanishing from the clinical scene, the prescription of TCAs seems to be achieving a more specific role definition. When major depression is severe (and, for example, is treated on an inpatient basis), imipramine and its classmates—desipramine, amitriptyline, nortriptyline, and doxepin—are often chosen first. When major depression is treated in the elderly, a secondary amine tricyclic (particularly nortriptyline) is often prescribed. Research studies with lengthy follow-ups to determine the role of antidepressants in the prevention of future depressive episodes have utilized imipramine and amitriptyline for recurrent depression. There had not yet been time for studies with SSRIs to establish their efficacy in maintenance.

With outpatients, often presenting with milder forms of depression, SSRIs are supplanting TCAs as the initial approach. The likelihood of side effects with TCAs, their potential for lethality with overdose, and the relative unpredictability of TCA dose level needed for response—all favor the newer SSRIs over the older TCAs.

While the prescription of 150 mg per day of imipramine (Tofranil and others) or amitriptyline (Elavil and others) was once considered routine, it is now common to increase the dose gradually, observing the patient for therapeutic response, as well as for side effects requiring management. Doses of 300 mg and beyond are no longer uncommon. At times, the secondary amine drugs (desipramine and nortriptyline) are favored over their parent compounds (imipramine and amitriptyline). Effective dosages for these drugs are often lower and might be guided by serum level determinations. For nortriptyline (Pamelor), a therapeutic window of 50 µg–140 µg is thought to be a guide to maximizing response. Later introduced antidepressants of this class (the second generation drugs)—maprotyline, amoxapine, and trazodone—

had little lasting impact, although amoxapine and trazodone each have indications for their use. Often employed for its sedative properties, trazodone
(Desyrel) might be prescribed at a low dose (25–100 mg), along with an SSRI,
as a sleep aid. It is also an option in treatment-resistant patients, particularly
women. (Some clinicians avoid prescribing trazodone to men because of concern for the infrequent side effect of priapism.) Amoxapine (Asendin) is utilized by some clinicians to treat psychotic depression.

As biological research identified receptors and their function as central
foci in the understanding of the affective disorders, TCA-SSRI differences
were highlighted. The older drugs, the TCAs, affected muscarinic receptors,
producing the anticholinergic side effects familiar to clinicians: dry mouth,
constipation, and sometimes blurred vision and urinary hesitancy. The TCA
effect on alpha-adrenergic receptors is responsible for the side effect of orthostatic hypotension (a fall in blood pressure upon standing), which could lead
to dizziness and falls, an especial concern in the elderly. The TCA effect on
histaminergic receptors is thought to be responsibile for the sedation
observed with some tricyclics. Sexual dysfunction, now recognized as a side
effect of SSRIs, had not been an issue raised with TCAs because in the past
patients rarely raised the issue and clinicians rarely inquired about it. There
appear to be no real differences between the two drug classes in this regard.

As experience grew over the years with the prescription of TCAs, reports
abounded of significant, unwanted weight gain. With the introduction of the
weight-sparing (or at least as "weight-neutral") SSRIs, this became a significant factor favoring the newer drugs. A swing back to the TCAs, however,
has been encouraged by the practice of some managed care plans to favor the
older, "off-patent" drugs, due to their lower cost. This is balanced by the
greater risk of mortality in overdose with TCAs, as well as by the morbidity
due to cardiac (e.g., conduction) effects sometimes seen with the TCA group.

Based upon the two-amine theory (discussed in chapter 7), the TCAs can
be subclassified by their respective effects on norepinephrine and serotonin
reuptake. Clomipramine, amitriptyline, imipramine, and the second-generation cyclic drug trazodone all exert more potent effects on the serotonergic system. Desipramine, nortriptyline, and maprotyline are predominantly noradrenergic in their reuptake blockage. With no clear method enabling a differentiation of norepinephrine depression from serotonin depression, clinicians of the
1970s and early 1980s would follow an unsuccessful trial of a drug in one group
by a a trial of an agent in the other group.

Bupropion (Wellbutrin)

Wellbutrin was introduced as an antidepressant in 1989. When an unacceptable occurrence of seizures was noted, it was removed from the American market. It was reintroduced with clear dosage guidelines for its prescription. Available in both 75 mg and 100 mg tablets, about 300 mg per day in two or three separate doses provides the effective dose for most patients. The suggested upper limit of 450 mg per day requires three separate doses so that no single dose exceeds 150 mg. It is further suggested that dosage increases and decreases be gradual. The introduction in early 1997 of a sustained-release preparation of Wellbutrin may provide clinicians with another option.

An aminoketone, bupropion has a structure unlike that of any other antidepressant compound. It is a weak inhibitor of norepinephrine and serotonin reuptake. It does not inhibit monoamine-oxidase. While it does affect the biogenic amine dopamine, this is not thought to be sufficient to account for its efficacy. It has no significant effect on muscarinic, histaminergic, or alpha-adrenergic receptors. Although one of bupropion's major metabolites has greater noradrenergic effect, it has not been established that this is relevant to its mechanism of action. To date, the compound's mode of action remains unknown.

While Wellbutrin is selected at times as an antidepressant of first choice, its value increased when reports of sexual dysfunction surfaced in a percentage of SSRI users. For some, a switch to bupropion results in similar antidepressant efficacy without sexual function interference. For others, the sexual dysfunction disappears, but their depression returns. This led some clinicians to experiment with a regimen combining both antidepressant drugs, often in reduced dosages. Some SSRIs (e.g., fluoxetine) can raise serum levels of bupropion, posing a renewed risk of seizures. (For additional strategies for dealing with antidepressant induced sexual dysfunction, see the section Issues in Drug Prescription.)

Selective Serotonin Reuptake Inhibitors (SSRIs)

By the mid-1980s, the TCAs and the MAOIs were the established pharmacotherapy for an acute depressive episode. Clinician and patient dissatisfaction focused on bothersome (and, at times, unacceptable) side effects, unpredictable therapeutic doses, and a three- to six-week waiting period before an effect was evident. Side effects likely prevented some patients from achieving a sufficient dose for effectiveness. Some may have terminated trials prematurely, and others may not have complied in the first place. When the second generation of cyclic drugs did not effectively remedy these problems, the marketplace was ready for a new antidepressant option.

Fluoxetine (Prozac) Rachel, a 32-year-old optometrist, came to see me after leaving her husband of five years. They had no children. She suffered medically from migraine headaches, irritable bowel syndrome, and lower back pain, seemingly all bearing some relationship to stress. She had never before consulted a psychiatrist.

Her chief complaint was: "I want to be able to have a happy life. I want to change how I think about myself. Especially for the six months that I've been separated from my husband, I've felt like a failure, but the feeling goes back to when I was a teenager."

She had decided to take an attractive job offer in Washington, with the expectation that her husband (an accountant in Orlando) would follow in several months. When he said "no," they agreed to separate. She described him as "alcoholic, workaholic, and unwilling to consider changes." Their relationship had been fraught with conflict and dissatisfaction.

Her parents had always had a "rocky relationship" growing up, and she felt that she had helped keep them together. She was an only child. She graduated from high school with Honors, and was president of her senior class. She was also a school beauty queen. At college, she had a 4.0 grade-point average after two years, when she left to attend optometry school.

She believed that her migraines were "punishment for sin." She believed that "no man would accept her" and was quite surprised when her husband married her. She saw herself as unattractive and had expected never to marry or have children. She remain wedded to a need for her parents' approval.

My diagnosis was dysthymic disorder. Psychotherapy was mostly supportive and brief. The major intervention was the prescription of Prozac (fluoxetine), 20 mg. After four weeks, there was a sharp change in her mood and the beginning of noticeable shifts in her expressed views.

She became less confrontative with her mother and orchestrated a change in their relationship around a request that her mother come to Washington to be with her during a surgical procedure. Concurrently, she began reporting to me significant positive feedback to her at work. Her sense of humor returned. She felt more and more "in control" of her life. She became less preoccupied with her husband and began dating. She was now more willing to take risks and try new things.

There were fifteen treatment sessions and two follow-up visits. A telephone call one year later found her engaged to be married and experiencing continued satisfaction about a job with expanding opportunities.

In December 1987, Prozac was introduced as the first SSRI available in the U.S. Its efficacy is at least equal to the standard (60–70%) set by the TCAs. Its selectivity results in a lack of anticholinergic, alpha-adrenergic, or histaminergic side effects. The side effect profile emphasizes nausea, diarrhea, insomnia, agitation, and anxiety, but none was as common as the anticholinergic effects typically observed with TCAs. Some patients claimed to experience no side effects. While the waiting period for response (three to six weeks) is no shorter than that of the TCAs, weight gain is rare. If there is a weight change with Prozac, typically it is a small weight loss. Prescription is simplified, since one 20 mg capsule is adequate treatment for most depressions that would respond.[13] There was generally no need for serum level determinations. Fluoxetine is markedly safer in overdose than the TCAs.

Prozac is thought to exert its major effect by inhibiting the reuptake of serotonin from the synaptic cleft. It has little to no affinity for other neurotransmitters. The half-life of fluoxetine was found to be one to three days, and steady state concentrations occur about 30 days after drug therapy begins. A major metabolite (norfluoxetine) has an even longer half-life (seven to fifteen days). These long half-lives have benefits and liabilities. A switch from Prozac to an MAOI requires a five- to six-week waiting period to ensure that the fluoxetine has cleared. Failure to do this could lead to an overaccumulation of serotonin, leading to the serotonin syndrome marked by confusion, restlessness, sweating, shivering, and myoclonus.[14] Meanwhile, withdrawal regimens are simplified by the gradual decline, and complaints upon discontinuation are infrequent. When a dose or two is missed, there is little serum level change, so loss of efficacy is unlikely. This lends itself to "weekend drug holidays" as a usually safe approach to ameliorating some cases of sexual dysfunction. For some with this side effect, a drug holiday is met with a return to normal functioning over the weekend period without drug use.

Initially, it was thought that fluoxetine was more likely to be effective in milder depression. More recent studies support little difference in (for example) fluoxetine-imipramine comparisons in severe depression, leaving the question unresolved. As Prozac surged in popularity, its success led to wide publicity being accorded to claims that there was a link between treatment with Prozac and the emergence of suicidal ideas in depressed patients.[15] The response from treating clinicians emphasized the known link between affective disorder, suicidal ideas, and suicidal behavior. It is known that about 15% of patients with recurrent depressive illness die by suicide and that the suicidal risk often persists until full recovery.[16] An analysis of clinical trials with fluoxetine revealed a rate of 1.2% for suicidal ideation emerging during treatment (less than half that seen with placebo!). There was no significant difference between depressed patients treated with fluoxetine and those treated with imipramine.[17] Finally, a survey of more than 1,000 depressed outpatients treated in 1989 found the incidence of suicidal ideas no different with Prozac than with other antidepressants.[18]

Despite research that seemed to indicate little additional likelihood of response to increasing dose, clinicians often experimented with doses of 40 mg, 60 mg, or 80 mg in patients unresponsive to the standard dose of 20 mg after the typical duration for response (four to six weeks) had passed. Whether success, when it occurred, was due to increasing the treatment duration or the dose level is unclear. But some additional successes did occur.

Sertraline (Zoloft) The F.D.A. (Food and Drug Administration) approved Zoloft for use as an antidepressant in December 1991. Controlled studies documented the efficacy of sertraline as an antidepressant.[19] There was some controversy over Zoloft's side effect profile and whether it differs significantly from that of Prozac. While the gastrointestinal complaints are similar, some clinicians believe that side effects of agitation and anxiety were somewhat less common with sertraline. There is consensus, however, that the half-life of sertraline (about one day) is much shorter than that of fluoxetine. The same is true for the time needed to achieve steady state (seven to ten days). Response is no quicker (still three to six weeks). Complaints upon withdrawal are more frequent. The real controversy focused on effective antidepressant dose. The dose range offered was 50–200 mg per day, leading some clinicians (myself among them) to increase the dose from a starting point of 50 mg at the rate of 50 mg per week to a final dose of 200 mg by week four. For most of my patients, this dose was well tolerated. However, it obscured the therapeutic dose generally needed for response. When the manufacturer, Pfizer, claimed that a 50 mg dose was adequate for most patients with major depression,[20] one prominent clinician disagreed in print.[21] The company spokesperson argued for a 50 mg dose trial for four weeks before concluding that more drug is needed. The company cited a study that showed response to 50 mg of Zoloft equivalent to response at higher doses.[22] The clinician (Dr. Charles

Nemeroff) countered with a study suggesting that doses of 50–150 mg of sertraline are no more effective than placebo but that a 200 mg dose is significantly better.[23] The issue remains unresolved and was raised anew in the midst of the "P450 controversy." As this problem of drug-drug interaction merits further discussion, it will be taken up in a separate section, Issues in Drug Prescription.

Paroxetine (Paxil) Rosemary, a 39-year-old married social worker with a 14-year-old son, was referred to me by her family doctor. She reported the onset of depression one year earlier. Once it began, it never left her "even for one day." Her husband and son constantly complained about her "negative thinking." She frequently cried without reason. She had become indecisive and without energy, constantly exhausted, in part because of severely disrupted sleep. She blamed herself for "all the family's troubles." She had gradually lost weight (she now weighed under 100 pounds), and that was not what she wanted to do.

Rosemary recalled an unhappy childhood in which nothing she did was ever "good enough" for her father. She became an adult whose self-standards were set at a perfectionistic level. Her depressive symptoms regularly worsened premenstrually. A letter or phone call from her father predictably led to a bad day and sometimes to a bad week. She felt "trapped" by her responsibilities at home and at work.

My diagnosis was major depressive disorder. I began a trial of increasing doses of Desyrel (trazodone), hoping to help her insomnia quickly and her depression over a brief time. By two months later, it was clear that there was no response, although Rosemary reported sleeping "somewhat better." I discontinued the drug and prescribed Paxil (paroxetine) at 20 mg each morning.

After three weeks, there was a clear response, with more restful sleep, considerably less anxiety, and less overreactivity to her son and husband. We terminated therapy six sessions later. I saw her twice more in monthly follow-up visits. She remained well.

Rosemary called me six months later to say that she had discontinued the Paxil and her symptoms were back. I saw her once and restarted the antidepressant. She called one month later to tell me that the drug "had kicked in," and she was feeling and functioning better.

I continued to refill her prescription and didn't hear from her until another year had passed. She had stopped the drug three months earlier, and now recognized a return of her depressive symptoms. I saw her four times and resumed the paroxetine at 20 mg. Within three weeks, Rosemary was once again stabilized.

Shortly thereafter, she called to set up a few joint sessions with her husband to talk about problem-solving. Now Paxil has continued for a total of about four years, and Rosemary reports "feeling fine." There has been no further recurrence of depression.

In December 1992 Paxil became the third SSRI approved for the treatment of depression. Paroxetine has no active metabolites, the shortest half-life (21 hours), and the quickest time to steady state (five to seven days).

A once-daily dose of 20 mg is recommended (similar to fluoxetine) and a range of 20–50 mg is advised. The short half-life of Paxil suggests benefits and liabilities similar to those of sertraline. Patient complaints upon withdrawal from Paxil are more frequent than from fluoxetine.

The effectiveness of paroxetine has been established against placebo.[24] Its comparative efficacy with other antidepressants has been demonstrated as well, both for TCAs[25] and other SSRIs.[26] It has been suggested that paroxetine has slightly more affinity than fluoxetine or sertraline for muscarinic receptors, resulting in occasional anticholinergic side effects.[27] Frequency and severity, however, are still markedly below that of the TCAs.

There is little solid basis to dictate a clinical choice among the three available SSRIs. Each is an effective antidepressant and none works predictably more often than another. For some patients (for reasons yet unknown), response to one drug occurs after response to a different SSRI was absent.

The Newer Antidepressants

Venlafaxine (Effexor) Following on the heels of the SSRIs, Effexor, a structurally novel antidepressant, was offered in 1994 as an inhibitor of both norepinephrine and serotonin reuptake.[28] It has little to no affinity for muscarinic, histaminergic, or alpha-adrenergic receptors, thus avoiding the side effects common to the TCAs. It is a weak inhibitor of dopamine reuptake.

Effexor's major problem is a demonstrated, sustained, dose-dependent increase in blood pressure in some patients, most evident at dose levels above 200 mg per day. Regular monitoring of blood pressure is advised.

The suggested dosage range is 75–375 mg per day, prescribed in divided doses, two to three times a day. In contrast to fluoxetine and paroxetine, venlafaxine has an ascending dose-response curve (increased efficacy at higher doses), much like the TCAs. Therefore, patients unresponsive to lower doses (150–225 mg) should be treated with higher doses (up to 375 mg per day). Common side effects are nausea, sleepiness, dry mouth, dizziness, headaches, nervousness, sweating, and tremor. Sexual dysfunction is no more (but no less) frequent than with the SSRIs. At lower doses (75–225 mg), inhibition of serotonin reuptake is thought to predominate, with side effects (chiefly gastrointestinal) similar to the those of the SSRIs. At higher doses, elevation in blood pressure, sweating, and tremor are consistent with norepinephrine reuptake inhibition.

Placebo-controlled trials demonstrated Effexor's efficacy in depression.[29] Venlafaxine has an elimination half-life of only three to five hours (leading to the need for divided doses), with a metabolite having a half-life of nine to eleven hours. It is recommended that the drug be tapered on discontinuation to prevent withdrawal symptoms. Because Efflexor is only a weak inhibitor of the cytochrome P450 enzyme 2D6, drug-drug interactions on this basis were expected to be minimal, but there is an exception: when switching antidepressants from fluoxetine to venlafaxine, clinicians should note that the conversion of venlafaxine to its major metabolite (O-desmethylvenlafaxine) is dependent upon the liver enzyme 2D6. Fluoxetine will likely block this conversion, resulting in an increase in levels of Effexor. Due to the lengthy half-life of fluoxetine, it is advisable to start a subsequent trial of venlafaxine at one-half to one-quarter of the usual starting dose of 75 mg. A similar 2D6 effect would be anticipated with paroxetine; however, with its shorter half-life a wait of one week should eliminate the potential problem. Similar to the SSRIs, venlafaxine should not be started until a prior trial with an MAOI has cleared.

Nefazodone (Serzone)   In a commercial message well known in the United States of the mid-1990s, a stage actor, equally well known, extolls the virtues of "having choices." The concept was not lost on the pharmaceutical industry, which had entered the realm of treating depression some 40 years earlier with the serendipitous discovery of the therapeutic value of iproniazid (the first MAOI) and imipramine (the first TCA). Four tricyclics followed, each achieving a place in some clinician's bag. Phenelzine (Nardil) and tranylcypromine (Parnate) had already gained attention among the MAOIs, lost favor, and then returned as their usefulness became more selectively defined. These seven drugs were augmented by two second-generation antidepressants, trazodone (Desyrel) and amoxapine (Asendin). Nomifensine (Merital) came, and then departed, a victim of reported intolerable side effects.

Wellbutrin came, was withdrawn, and then reintroduced. The SSRIs brought the generally accepted antidepressant drug choices to a baker's dozen (thirteen). Effexor was number fourteen. The year 1995 produced the fifteenth, nefazodone (Serzone).

Chemically a phenylpiperazine, nefazodone bears a structural relationship to trazodone. This compound has three active metabolites: hydroxynefazodone, triazolodione, and meta-chlorophenyl piperazine (MCPP). Plasma levels of the first and the third are considerably less than that of the parent compound, but triazolodione levels are ten times greater (in part because their half-life, 18–33 hours, is longer than the parent's). The elimination half-life of Serzone is the shortest of all the available choices: only four hours.

In vitro studies have shown that nefazodone is metabolized by the liver's P450 cytochrome enzymes 3A3/3A4. Drugs that affect these enzymes may therefore alter the metabolism of Serzone. Two such drugs are the commonly prescribed alprazolam (Xanax) and the sedative triazolam (Halcion). When these are prescribed with Serzone, there may be a 400% increase in the plasma levels of these benzodiazepines. In addition, the commonly prescribed antihistamines terfenadine (Seldane) and astemizole (Hismanal), the antifungal agent ketoniazole, and the antibiotic erythromycin all affect the 3A3/3A4 enzyme system. Potentially serious accumulations of each of these compounds may occur when they are used in combination with nefazodone. When antihypertensive agents are administered along with Serzone, a reduction in their dosage may be required due to the possibility of orthostatic hypotension and syncope. Clinicians are urged to be aware of these drug-drug interactions.

The most significant known action of nefazodone (like trazodone) is its serotonin reuptake blockade. It seems clear that the second metabolite (triazolodione) contributes significantly to the drug's effect. Nefazodone is not as specific for serotonin as are the SSRIs, but its effect on muscarinic, alpha-adrenergic, and histaminergic receptors, while greater than the SSRIs and venlafaxine, is significantly less than that of the TCAs and trazodone. It is recommended that combined use with the MAOIs be avoided.

Dosing recommendations begin at 100 mg twice daily. The anticipated effective dose is 300 mg, with a range to 500 mg. There is, as with venlafaxine, an ascending dose-response curve. Serzone is thought to be less sedating than trazodone. Like the SSRIs and venlafaxine, Serzone differs from the TCAs by its relative safety in overdose.

Frequent side effects are dizziness, nausea, drowsiness, headache, dry mouth, and constipation. Serzone may aid sleep and may reduce anxiety. Most significant, however, is its low incidence of sexual dysfunction. This has led clinicians to substitute Serzone for other antidepressant drugs when sexual side effects are present, unresponsive to other approaches, and intolerable to the patient. Despite its resemblance to trazodone, priapism has not been observed with nefazodone.

The antidepressant efficacy of nefazodone has been demonstrated,[30] and it has been found to be equivalent in effect to that of imipramine.[31] Some clinicians believe that agitation and anxiety respond more readily to Serzone. Serzone's efficacy and tolerability are similar to those of paroxetine[32] and sertraline.[33]

Fluvoxamine (Luvox)   The sixteenth choice for the treatment of acute depression has not yet been approved for this indication by the F.D.A., but approval is anticpated shortly. It is approved for OCD (1994), however, and some clinicians are already using it for depression. Luvox would be the fourth SSRI available. It is chemically distinct from other antidepressants on the market. Its mean elimination half-life is 19–22 hours. Premarketing trials suggest its efficacy is superior to placebo and equivalent to imipramine. Dosing begins with 25–50 mg at bedtime and may be increased in 25–50 mg increments every four to seven days. The recommended dose range is 50–150 mg per day. The most common effective antidepressant dose in trials was 100 mg per day. Typical SSRI side effects of nausea, sleepiness, or insomnia have been noted in trials, along with headache, nervousness, and sexual dysfunction.

Fluvoxamine inhibits the activity of three cytochrome P450 isoenzymes— 1A2, 2C9, and 3A4—slowing the metabolism of concurrently taken drugs that act on these systems. Because of some reports of seizures, fluvoxamine should be avoided in patients with a history of epilepsy. Lithium and fluvoxamine prescribed together have reportedly been associated with seizures as well. The caution against concurrent prescription of an MAOI and an SSRI obviously applies to fluvoxamine.

Issues in Drug Prescription

The P450 Controversy   The mid-1990s found the antidepressant drug marketplace crowded, with few significant parameters available to aid clinicians in choosing among the SSRIs and the newer antidepressants. It was in this context that the P450 controversy arose. No one challenged the caution that patients taking multiple drugs for differing purposes entailed risks that single drug prescription avoided. And, as the patient aged, the likelihood increased of any number of medical problems coexisting with acute depression—for example, asthma, hypertension, or seasonal allergy. As a consequence, the patient might present to the mental health worker already taking a number of medications.

It was equally well known to most clinicians that most drugs (including most psychotropic drugs) undergo their first metabolic steps (usually oxidation) in the liver. It came as no surprise, therefore, when we began to be deluged with research data relevant to the cytochrome P450 enzyme system. These isoenzymes are located largely in the endoplasmic reticulum of liver cells, and they are responsible for this first metabolic step for many drugs. We learned that there were at least 30 isoforms of the cytochrome P450 system. Some of these drugs form the substrate (are metabolized by) these enzymes. Some of the same drugs inhibit isoforms different from the ones responsible for their metabolism.[34] Therefore, the P450 enzyme system may hold the key to understanding many drug-drug interactions, some of them with potentially serious clinical consequences.

As each compound interacted with this system somewhat differently, "P450" provided the pharmaceutical companies with a rich field for claiming superiority for their particular antidepressant drug over the competition. One well known clinician, taking notice of the unusual publicity given to this issue, questioned its clinical significance, measured against its marketing potential.[35]

Interest was initially piqued by the reported inability of some patients to metabolize the antihistamines Seldane (terfenadine) or Hismanal (astemizole) while taking erythromycin (an antibiotic) or ketoconazole (an antifungal agent). The interaction reportedly led to an increase in the serum level of the antihistamine, with potentially adverse cardiac consequences. All three drugs now carried a warning label contraindicating the prescription of the drugs in combination. The mechanism of the drug-drug interaction is that ketoconazole is a potent inhibitor of cytochrome P450 isoenzyme 3A3/4, while terfenadine, astemizole, and erythromycin are substrates of the same enzyme.

As the field became energized to look into these interactions further, it was found that the antidepressants Serzone, Luvox, Prozac, and Zoloft, along with the benzodiazepines Xanax, Halcion, and the anesthetic Versed, were all metabolized significantly by 3A3/4.[36] This led to published contraindications for the co-prescription of any of these drugs (especially with Serzone or

Luvox). How to resolve the need for an antihistamine in a patient already taking a drug metabolized by 3A3/4? One choice would be to substitute a nasal steroid for the antihistamine. A second choice would be to use a different antihistamine, for example chlorpheniramine (Chlor-Trimeton) or loratidine (Claritin).

Many antidepressants and antipsychotic drugs are initially metabolized by the 2D6 isoenzyme. SSRIs (among other drugs) inhibit 2D6, leading to accumulations of other drugs usually metabolized by 2D6. Three potent inhibitors of 2D6 (for example) are thought to be paroxetine, fluoxetine, and sertraline. Substrates for this enzyme include secondary amine tricyclic antidepressants (nortriptyline, desipramine), some antipsychotic drugs (e.g., haloperidol) and some anti-arrythmic drugs (e.g., flecanide), codeine, and beta blockers. There was the concern that any of these drugs could receive an unwanted boost in serum level from their co-prescription with the antidepressants. Some clinicians treating depression combined nortriptyline (a TCA) with an SSRI. Since both were involved with the 2D6 system, there was the potential for increasing the serum level of the TCA, with the risk of cardiac arrhythmia.

Aside from the contraindications, it is not yet clear which interactions are likely to be insignificant clinically, and which are more worrisome. When the substrate drug had a narrow therapeutic index (short distance between therapeutic effect and toxic effect), the stakes are higher for the potential consequences of drug interaction. As if this were not already uncertain and complicated enough, there is an additional factor to consider. People apparently differed in the activity level for the P450 enzymes, producing marked inter-patient variability.[35] Therefore, even an up-to-date knowledge of potential interactions did not always allow an accurate prediction to be made for the individual patient.

The bottom line for now, until more definitive information is available, is that the clinician should make him- or herself aware of these potentials for drug-drug interactions and then make individual decisions for individual patients, based upon the range of relevant considerations for drug choice in each case. Lists of potential drug interactions are widely available.[34, 35] In addition, there is a special reprint edition of the *Psychiatric Times* that presents a useful table (November 1995, Vol. XII, No. 11).

Treatment-Emergent Sexual Dysfunction A useful understanding of the complaint of sexual side effects attributed to antidepressant medication requires the consideration of factors ranging from cultural to pathological to research findings. If the drug is indeed the culprit, there is much that can be done to help. *Sexual Pharmacology*[81] gives an in-depth review of the options.

For some older clinicians, sexual dysfunction may be a "new" problem, not because it never occurred before, but rather due to conspiracy of silence between doctor and patient. In some circles, patients will still not offer a sexual complaint because it isn't "proper"; today, however, doctors are being strongly urged to overcome their own discomfort (if it's there) and inquire.

Closely related to the office situation is that of the clinical trial of a new drug. Clinical trials rely on spontaneous reports of side effects of new drugs rather than active questioning, likely leading to an underreporting of sexual dysfunction.[37]

Most clinicians are aware of the effect a depressive disorder has in the sexual area. When previous pleasures and interests are lost in the depressed person, decreased sexual desire is a common finding. Both men and women may have, as well, an impaired capacity to achieve orgasm. Decreased sexual activity is the norm, too. Is the sexual dysfunction related, therefore, to the problem (depression) or to the treatment (the drug)? A careful history of when the symptoms began can usually resolve this dilemma.

There is relatively little controlled research available in this area. A majority of reports are anecdotal and not systematic.[38] It is a valid speculation that sexual dysfunction, when attributed to a treatment, may lead to noncompliance with that treatment.

All the antidepressants (TCAs, MAOIs, SSRIs) and lithium carbonate have, at some point, been associated with sexual dysfunction. (Two compounds, bupropion and nefazodone, appear so far to be exceptions to this finding.) The mechanism by which the dysfunction is wrought is not yet clear.[39] It is known, however, that alpha-adrenergic mechanisms are central to erection and ejaculation, while inhibition of orgasmic function may be associated with serotonin.[37]

Estimates of the magnitude of the problem vary widely, from less than 2% of antidepressant users to over 90%.[38] In one study, utilizing a structured questionaire, 37% of patients with mood disorders treated with a variety of agents reported sexual dysfunction.[39] Interestingly, 16% reported increased libido as well, likely due to diminution of depression. An older, but systematic, study found that 30% of patients taking imipramine and 40% of patients taking phenelzine acknowledged sexual side effects.[40] A later study investigating fluoxetine found a figure of 8.3%.[41]

It is evident, then, that treatment-emergent sexual dysfunction is a real concern, but what can the clinician do about it? First, *inquire* about your patient's sexual functioning. Second, *document* whether the problem is likely related to the treatment. Third, consider a *dose reduction* of the antidepressant in question. Fourth, consider a *change* to an antidepressant less likely to interfere with sexual functioning (currently, bupropion or nefazodone). The literature is accumulating that bupropion (which, you will recall, has little to no serotonergic activity) is only rarely associated with sexual complaints.[37, 42, 43]

If you decide to continue the antidepressant associated with sexual side effects, there remain multiple options in the form of drugs to add. For anorgasmia, bethanechol (urecholine) 10–20 mg has worked.[44] Additional choices are cyproheptadine (Periactin) 4–12 mg,[45] yohimbine (Yocon) 10 mg,[46] amantidine,[47] methylphenidate,[48] and buspirone.[49]

Apparently, no one treatment resolves the problem for all people all the time. But there are today a multitude of choices. And at times the sexual problem does resolve "spontaneously."

ELECTROCONVULSIVE THERAPY (ECT)

While ECT is not today a first-line treatment for an uncomplicated major depressive episode, it remains a useful alternative for the clinician. The controversy that has surrounded convulsive therapy is not about its efficacy or safety. It works as well or better than drug treatment and, for many clinical situations, it is as safe or safer than antidepressant medications. It has been portrayed to the public, however, as potentially invasive and brain-damaging.

Max Fink, a long-time advocate of ECT, has reviewed the perilous journey the treatment has taken with general public opinion and documented its negative impact on research as well as clinical receptivity.[50] He notes how the terminology ("electroshock") calls to mind "electrocution," one application of the legal death penalty. ECT has been a focus of the so-called antipsychiatry movement because it has formed a vulnerable target in the public mind. Some mental health professionals oppose the use of ECT because it is inconsistent with their psychological view of the causality of emotional disorder or antithetical to their preferred psychotherapeutic approach to every patient. The media presentation of shock therapy as "punishment" or as a way of imposing control over another has made the acceptance of ECT as a therapeutic option more difficult.

In response, the American Psychiatric Association formed a task force to evaluate ECT and issued a report in 1978.[51] They found a role for convulsive therapy in the treatment of major depression, intractable mania, and therapy-resistant schizophrenia. A British survey by the Royal College of Psychiatrists (1980) offered similar indications and support.[52] ECT was the focus of a 1985 NIH/NIMH Consensus Development Conference, which concluded that the treatment is effective and safe.[53] Finally, a detailed review was presented by a second A.P.A. task force in 1990, supporting similar conclusions.[54] A journal (*Convulsive Therapy*) and a society (The Association for Convulsive Therapy) have arisen to support and enhance communication about the treatment technique.

History

Electroconvulsive therapy is not new; it predates the introduction of antidepressant drugs by two decades. Ladislas von Meduna first found that pharmacological (camphor-induced) seizures mitigated psychotic symptoms in schizophrenics (Hungary, 1934). The formal introduction of therapeutic use of electrical seizures is attributed to Ugo Cerletti and Luigi Bini in 1938 in Rome, Italy.[55] Cerletti was studying the brains of animals with epilepsy. He noted that the duration of exposure to electricity was the potentially lethal element, rather than the amplitude of the voltage. It was Bini who found that the high rate of fatality from shock therapy in animals was due to current going through the heart. He determined that electrode placement would be best on the temples.

Initially, ECT was applied to the treatment of schizophrenia. Later, it was found that it produced even better results in depression. Lothar B. Kalinowsky was the first to use shock therapy in the U.S., in 1940 at the Pennsylvania Hospital. Soon after its introduction, it was applied to a broad range of psychiatric disorders. A. E. Bennett was the first (also in 1940) to suggest spinal anesthesia to prevent fractures, which were not uncommonly seen with convulsive therapy.[56] He worked with curare and recommended this muscle relaxant as a fracture preventative. In 1951, succinyl choline became available as a safe muscle relaxant for use with ECT.[55] Short-acting barbiturate anesthesia protected the patient from distress related to paralysis of the respiratory muscles during the procedure.

When the antidepressant drugs were introduced in the 1950s, enthusiasm for ECT waned, and its use declined. Its rebirth occurred 20 years later, in the context of the identification of depressed patients unresponsive to drug therapy as well as to psychotherapy.[50]

Research

Newer brain-imaging techniques have allowed a scientific answer to critics associating brain damage with ECT. Studies utilizing computed tomography (CT) scanning have found no morphological changes attributable to convulsive therapy.[57] A major researcher, C. Edward Coffey, showed, utilizing magnetic resonance imaging (MRI), that preexisting brain abnormalities are common in patients receiving ECT.[58] These are attributable to normal aging, medical conditions, or psychiatric disorders.

In a field diverse enough to encompass most mental health care providers, some pretty wild theories have been offered to explain the effects of convulsive therapy. O'Connor reviewed the hypotheses, along with any relevant data in the literature.[59] Some have claimed that ECT works because it satisfies the depressed patient's need for punishment, or due to another form of placebo effect. Controlled studies utilizing "sham ECT" (treatment without the electric current) have demonstrated that this hypothesis is inaccurate. Some have claimed that ECT induces amnesia (true) and that patients forget the reasons they became depressed. Interestingly, the degree and duration of memory loss vary with unilateral and bilateral electrode placement. No association, however, has ever been shown between the amnesic effect and therapeutic benefit. Finally, some have hypothesized the existence of a peptide ("anti-depressin") and suggested that ECT stimulates its release. This has never, however, been demonstrated.

Indications and Contraindications

It is generally agreed that the endogenous type of acute depression responds to ECT.[60] This conforms to a symptom picture of severe depressed mood, psychomotor retardation, early morning awakening, excessive guilt, and diurnal mood variation. A history of previous depressive episodes (recurrence) and/or the presence of delusions are signs that favor a good response to ECT. ECT may be indicated in the older patient with concurrent medical illness or one likely to be intolerant to drug side effects. ECT may be indicated early in a woman's pregnancy when drug use is discouraged. ECT is typically prescribed somewhere in the sequence of treatment for the resistant patient (discussed in the section, Resistant Depression.)

Response is the same in both genders.[61] Response may be slower in the older patient.[62] When the depressed patient is dangerously suicidal, ECT may be the fastest-acting treatment alternative. In the treatment of the bipolar patient, convulsive therapy is thought to have a place in the management of intractable mania, as well as among the different options for treating patients with mixed states.

While there are clinical situations in which caution is strongly advised in the prescription of ECT, there may well be no absolute contraindications.[1] Space-occupying lesions (brain tumors) and recent myocardial infarctions with unstable cardiac function have long been "relative" contraindications. Cerebral and aortic aneurysms, a past history of cerebral hemorrhage, pheochromocytoma, and retinal detachments would each seem to pose relevant risk. Since the modified convulsion is usually accompanied by a transient rise in blood pressure, in ECT with the hypertensive patient risks must be weighed against benefits.[60]

Procedure, Side Effects, and Maintenance

Typically a short-acting anesthetic—e.g., methohexitol (Brevitol)—is administered prior to a muscle relaxant—e.g., succinyl choline. The use of benzodiazepines, barbiturates, or anticonvulsants all seem to hinder the capacity to induce a seizure.[63] In 1958, Lancaster et al. coined the term "unilateral ECT."[64] With one-sided electrode placement, memory loss was found to be diminished; however, efficacy may be less as well. As a result, bilateral ECT continues to dominate clinical practice.[63]

It is commonly observed that loss of consciousness following a treatment may last for up to 20 minutes. This state resolves with gradual recovery of mental functioning. The speed of recovery is thought to vary with electrode placement (unilateral effects more rapid recovery than bilateral), age (older patients may take longer to recover), and number of treatments (there appears to be a cumulative effect, with slower recovery observed as the course of treatment goes on).

Once the depressed patient treated with ECT recovers from the acute episode, it is not clear how long-lasting the recovery is.[63] To prolong recovery, both maintenance ECT and maintenance antidepressant medication have been suggested. Some have recommended lithium carbonate.[65] Others have favored an antidepressant drug with a purported mechanism of action different from one previously administered to the patient.[63] Kramer (among others) has suggested maintenance ECT.[66] Depressed patients with the psychotic subtype may require both a neuroleptic and an antidepressant to prevent relapse.[67]

It seems like good clinical practice today for the clinician treating depression to know where in his or her community electroconvulsive therapy is administered. In addition, the clinican must determine where ECT fits in his or her individual approach to the depressed patient. The clinician must be able to discuss convulsive therapy with patients and their families when it is an option. Finally, the practitioner should keep up with new developments relevant to this treatment option.

PSYCHOTHERAPY

Psychotherapy may be considered as the sole intervention provided for some patients with an acute depressive episode. As our biological knowledge base has increased and managed care plans have dictated more rapid and less expensive treatment, psychotherapy for acute depression may also be utilized as an adjunct to somatic treatment. One aspect of this procedure was referred to in the past as "supportive therapy." Today, we call it psychotherapeutic management. As such, it integrates many aspects of good clinical care. It combines the value of the therapeutic relationship with the vigilance of a good clinician, the instruction of a good teacher, and the structuring of a skilled therapist. Its major elements are summarized in Table 10.5.

A third application of psychotherapy in acute depression combines its power to effect change with that of a somatic treatment. Today, a psychiatrist may deliver both components, or a psychotherapist may work with a pharmacologist and each may focus on a separate aspect of the patient's problem.

Table 10.5
PSYCHOTHERAPEUTIC MANAGEMENT OF THE
ACUTE DEPRESSIVE EPISODE

• Establish a therapeutic relationship.	• Provide a prescription for relief.
• Strengthen hope.	• Educate the patient about depression.
• Set realistic goals.	• Discourage major life changes.
• Be vigilant for destructive impulses.	• Enlist the support of significant others.
• Provide an explanation for symptoms.	• Encourage success experiences.

Modified from American Psychiatric Association, 1993[1]

It appears that the future will support, at best, short-term psychotherapy interventions for acute depression. Choices will span the psychodynamic, cognitive, interpersonal, and behavioral therapy spectrum. In practice, psychotherapists form their own integration and interpretation of these systems into individual styles of therapeutic intervention. The specific techniques and the more general relationship elements join together to make up the therapist's offering.

Let's now briefly consider in more detail the choices available for the psychotherapeutic treatment of acute depression, emphasizing relevant theory, usual focus, therapy aims, and typical format.

Psychodynamic Psychotherapy

Although there are multiple psychoanalytic understandings relevant to depression, the major theoretical concepts describe the loss of an ambivalently held object, resulting in repressed, self-directed rage. The focus spans psychological vulnerability, externally dependent self-worth, early lack of love, guilt based upon a harsh conscience, repressed wishes, and frustration due to high ego ideals. Therapy aims to bring the unconscious factors into awareness and help the patient to master the relevant conflicts or to neutralize them with insight. A concurrent aim is to utilize the transference relationship to promote change in thoughts, feelings, and actions.

While I know of no specific guide to doing psychodynamic psychotherapy with the depressed patient, there are a number of systems of short-term psychoanalytic therapy worth exploring.[68-70]

Cognitive Therapy (CT)

Cognitive theory centers upon the irrational beliefs and distorted attitudes that underlie the depression. The focus is on thoughts, attributions, and meanings. Therapy is an active, often structured, problem-solving dialogue. It employs homework to reinforce in-session learning. There are no interpretations made and no specific utilization of the concept of transference or the unconscious. The relationship may be discussed within the structure of a cognitive agenda (not unlike other material). The format is for brief therapy, generally once-weekly meetings, and is rooted in the here-and-now. The original manual for teaching cognitive therapy is available,[71] along with the author's practical guide for clinicians[72] and a status report.[73]

Interpersonal Therapy (IPT)

This model views depression as a disruption of attachment bonds. Four foci are offered: grief reactions, role disputes, role transitions, and interpersonal deficits. The therapist begins by defining the problem focus and setting goals, then selects relevant treatment strategies. The format is brief therapy that is present-oriented. The original manual describing IPT is available,[74] as well as a modification that applies the original principles more broadly [75] and a status report.[76]

Behavior Therapy (BT)

Relevant theoretical considerations in depression are a sustained reduction in response-contingent positive reinforcement and the presence of social skill deficits. The focus is on habit, behavior, and action. It may involve problem-solving and self-control issues. Treatment techniques include desensitization, skills training, activity scheduling, and assertiveness training. The format is both brief and rooted in the present.

Suggestions for designing a behavior therapy program for the depressed patient are available.[77, 78] A review of relevant research data by Becker and Heimberg[79] and a comparative study by Bellack et al.[80] should be helpful to the clinician seeking to apply the behavioral model to depression.

POSTSCRIPT

In addition broadening the range of treatment models, the clinician may broaden the range of participants. When one member of a couple is acutely depressed, psychotherapy may take the form of marital therapy. Some clinicians will offer family therapy to approach depression from a systems theory perspective. When the focus of the patient's problem is interpersonal, group therapy may offer approaches lacking in the standard two-person interaction.

Since there is not yet general agreement or scientific basis for prescribing a specific form of psychotherapy for depression, patient preference often determines the selection. As the influence of managed care grows, the predilection of the therapist to which the patient is assigned may more often dictate how he or she is treated. Management needs may more often determine the frequency of visits, along with guidelines established by the managed care company. When there is no response to psychotherapy, somatic treatment may be considered even in mild cases.[1]

Notes

1. American Psychiatric Association. (1993). *Practice guideline for major depressive disorder in adults.* Washington D.C.: American Psychiatric Association.

2. American Psychiatric Association. (1994). Practice guideline for the treatment of patients with bipolar disorder. *American Journal of Psychiatry, 151*(Suppl. 12), 1.

3. English, J. T. (October 20, 1996). *Resolved: Is there a future for psychiatry in the emerging health delivery system? (Affirmative position).* Presented at the Institute on Psychiatric Services, Chicago, IL.

4. Michels, R. (October 20, 1996). *Resolved: Is there a future for psychiatry in the emerging health delivery system? (Negative position).* Presented at the Institute on Psychiatric Services, Chicago, IL.

5. Stone, A. A. (1995). Paradigms, pre-emptions and stages: Understanding the transformation of American psychiatry by managed care. *International Journal of Law and Psychiatry, 18*(4), 353.

6. Eist, H. Quoted in 3, 4.

7. Blackwell, B. (1963). Hypertensive crisis due to monoamine oxidase inhibitors. *Lancet, 2,* 849.

8. Kaplan, H. I., Sadock, B. J., & Grebb, J. A. (1994). *Synopsis of psychiatry* (7th ed.). Baltimore: Williams & Wilkins.

9. Liebowitz, M. R., Quitkin, F. M., Stewart, J. W., et al. (1988). Antidepressant specificity in atypical depression. *Archives of General Psychiatry, 45,* 129.

10. Thase, M. E., Frank, E., Mallinger, A. G., et al. (1992). Treatment of imipramine-resistant recurrent depression, III: Efficacy of monoamine-oxidase inhibitors. *Journal of Clinical Psychiatry, 53*(1), 5.

11. Clary, C., Mandos, L. A., & Schweizer, E. (1990). Results of a brief survey on the prescribing practices for monoamine-oxidase inhibitor antidepressants. *Journal of Clinical Psychiatry, 51*(6), 226.

12. Gardner, D. M., Shulman, K. I., Walker, S. E. et al. (1996). The making of a user friendly MAOI diet. *Journal of Clinical Psychiatry, 57*(3), 99.

13. Wernicke, J. F., Dunlop, S. R., Dornseif, B. E., et al. (1987). Fixed dose fluoxetine therapy for depression. *Psychopharmacolgy Bulletin, 23,* 164.

14. Sternbach, H. (1991). The serotonin syndrome. *American Journal of Psychiatry, 148,* 705.

15. Teicher, M. H., Glod, C., Cole, J. O. (1990). Emergence of intense suicidal pre-occupation during fluoxetine treatment. *American Journal of Psychiatry, 147,* 207.

16. Stokes, P. E. (1993). Fluoxetine: A five year review. *Clinical Therapeutics, 15*(2), 216.

17. Beasley, C. M., Dornseif, B.E., Bosomworth, J. C., et al. (1991). Fluoxetine and suicide: A meta-analysis of controlled trials of treatment for depression. *British Medical Journal, 303,* 685.

18. Fava, M., & Rosenbaum, J. F. (1991). Suicidality and fluoxetine: Is there a relationship? *Journal of Clinical Psychiatry, 52*, 108.
19. Reimherr, F. W., Chouinard, G., Cohn, C. K., et al. (1990). Antidepressant efficacy of sertraline: A double-blind, placebo-and amitryptiline-controlled, multicenter comparison study in outpatients with Major Depression. *Journal of Clinical Psychiatry, 51* (Suppl. 12B), 18.
20. Lane, M. (1996). [Letter to the editor]. *Journal of Clinical Psychiatry, 57*(6), 265.
21. Nemeroff, C. B. (1996). [Letter to the editor]. *Journal of Clinical Psychiatry, 57*(6), 267.
22. Fabre, L .F., Abuzzahab, F. S., Amin, M., et al. (1995). Sertraline safety and efficacy in major depression: A double-blind, fixed-dose comparison with placebo. *Biological Psychiatry, 38*, 592.
23. Amin, M., Lehmann, H., & Mirmiran, J. (1989). A double-blind, placebo-controlled, dose-finding study with sertraline. *Psychopharmacology Bulletin, 25*, 164.
24. Rickels, K., Amsterdam, J., Clavy, C., et al. (2992). The efficacy and safety of paroxetine compared with placebo in outpatients with major depression. *Journal of Clinical Psychiatry, 53*(Suppl. 2), 30.
25. Fabre, L. F. (1992). A six-week, double-blind trial of paroxetine, imipramine, and placebo in depressed outpatients. *Journal of Clinical Psychiatry, 53*(Suppl. 3), 40.
26. Dewilde, J., Spiers, R., Mertens, C., et al. (1993). A double-blind, comparative, multi-center study comparing paroxetine with fluoxetine in depressed patients. *Acta Psychiatrica Scandinavica, 87*(2), 141.
27. Thomas, D. R., Nelson, D. R., & Johnson, A. M. (1987). Biochemical effects of the antidepressant paroxetine, a specific 5-hydroxytryptamine uptake inhibitor. *Psychopharmacology, 93*, 193.
28. Muth, E. A., Haskins, J. T., Moyer, J. A., et al. (1986). Antidepressant biochemical profile of the novel bicyclic compound WY-45,030, an ethyl cyclohexamol derivation. *Biochemical Pharmacology, 35*, 4493.
29. Ballenger, J. C. (1996). Clinical evaluation of venlafaxine. *Journal of Clinical Psychopharmacology, 16*(3 Suppl. 2), 298.
30. Rickels, K., Robinson, D. S., Schweizer, E., et al. (1995). Nefazodone: Aspects of efficacy. *Journal of Clinical Psychiatry, 56*(Suppl. 6), 43.
31. Rickels, K., Schweizer, E., Clary, C., et al. (1994). Nefazodone and imipramine in major depression: A placebo-controlled trial. *British Journal of Psychiatry, 164*, 802.
32. Baldwin, D. S., Hawley, C. J., Abed, R. T., et al. (1996). A multi-center, double blind comparison of nefazodone and paroxetine in the treatment of outpatients with moderate-to-severe depression. *Journal of Clinical Psychiatry, 57*(Suppl. 2), 46.
33. Feiger, A., Kiev, A., Shrivastava, R. K., et al. (1996). Nefazodone versus sertraline in outpatients with major depression: Focus on efficacy, tolerability and

effects on sexual function and satisfaction. *Journal of Clinical Psychiatry*, *57*(Suppl. 2), 53.

34. Gelenberg, A. J. (1995). The P 450 family. *Biological Therapies in Psychiatry Newsletter*, *18*(8), 29.

35. Nemeroff, C. B., Devane, C. L., & Pollock, B. G. (1996). Newer antidepressants and the cytochrome P 450 system. *American Journal of Psychiatry*, *153*(3), 311.

36. Swims, M. P. (1993). Potential terfenadine-fluoxetine interaction. *Annals of Pharmacotherapy*, *27*, 1404.

37. Walker, P. W., Cole, J. O., Gardner, E. A., et al. (1993). Improvement in fluoxetine-associated sexual dysfunction in patients switched to bupropion. *Journal of Clinical Psychiatry*, *54*, 459.

38. Balon, R., Yeragani, V. K., & Pohl, R. (1993). Sexual dysfunction during antidepressant treatment. *Journal of Clinical Psychiatry*, *54*, 209.

39. Segraves, R. T. (1992). Sexual dysfunction complicating the treatment of depression. *Journal of Clinical Psychiatry*, *10*(1), 75.

40. Harrison, W. M., Rabkin, J. G., Ehrhardt, A. A., et al. (1991). Effects of antidepressant medication on sexual function: A controlled study. *Journal of Clinical Psychopharmacology*, *52*, 461.

41. Herman, J. B., Brotman, J. W., Pollack, M. H., et al. (1990). Fluoxetine-induced sexual dysfunction. *Journal of Clinical Psychiatry*, *51*, 25.

42. Gardner, E. A., & Johnston, J. A. (1976). Bupropion: An antidepressant without sexual pathophysiological action. *Journal Clinical Psychopharmacology*, *5*, 24.

43. Gelenberg, A. J. (1996). Sexual effects of bupropion. *Biological Therapies in Psychiatry Newsletter*, *19*(8),29.

44. Yager, J. (1986). Bethanechol chloride can reverse erectile and ejaculatory dysfunction induced by tricyclic antidepressants and mazindol: A case report. *Journal of Clinical Psychiatry*, *47*, 210.

45. McCormick, S., Olin, J., & Brotman, A. W. (1990). Reversal of fluoxetine-induced anorgasmia by cyproheptadine in two patients. *Journal of Clinical Psychiatry*, *51*, 383.

46. Hollander, E., & McCarley, A. (1992). Yohimbine treatment of sexual side effects induced by serotonin reuptake blockers. *Journal of Clinical Psychiatry*, *53*, 207.

47. Bartlik, B. D., Kaplan, P., & Kaplan, H. S. (1995). Psychostimulants apparently reverse sexual dysfunction secondary to selective serotonin reuptake inhibitors. *Journal of Sex and Marital Therapy*, *21*, 262.

48. Balogh, S., Hendricks, S. E., & Kang, J. (1992). Treatment of fluoxetine-induced anorgasmia with amantadine [Letter]. *Journal of Clinical Psychiatry*, *53*, 212.

49. Nordon, M. J. (1994). Buspirone treatment of sexual dysfunction associated with selective serotonin reuptake inhibitors. *Depression*, *2*, 109.

50. Fink, M. (1991). Impact of the anti-psychiatry movement on the revival of electroconvulsive therapy in the United States. *Psychiatric Clinics of North America*, *14*(4), 793.

51. American Psychiatric Association. (1978). *Electroconvulsive therapy: Task force report #14.* Washington D.C.: American Psychiatric Association.
52. Pippard, J., & Ellam, L. (1980). *Electroconvulsive treatment in Great Britain.* London: Gaskell.
53. NIH/NIMH Consensus Development Panel. (1985). Electroconvulsive therapy. *Journal of the American Medical Association, 254,* 103.
54. American Psychiatric Association. (1990). *The practice of electroconvulsive therapy: Recommendations for treatment, training, and privileging.* Washington D.C.: American Psychistric Association.
55. Kalinowsky, L. B. (1991). History of convulsive therapy. *Psychiatric Clinics of North America, 14*(4), 1.
56. Bennett, A. E. (1940). Preventing traumatic complications in convulsive shock therapy by curare. *Journal of the American Medical Association, 141,* 322.
57. Black, J. L. (1993). ECT: Lessons learned about an old treatment with new technologies. *Psychiatric Annals, 23*(1), 7.
58. Coffey, C. E., Weiner, R. D., Djang, & W. T. et al. (1991). Brain anatomic effects of electroconvulsive therapy: A prospective magnetic resonance imaging study. *Archives of General Psychiatry, 48,* 1013.
59. O'Connor, M. K. (1993). Hypotheses regarding the mechanism of action of electroconvulsive therapy, past and present. *Psychiatric Annals, 23*(1), 15.
60. Hamilton, M. (1986). Electroconvulsive therapy: Indications and contraindications. *Annals of the New York Academy of Science, 462,* 5.
61. Zetin, M., Sklansky, G. J., & Cramer, M. (1984). Sex differences in inpatients with major depression. *Journal of Clinical Psychiatry, 45,* 257.
62. Rich, C. L., Spikles, D. G., Jewell, S. W., et al. (1984). The efficiency of ECT: 1. Response rate in depressive episodes. *Psychiatry Research, 11,* 167.
63. Khan, A., Mirolo, M. H., Hughes, D., et al. (1993). Electroconvulsive therapy. *Psychiatric Clinics of North America, 16*(3), 497.
64. Lancaster, N. P., Steinert, R. R., & Frost, I. (1958). I. Unilateral electro-convulsive therapy. *Journal of Mental Science, 104,* 221.
65. Coppen, A., Abou-Saleh, M. T., Millen, P., et al. (1981). Lithium continuation therapy following electroconvulsive therapy. *British Journal of Psychiatry, 139,* 284.
66. Kramer, B. A. (1990). Maintenance electroconvulsive therapy in clinical practice. *Convulsive Therapy, 6,* 279.
67. Aronson, T. A., Shukla, S, Gujavarty, K., et al. (1988). Relapse in delusional depression: A retrospective study of the course of treatment. *Comprehensive Psychiatry, 29,* 12.
68. Sifneos, P. E. (1987). *Short-term dynamic psychotherapy: Evaluation and technique.* New York: Plenum.
69. Malan, D. H. (1976). *The frontier of brief psychotherapy: An example of the convergence of research and clinical practice.* New York: Plenum.

70. Mann, J., & Goldman, R. (1982). *A casebook in time-limited psychotherapy.* New York: McGraw-Hill.

71. Beck, A. T., Rush, A. J., Shaw, B. F., et al. (1979). *Cognitive therapy of depression.* New York: Guilford.

72. Schuyler, D. (1991). *A practical guide to cognitive therapy.* New York: Norton.

73. Robins, C. J., & Hayes, A. M. (1993). An appraisal of cognitive therapy. *Journal of Consulting and Clinical Psychology, 61*(2), 205.

74. Klerman, G. L., Weissman, M. M., Rounsaville, B. J., et al. (1984). *Interpersonal therapy of depression.* New York: Basic.

75. Klerman, G. L., & Weissman, M. M. (1993). *New applications of interpersonal psychotherapy.* Washington D.C.: American Psychiatric Association.

76. Weissman, M. M., & Markowitz, J. C. (1994). Interpersonal psychotherapy: Current status. *Archives of General Psychiatry, 51,* 599.

77. Foa, E. B., Rothenbaum, B. O., & Kozak, M. J. (1989). Behavioral treatments for anxiety and depression. In P. C. Kendall & D. Watson, *Anxiety and depression: Distinctive and overlapping features.* New York: Academic Press.

78. Becker, R. E., Heimberg, R. G., & Bellack, A. S. (1987). *Social skills training treatment for depression.* New York: Pergamon.

79. Becker, R. E., & Heimberg, R. G. (1984). Cognitive-behavior therapies for depression: A review of controlled clinical research. In A. Dean (Ed.), *Depression in multidisciplinary perspectives.* New York: Brunner/Mazel.

80. Bellack, A. S., Hersen, M., & Himmelhoch, J. M. (1983). A comparison of social skills training, pharmacotherapy and psychotherapy for depression. *Behavioral Research and Therapy, 21,* 101.

81. Crenshaw, T. L. & Goldberg, J. P. (1996). *Sexual pharmacology: Drugs that affect sexual function.* New York: Norton.

Chapter 11

Tailoring Treatment to the Illness
Dysthymia, MDD, Bipolar Depression, and Resistant Depression

Over the past two decades, there have been significant changes that affect how we treat the depressive disorders. Clearly, the progression from *DSM-II* to *DSM-III* and *DSM-IV* has been one engine that has driven change in treatment prescription. Dysthymia, for example, is more clearly defined, and treatment is more often expected to include drugs in addition to psychotherapy. Bipolar depression is better researched and better understood; as a result, patients often have a better understanding of it, and clinicians have a braoder range of treatment options. New drugs have been added to the armamentarium for treating mania and altering the course of bipolar and unipolar disorders. For major depression there is a larger collection of pharmacological choices, allowing the clinician to more selectively tailor the drugs to the needs of the individual patient. The subsyndromal and the less frequently encountered forms of depression are better defined, more often recognized, and therefore more amenable to intervention. New treatment algorithms are being developed and tried for resistant depression, the clinically most challenging depression.

TREATING DYSTHYMIA

The one-two punch of *DSM-III*'s redefinition of dysthymia as a mood disorder and managed care's stimulus favoring short-term treatment has led to new clinical approaches for what many clinicians see as "garden-variety" depression. This subsyndromic form makes up a significant part of the practice of most clinicians and, in the past, was treated almost exclusively with long-term psychotherapy.

Research in the late 1980s and '90s has shown that significant numbers of dysthymics improve with antidepressant medication.[1] Table 11.1 summarizes the research studies, which began by testing the efficacy of imipramine against placebo in 1988 and by 1993 were matching the SSRIs against TCAs and placebo. All three drug classes have demonstrated effectiveness with some dysthymics. The placebo response in treating this subsyndromic disorder is surprisingly low. The second surprise is the lengths to which clinicians are willing to go in treating resistant dysthymia. The sequence illustrated in Table 11.2 is little different from somatic treatments offered for full syndrome major depressive disorder.[2]

I have combined the provision of psychotherapy with the prescription of antidepressant medication for the majority of my dysthymic patients over the past decade. Being a clinician (and not a researcher), I focus on providing for each patient the greatest probability of a successful outcome, and only secondarily on understanding why an intervention worked. As a consequence, when there is recovery from depression, the active ingredient in change may be elusive. However, for one dysthymic patient I can recall the active ingredient was surely the antidepressant drug.

Pharmacotherapy

Rick, a 49-year-old computer specialist was referred to me by his wife, who is a clinical psychologist. He was "unhappy with his situation at work and at home," and his therapist-spouse saw him as depressed. In addition, Rick was

Table 11.1
ANTIDEPRESSANTS FOR DYSTHYMIA: RESEARCH REPORTS

- Kocsis et al. (1988)[66]:   Imipramine (59%) Placebo (13%)

- Stewart et al. (1989)[67]:   Imipramine (78%) Phenelzine (58%) Placebo (33%)

- Nardi et al. (1992)[68]:   Moclobemide (75%) Imipramine (73%) Placebo (26%)

- Hellerstein et al. (1993)[69]: Fluoxetine (62.5%) Placebo (18.8%)

- Thase and Holland (1995)[2]: Sertraline (54%) Imipramine (56%) Placebo (39%)

Modified from Harrison and Stewart, 1993[1]

Table 11.2	
AN ALGORITHM FOR THE ANTIDEPRESSANT	
TREATMENT OF DYSTHYMIA	
1. SSRI	**5.** TCA + SSRI
2. second SSRI	**6.** augment with Li or T3
3. Effexor or Wellbutrin	**7.** MAOI
4. TCA	**8.** ECT
From Thase and Howland, 1995[2]	

"passed over" for a promotion at work and became so angry that he found himself withdrawn and inaccessible on the job, where he had previously been gregarious and open. He replayed this work event over and over again in his mind. There were, however, few vegetative changes. Although tired and having less than his usual amount of energy and enthusiasm, Rick slept and ate normally. There was no weight change. He felt sad and "detached," but didn't cry.

It was unclear whether his emotional state represented an early stage of a major depression or a more chronic condition being interpreted within the context of an acute event. Regardless, the diagnosis appeared to me to be dysthymia. There was no previous history or any family history of major depression.

My judgment was that psychotherapy as a sole intervention was not likely to engage Rick, so I prescribed Prozac (fluoxetine) at the outset. There was no change noted for four weeks. At week five, he reported "doing better at home" for the first time and beginning to tackle his work situation "as a problem" rather than "just staying angry about it." I saw Rick next one month later and he told me that he was back to his usual self. He was outgoing at home and at work. He had talked to his boss about the work event and received an acceptable response. He eagerly anticipated the resumption of some activities that were fun for him and for his wife as well. We met for a total of seven sessions.

The recommendation, therefore, is to consider a trial of an SSRI for most patients with dysthymia.

Psychotherapy

Rebecca was unmarried and the elder of two daughters in a middle-class Florida family. She had been depressed for as long as she could remember. Recently, her younger sister Ellen had died suddenly of a heart attack. Her mother died young from complications of hypertension, and her father had died two years earlier of lung cancer. Rebecca was "alone," but the story wasn't that simple. Her memories of childhood were dominated by her father's constant physical abuse of her mother and his constant negative and critical commentary to Rebecca. Her sister, too, was "mean and inaccessible." Rebecca concentrated on her schoolwork, and she did extremely well. After college, she took and passed a challenging CPA exam and began to pursue her career. She described an "inner voice" that was constantly belittling her and blaming her. Relationships with men had always ended badly, with Rebecca believing "there was something wrong with me—that's why I always end up alone." One example of a disappointment was enough for her to overgeneralize—"All men criticize me"—and then to personalize—"So, I must be bad."

Prior to consulting me, Rebecca had been treated by two psychiatrists with an assortment of TCAs, an MAOI, and fluoxetine—all to no avail despite good trials at good doses. For the previous ten years, she had had psychodynamic psychotherapy with a competent therapist with whom she had a wonderful relationship. She had learned a lot about herself, but little had changed. After a lengthy evaluation session, the diagnosis was clearly dysthymia.

At session two, I taught her the cognitive method for identifying automatic thoughts when feeling distressed. She talked in detail about a year-long love relationship that was ending. By the fourth session, she reported using the method regularly and finding she was "no longer accepting the conclusions I usually jump to." Also, when she responded differently to people, she noted, they reacted differently to her as well. She was beginning to feel "empowered." At session ten, she announced that she "was no longer depressed." She had had an epiphany, and everything became "crystal clear" to her for the first time in 20 years. It was all within her and not outside her. She had kept herself in a "perpetual state of feeling diminished and victimized." She was no longer doing that, and life looked very different to her now. She was reformulating her view of her family and herself. I saw her twice more (a total of twelve sessions) and we terminated therapy.

In a 180-degree shift from the past, the question today may be: "Why recommend psychotherapy?" There are several credible answers. Roughly 50%

of dysthymics do not respond to antidepressant drugs. For some of the remainder, the response may be partial, with residual symptoms.[3] Furthermore, dysthymics often have significant psychosocial impairment, marital and vocational problems, adverse life events, and self-defeating personality traits—typically good reasons to prescribe psychotherapy.

Although there are no research data to support long-term psychotherapy with this group, studies of short-term therapy are beginning to appear. Markowitz reports on a small group of preliminary studies that suggest that cognitive therapy is helpful to some dysthymic patients.[3] I have been doing psychotherapy with dysthymics for many years. When you work with a patient in the context of a long-standing problem with depression and achieve change in a short period of time, the results can be quite dramatic. This does not represent my clinical experience with every dysthymic patient, nor is it intended to endorse my therapy model, cognitive therapy, over other models. However, since the research answers about psychotherapy and dysthymia are not yet in, it may serve to bolster the clinician approaching these chronic patients with a short-term intervention.

The desired outcomes of psychotherapy are usually easy to describe: to change one's attitude about oneself, significant others, and the future; to change one's dominant mood; to act in different ways from usual. Unfortunately, the desired outcomes are not often easy to achieve. Occasionally, though, a motivated patient arrives who is indeed ready to do the work of psychotherapy. Such was the case with Rebecca.

Medication had played no role in this change; Rebecca had discontinued it months before coming to my office. What part had prior therapy played? Was she somehow "ready" to change now, where that had not been the case before? Our relationship was a warm, dialoguing one of mutual respect. How important was that component? Finally, how central to change was the cognitive focus of the intervention? I must leave you to form your own opinions on these objectively unanswerable questions.

THE TREATMENT OF BIPOLAR DISORDER

Treating Mania

Mania and suicide are the mental health practitioner's two most urgent situations. The acutely manic patient is often unable to control his or her impulses—unable to regulate behavior. Manic patients may be dangerous to themselves, may damage property, spend money unwisely, or act impulsively, with little regard for consequences. Acute treatment may be rendered in a hospital emergency room, with admission or legal commitment to an inpatient ward of a hospital to follow. The experience of a manic episode can wreak havoc with a marital relationship, jeopardize a job, and alienate family and friends. The stakes for therapeutic intervention here (as in suicide) are high.

When mania is mild, the intervention priority is to begin a mood-stabilizing drug (typically lithium carbonate) and to prescribe a sedative (e.g., clonazepam or lorazepam) to ensure that insomnia does not worsen mania. When mania is severe, the first priority is to stabilize the patient's mood and behavior. Over 50% of manias have psychotic symptoms.[4]

In the past, neuroleptic (antipsychotic) drugs were the mainstays of treatment. Chlorpromazine (Thorazine) was a standard approach to mania in the 1950s. A decade later, haloperidol (Haldol) proved able to control psychotic behavior with less sedation and risk of hypotension than Thorazine. The discovery of the effect of lithium carbonate was a watershed in the treatment of bipolar disorder in general and mania in particular.

One problem with using lithium as the sole intervention for mania is the length of time it takes to achieve stabilization (from five days to two or three weeks). It is thought that one factor that determines this slowness of stabilization may be the relatively long time needed to achieve an effective steady state concentration.[5] When behavior control is a priority, a neuroleptic is often utilized to achieve it. The advantage of a high-potency neuroleptic (haloperidol, thiothixene) is the low level of hypotension and sedation. Unfortunately, sedation may initially be desirable, leading to the prescription of a low-potency neuroleptic (e.g., chlorpromazine or thioridazine). These drugs are more sedating and carry a higher risk of hypotension, but they are less likely to cause extrapyramidal symptoms and neurotoxic reactions.

An uncommon, but dangerous, reaction to neuroleptic use is the neuroleptic malignant syndrome (NMS). Its symptoms include lethargy, tremulousness, muscular rigidity, hyperthermia, impaired consciousness, and even irreversible brain damage.[6] A good strategy, therefore, is to prescribe only the amount of neuroleptic needed for behavioral control and then, once control is achieved, taper the drug and start a mood stabilizer.

By the mid-1990s, the number of drug options for treating mania had increased considerably. In addition to lithium carbonate, there were divalproex sodium (Depakote), carbamazepine (Tegretol), and clonazepam (Klonopin). The latter three are anticonvulsants, with demonstrated antimanic effect. They offer mood stabilization without much sedation and with little risk of tardive dyskinesia.[4] Although lithium has a *narrow margin of safety* between therapeutic and toxic dosages, for the other three drugs the margin is much broader.

Concern has been raised about concurrent usage of lithium and a neuroleptic drug. A report appeared in 1974 describing irreversible encephalopathy in a number of patients treated with both lithium and high-dose haloperidol.[7]

The anticonvulsants have been employed to treat mania for two decades, but in recent years they seem to have made real inroads into widespread clinical use. Risperidone and clozapine, primarily useful in treating schizophrenia, have become therapeutic options for resistant mania, along with convulsive therapy, which has been used to treat mania for decades.

With the demonstration that lithium carbonate is relatively less effective in mixed mania, rapid cycling, secondary mania, and mania with comorbid substance abuse, valproate may be a clinician's first choice in treating the nonresponsive acutely manic patient.[8] Studies by Bowden et al.[9] and Pope et al.[10] suggest equivalent efficacy for valproate and lithium even in pure mania. So, the treatment algorithm begins with lithium or valproate[11] (see Table 11.3).

The therapeutic blood level for lithium is thought to be in the range of 0.8–1.2 mEq/l Above 1.5 mEq/l is thought to be generally in the toxic range. A serum level of 1.2–1.5 meq/l requires caution. The typical dose required to reach the therapeutic range for treating mania is 900–1,800 mg per day, but serum levels must be done in coordination with the prescription of lithium, and dosages determined accordingly. When mania subsides, it is necessary to reduce lithium dosage, since the manic state requires more lithium than does euthymia.

Table 11.3
AN ALGORITHM FOR THE TREATMENT OF MANIA IN BIPLOAR DEPRESSION

1. lithium or valproate

2. augment with benzodiazepine

3. lithium + valproate combination or carbamazepine (Tegretol)

4. augment with neuroleptic drug

5. augment with low-dose risperidone

6. Tegretol + Depakote

7. lithium + Tegretol + Depakote

Valproate was approved by the F.D.A. for the treatment of acute mania in the fall of 1995. First studied as a mood stabilizer in France by Lambert,[8] valproate has been marketed as an antiseizure drug in the U.S. since 1983. It is available in two forms: divalproex sodium (Depakote) and valproic acid (Depakene). The former is better tolerated by the G.I. tract and is the form generally prescribed. Since the half-life of valproate is nine to sixteen hours, typical dosing is two to three times daily. The serum level range for efficacy is 50–100 $\mu g/$ ml.

If there is no response to either drug in sequence, Tohen suggests adding a benzodiazepine (e.g., clonazepam).[11] The next step is the combination of lithium with valproate, or the introduction of another anticonvulsant, carbamazepine (Tegretol). Some believe that Tegretol is a better drug for severe, psychotic mania.[12] It may work faster than lithium, may have some antidepressant properties, and may reduce aggression.[4]

The following step is the addition of a neuroleptic drug. The step after that is the addition of low doses of risperidone.[13] If there is still no response, the next step is a combination Tegretol and Depakote. (With this combination, serum levels need to be followed carefully.) The final step is the combination of all three mood stabilizers: lithium, Tegretol, and Depakote.

Some resistant manias respond to clozapine.[14] There are data to support the use of ECT in mania,[15, 16] although there is danger of neurotoxicity with the use of convulsive therapy in a patient concurrently taking lithium.[17]

Treating Bipolar Depression

When an acute depressive episode occurs in the course of a bipolar disorder, is it any different from depression in the course of a unipolar disorder? Theoretically, the answer is no, aside from an increased likelihood of an anergic (psychomotor-slowed) picture. Practically, however, there are two major consequences of treatment that earn "bipolar depression" separate consideration. First, there is a tendency (in up to one-third of treatment-refractory bipolar patients) for antidepressant treatment to induce mania.[18] Second, there is a tendency (in up to one-quarter of treatment-refractory bipolar patients) for antidepressant treatment to induce a rapid cycling course pattern.[18]

These findings are not new.[19, 20] The phenomena are real, and the unresolved questions relate to prevention. Let's review the treatment of an acute depressive episode (with a focus on the bipolar patient) and explore the questions as they arise in context.

In some bipolar patients, acute depression will respond to lithium alone, but it may take up to a month.[4] Theoretically, all classes of antidepressants (TCA, MAOI, SSRI) are available as options for bipolar depression. Some think that MAOIs may be more effective than TCAs in these cases,[21] especially when there is a past history of nonresponse to TCAs.[22] Response to antidepressants in bipolars is thought to take longer than in unipolar depressives.[4] Potentiators (e.g., thyroid hormone taken for three to five days) may be useful in bipolars; however, the use of methylphenidate (Ritalin) is complicated by the possibility that it may precipitate mania (as well as carry a risk of dependency).

The antidepressant bupropion (Wellbutrin) may have special utility here because it may be less likely to precipitate mania,[23] may be more effective against psychomotor retardation,[24] and may be less likely to induce rapid cycling.[25]

The anticonvulsant carbamazepine has some antidepressant effect, so it might be a useful option in these cases. When would you prescribe convulsive therapy? Goodwin and Jamison make four suggestions:[4]

- when the patient is severely ill
- when the patient is delusional
- when there is a high risk of suicide
- when there is a history of previous response to ECT.

It is not easy to discriminate clinically between pharmacologically induced mania and the natural course of the bipolar process. Life-charting (a careful written review of past events on a timeline) may help the clinician discern a pattern. Many doctors will "cover" the prescription of an antidepressant for a depressive episode with a course-altering drug (discussed in the next section, Altering the Course of Depressive Illness), expecting that this approach will make both course acceleration (more frequent episodes) and pharmacological mania less likely. One well known study validates this approach.[26] However, the issue is not considered resolved. Furthermore, the phenomenon of antidepressant-induced mania appears to increase the likelihood of cycle acceleration at some point.[18] A study by Altshuler et al. finds increased vulnerability to cycle acceleration for both women and bipolar II patients.[18] It also provides an up-to-date review of both rapid cycling and pharmacological mania in the drug therapy of bipolar depression.

ALTERING THE COURSE
OF DEPRESSIVE ILLNESS

The clinician treating a patient with recurrent depressive illness simultaneously faces two agendas. The more immediate concern is terminating an acute episode of depression, mania, or a mixture of the two. The more distant, but often more daunting task, is to alter the course of the depressive illness.

This task has been referred to as *prophylaxis*, or prevention. The revolutionary discovery in this regard has been attributed to Noack and Trautner,[27] Schou,[28] and Baastrup.[29] It is that the naturally occurring element lithium, typically prescribed as lithium carbonate, alters the course of bipolar illness. Episodes of mania and depression may be eliminated entirely for some patients. Although they may continue in other patients, their duration is shortened and their intensity is diminished. Since bipolar illness is marked by multiple relapses and recurrences, this discovery was revolutionary indeed.

Although lithium is a naturally occurring element, it is not a benign one. It was once used in medicine as a salt substitute, but this practice was discontinued when some people died of cardiac complications caused by the ion. When lithium carbonate was reintroduced as an acute treatment for mania (and for some depressions), as well as a prophylactic approach to the course of manic-depression, it came with a protocol for serum-level monitoring, identification of situational concerns, lists of side effects and long-term effects, and signs of toxicity.

A wonderful primer in lithium management is offered by Goodwin and Jamison in their classic work, *Manic-Depressive Illness*.[4] I will extract from their presentation only a few clinical highlights, which will be presented in tabular form. For most patients, the prescription of prophylactic lithium carbonate begins at a dose of 900 mg per day. Serum level determinations guide the practitioner to a dosage in the range of 0.8–1.0 mEq/l of lithium. (Some patients maintain prophylaxis at lower serum levels.) The long-term concerns with lithium therapy involve the thyroid gland, the kidneys, the heart, and the central nervous system (see Table 11.4). These concerns form the rationale for medical monitoring of thyroid function, kidney function, and cardiac function, in addition to serum lithium levels (see Table 11.5).

Since lithium forms a part of the body's fluid and electrolyte balance and is affected by changes in it, a number of situational concerns involve nutrition and electrolyte balance (see Table 11.6). In addition, it is known that in

Table 11.4
LONG-TERM CONCERNS WITH LITHIUM MAINTENANCE

1. Thyroid function

2. Kidney concentrating ability

3. Cardiac function

4. Central nervous system function

    a. Tremor

    b. Motor coordination

    c. Muscle weakness

    d. Memory problems

    e. Blunted creativity

From Goodwin and Jamison, 1990[4]

Table 11.5
MEDICAL MONITORING FOR LITHIUM MAINTENANCE

Serum Lithium Level • T4, free T4, TSH

Creatinine; urinalysis • EKG

From Goodwin and Jamison, 1990[4]

depression serum lithium rises and in hypomania and mania it falls. Therefore, an awareness of the patient's current mood state is another specific concern. Finally, there is a long-standing caution relevant to the prescription of lithium in pregnancy. It is based upon the finding of Ebstein's cardiac anomaly in 1 out of 1,000 fetal exposures to lithium. The prescription of lithium to pregnant bipolar women is in the process of being reviewed.

There is a commonly encountered group of side effects that accompany treatment with lithium. They range from the annoying to the unacceptable, depending upon the patient's sensitivity to, and tolerance for, them. These common side effects are listed in Table 11.7. In a treatment with a narrow margin of safety between therapeutic and toxic dose, as well as a series of internal and external factors that can upset the balance, it becomes clinically

Table 11.6
SITUATIONAL CONCERNS WITH LITHIUM MAINTENANCE

• Medical illness	• Changes in mood state
• General anesthesia	• Decrease in renal clearance with age
• Dieting	• Pregnancy

• Changes in physical activity

From Goodwin and Jamison, 1990[4]

crucial to be knowledgeable about toxic effects. These toxic effects may begin with difficulty concentrating, nausea, or irritability, and may progress to impaired consciousness or seizures. Other symptoms of toxicity are summarized in Table 11.8.

When lithium was introduced in the late 1960s, our attention focused on the therapeutic potential it offered. As time has gone by, that attention has inevitably shifted to those bipolar patients for whom it has little to no prophylactic value.[30] Meanwhile, pharmacological research has begun to document the efficacy of the anticonvulsants valproate and carbamazepine for some types of bipolar illness.[31]

Over two decades ago, *rapid cycling* was identified as a predictor of nonresponse to lithium prophylaxis.[32] Since patients with rapid cycling may make up as much as 20% of the bipolar population, and 72–82% may exhibit a poor response to lithium, this is not a finding to be dismissed.[33] A significant portion of these patients may have bipolar II disorder. When manic and depressive symptoms occur simultaneously (mixed episode; dysphoric mania), this too predicts poor lithium prophylactic response.[34]

Table 11.7
LITHIUM'S COMMON SIDE EFFECTS

• Lethargy	• Tremor
• Polydipsia (excess thirst)	• Memory problems
• Polyuria (excess urine volume)	• Diarrhea
• Weight gain	

From Goodwin and Jamison, 1990[4]

Table 11.8 LITHIUM TOXICITY	
• Drowsiness	• Unsteady gait
• Confusion	• Restlessness
• Disorientation	• Vomiting
• Slurred speech	
From Goodwin and Jamison, 1990[4]	

Post et al. have suggested that frequent episodes early in life may facilitate *kindling* (discussed in chapter 3) and, with it, poorer response to lithium.[35]

In addition to these "internal" factors that make response to lithium less likely, there are some external factors. The most evident is *noncompliance.*[31] When psychotherapy is available and the patient engages in it, it can deal well with this issue. A second factor is the maintenance of a serum level of 0.8–1.0 mEq/l. This requires periodic monitoring, as well as responding to events that can affect lithium levels. A third factor is the degree of *clinician-patient contact.* In a managed care environment, this may require a savvy case manager who will underwrite a level of care appropriate to the patient's need.

Probably the most common circumstance that may lead to noncompliance and poor response is inconsistent medication-taking due to side effects. Once again, a good clinician-patient relationship can define this as a problem to be overcome together rather than as an arena in which the patient takes unilateral action without considering consequences.

Comorbid substance abuse is a serious concern with bipolar patients. This, too, makes noncompliance more likely, which feeds a poorer outcome to lithium prophylaxis.[36] Finally, stress in family relationships, at work, or from adverse life events has been associated with poor prophylactic outcome as well.[37]

For the majority of bipolar patients, medications in addition to lithium carbonate (at least during acute episodes) are likely to be necessary.[38] The long-term use of neuroleptics is discouraged because of the risk of tardive dyskinesia (as in schizophrenia). It seems clear from surveys, however, that neuroleptics remain a component of some prophylactic treatments.[39] Finally, when lithium is to be stopped, it seems critical to avoid abrupt discontinuation and to withdraw the drug over several weeks. Sudden discontinuation may lead to relapse.[40]

What can be done for lithium nonresponders? The success observed with valproate and carbamazepine in the treatment of acute mania has raised the possibility of their prophylactic value in altering the course of bipolar illness.[41-44]
Controlled studies are not yet available, but the target populations are readily
identifiable: those with mixed manic episodes, rapid cycling, comorbid substance
abuse or (often borderline) personality disorders.[44] It is thought that drug combinations (e.g., valproate, carbamazepine, lithium, or a combination of two of the
three) may be effective for some resistant patients.[45]

Subsyndromal symptoms are commonly found even during seemingly
euthymic periods in bipolar patients.[46] Couple this finding with the now nearly 50% of bipolars thought to respond inadequately to lithium prophylaxis,[26]
and the necessity for adjunct psychotherapeutic management seems clear.
Little systematic study has been given to psychotherapy for bipolar disorder.
Preliminary work suggests a place for family therapy,[47] group therapy,[48] and
cognitive therapy.[49]

Bipolar II Disorder

Two approaches have been taken to altering the course of bipolar II disorder, and each may be inadequate to the task. The first is an array of treatments similar to that proposed for bipolar I disorder: lithium carbonate, the
anticonvulsant drugs, neuroletpics, and benzodiazepines. The second
approach is to view the disorder as a variant of normalcy and ignore it.

The perils of the latter course relate first to the comorbidity of bipolar II
disorder with eating disorders, substance abuse, and borderline personality.[50]
Second, the suspected high percentage of rapid cyclers among bipolar II disorder patients predicts treatment resistance in many patients.[51] Third, an
increased risk of suicidal behavior in this group lends an urgency to treatment.[4]

When treatment is offered, the same caution in prescribing antidepressants to bipolar I patients with concurrent use of a course-altering drug should
be observed in treating bipolar II disorder as well. In terms of selecting a drug
for prophylaxis, there is little research to date to guide the clinician.

Major Depressive Disorder

In the focus established on the use of lithium to alter the course of bipolar disorder, a similar need to deal with the course of unipolar illness is often

overlooked. For most, major depressive disorder is a recurrent illness. Therefore, prophylactic treatment is an important consideration for its management.[41] Therapeutic options include antidepressants, lithium, anticonvulsants, electroconvulsive therapy, and psychotherapy.

In a definitive maintenance study with imipramine, lasting benefit was demonstrated by a continuation of therapeutic doses of the antidepressant.[52] Although clinical practice several decades ago was to maintain patients at a lower (so-called "maintenance") dose (for which there was little research support), today most often antidepressant drugs are prescribed at the same level to which the patient responded. Lithium was found to have prophylactic value for recurrent unipolar as well as recurrent bipolar disorders.[26] The prophylactic usefulness of the anticonvulsants in major depression has not been studied to date.

When an acute depressive episode has been treated with convulsive therapy, and maintenance is desirable, the usual procedure is to start an antidepressant drug and/or lithium.[41] Maintenance (usually monthly) ECT has not been well studied, but is an alternative for those patients treated acutely with convulsive therapy.

The definitive study of maintenance psychotherapy supports the value of interpersonal psychotherapy for the patient with recurrent depression.[53] I have found in my practice that periodic psychotherapy for patients with unipolar recurrent depression has multiple benefits, among them: Patients are more likely to call during acute periods or times of high stress. Having learned a model of problem-solving, the patient is likely to utilize it continuously, and to call when obstacles to its use arise.

RESISTANT DEPRESSION

By this time in our discussion of the treatment of depression, it should be clear that we cannot predict, by either clinical diagnosis or a biological test, who will respond to a given treatment and who will not.[54] We don't even have a standard definition of "treatment resistance." Some have defined it as failure to respond to an adequate trial of one antidepressant or one course of ECT.[55] Others have required failure to respond to at least three heterocyclic antidepressants.[56] It is not surprising, therefore, that a protocol for treatment-resistant depression has not been established.[54]

The questions that must be answered to create such a protocol are, however, not hard to identify: How many trials? With what target doses? Followed by which augmentation strategies? Accompanied by what model of psychotherapy? And, finally, what place to assign to ECT?

It is also generally agreed that at least 20% of depressed patients do not respond readily to the initial treatment offered. In addition, perhaps 30% more get only partial relief. Some part of this disturbingly large number are labeled "resistant" due to clinical decisions, and some due to patient factors. When a patient with typical signs and symptoms of an acute depressive episode does not respond, first the diagnosis should be reviewed. Then the possibility of undertreatment should be considered, i.e., inadequate dosage[57] for an insufficient period of time.[58]

There is a debate about the virtue in increasing standard doses of fluoxetine (20 mg), paroxetine (20 mg), and sertraline (50 mg). It seems clear that some patients take eight to twelve weeks, instead of four, to respond to these starting doses. For others, an increase in dose (to 40 mg of fluoxetine, 30–40 mg of paroxetine, or 100–150 mg of sertraline) seems to produce a response. Fava found just such a result in a study with fluoxetine, in 1992.[59] The issue is unresolved.

A third contribution to the rolls of treatment resistance comes from the presence of clinically significant comorbid disorders (e.g., substance abuse, personality disorder, dysthymia). The final factor related to clinical decision-making comes from ignorance of special indications for particular classes of drug.[60] An example would be MAOIs for bipolar depression or atypical depression.

Patient contributions to treatment resistance rise first from noncompliance and second from a trial that is aborted due to intolerable side effects.[60] When a depressed patient does not respond to a standard drug trial, the clinician has several standard options: increase the dose of the drug, augment it with another drug, add a second antidepressant (drug combination), or discontinue the first drug and switch to another antidepressant.[61]

Typical augmentation strategies involve adding lithium carbonate to the antidepressant chosen[62] or adding thyroid hormone.[63] Buspirone (BuSpar) has been suggested as well.[64] Some have recommended the addition of a TCA to the initial SSRI chosen.[65] Caution must be observed here, due to the cytochrome P450 isoenzyme issue alluded to in chapter 10. Less common strategies involve stimulants, neuroleptics, carbamazepine, and benzodiazepines.[56]

When switching drug therapies, it is common to try a drug from a different class than that prescribed initially. Since the SSRIs have become the acknowledged first-line drugs, a TCA or bupropion may be next. An MAOI or ECT may follow, with observance of appropriate drug washout intervals.

In the past, by the time some patients had worked their way through a protocol for treating resistant depression, hospitalization was inevitable. Today, with the increased scrutiny of the managed care case worker, inpatient treatment is more often unavailable. Some common indications for hospital care are summarized in Table 11.9.

Table 11.9
HOSPITALIZATION FOR DEPRESSION

Hospitalization may be indicated when the patient:

- Is unable to cooperate with treatment

- Is at risk for suicide or homicide

- Lacks social supports

- Has complicated psychological or medical problems

- Needs detoxification from substance abuse

- Has psychosis endangering relationships, reputation, or assets

Modified from American Psychiatric Association (1993)[41].

POSTSCRIPT

The clearest progress in tailoring the treatment to the disorder has come in treating dysthmia, with the addition of effective pharmacotherapy to short-term psychotherapy. More clinically useful nosology has led to more specific treatments for subtypes of depression. The addition of the new SSRIs allows the generalist to play a significant role in the management of depression.

In the future, the advent of psychotherapy designed to meet the specific needs of the acutely or chronically depressed individual seems likely. Newer drugs, as effective in treating depressive disorders as today's but without the unwanted side effects, may also emerge.

Notes

1. Harrison, W. M., & Stewart, J. W. (1993). Pharmacotherapy of dysthymia. *Psychiatric Annals, 23*(11), 638

2. Thase, M. E., & Howland R. H. (1995). Assessment and treatment of chronic depression. *Clinical Advances in the Treatment of Psychiatric Disorders, 9*(3), 1.

3. Markowitz, J. C. (1994). Psychotherapy of dysthymia. *American Journal of Psychiatry, 151*(8), 1114.

4. Goodwin, F. K., & Jamison, K. R. (1990). *Manic-depressive illness.* New York: Oxford.

5. Bowden, C. L. (1996). Dosing strategies and time course of response to antimanic drugs. *Journal of Clinical Psychiatry, 57*(Suppl. 13), 4.

6. Levenson, J. L. (1985). Neuroleptic malignant syndrome. *American Journal of Psychiatry, 142,* 1137.

7. Cohen, W. J., & Cohen, N. H. (1974). Lithium carbonate, haloperidol and irreversible brain damage. *Journal of the American Medical Association, 230,* 1283.

8. Bowden, C. L. (1996). Efficacy of divalproex sodium and lithium in the treatment of acute mania. *Directions in Psychiatry, 16,* 1.

9. Bowden, C. L., Brugger, A. M., Swann, A. C., et al. (1994). Efficacy of divalproex vs. lithium and placebo in the treatment of mania. *Journal of the American Medical Association, 271,* 918.

10. Pope, J. G., McElroy, S. L., Keck, P. E., et al. (1991). Valproate in the treatment of acute mania: A placebo-controlled study. *Archives of General Psychiatry, 68,* 62.

11. Tohen, M. (September, 1996). An algorithmic approach to the pharmacologic treatment of acute mania. *Journal of Clinical Psychiatry.*

12. Post, R. M. (1990). Non-lithium treatment for bipolar disorder. *Journal of Clinical Psychiatry, 51,* 9.

13. Tohen, M., Zarate, C. A., Centorrilo, F., et al. (1986). Risperidone in the treatment of mania. *Journal of Clinical Psychiatry, 57,* 249.

14. Zarate, C. A., Tohen, M., & Baldessarini, R. (1995). Clozapine in severe mood disorders. *Journal of Clinical Psychiatry, 56,* 411.

15. Black, D. W., Winokur, G., & Nasrallah, A. (1987). Treatment of mania: A naturalistic study of electroconvulsive therapy versus lithium in 438 patients. *Journal of Clinical Psychiatry, 48,* 132.

16. Small, J. G., Milstein, V., Klapper, M. H., et al. (1986). Electroconvulsive therapy in the treatment of manic episodes. *Annals of the New York Academy of Science, 462,* 37.

17. Small, J. G., Kellams, J. J., Milstein, V., et al. (1980). Complications with elec troconvulsive treatment combined with lithium. *Biological Psychiatry, 15,* 103.

18. Altshuler, L. L., Post, R. M., Leverich, G. S., et al. (1995). Antidepressant-induced mania and cycle acceleration: A controversy revisited. *American Journal of Psychiatry, 152*(8), 1130.

19. Wehr, T. A. (1987). Can antidepressants cause mania and worsen the course of the affective illness? *American Journal of Psychiatry, 144,* 1403.

20. Wehr, T. A. (1993). Can antidepressants induce rapid cycling? *Archives of General Psychiatry, 50,* 495.

21. Himmelhoch, J. M., Thase, M. E., Mallinger, A.G., et al. (1991). Tranylcypromine versus imipramine in anergic bipolar depression. *Psychopharmacology Bulletin, 148,* 910.

22. Thase, M. E., Mallinger, A. G., McKnight, D., et al. (1992). Treatment of imipramine-resistant depression, IV: A double-blind, crossover study of tranylcypromine for anergic bipolar depression. *American Journal of Psychiatry, 149,* 195.

23. Stoll, A. L., Mayer, P. V., Kolbrener, M., et al. (1994). Antidepressant-associated mania: A controlled comparison with spontaneous mania. *American Journal of Psychiatry, 151,* 1642.

24. Fabre, L. F., Brodie, H. K. H., Garver, D., et al. (1983). A multi-center evaluation of bupropion versus placebo in hospitalized depressed patients. *Journal of Clinical Psychiatry, 44*(5), 157.

25. Haykal, R. F., & Akiskal, H. S. (1990). Bupropion as a promising approach to rapid cycling bipolar II patients. *Journal of Clinical Psychiatry, 51,* 450.

26. Prien, R. F., Kupfer, D. J., Mansky, P. A., et al. (1984). Drug therapy in the prevention of recurrences in unipolar and bipolar affective disorders. *Archives of General Psychiatry, 41,* 1096.

27. Noack, C. H., & Trautner, E. M. (1951). The lithium treatment of maniacal psychosis. *Medical Journal of Australia, 2,* 219.

28. Schou, M., Juel-Nielson, N., Stromgren, E., et al. (1954). The treatment of manic psychoses by administration of lithium salts. *Journal of Neurology, Neurosurgery, and Psychiatry, 17,* 250.

29. Baastrup, P. C. (1964). The use of lithium in manic-depressive psychosis. *Comprehensive Psychiatry, 5,* 396.

30. Moncrieff, J. (1995). Lithium revisited: A re-examination of the placebo-controlled trials of lithium prophylaxis in manic-depressive disorder. *British Journal of Psychiatry, 167,* 569.

31. Goldberg, J. F., Harrow, M., & Sands, J. R. (1996). Lithium and the longitudinal course of bipolar illness. *Psychiatric Annals, 26*(10), 651.

32. Dunner, D. L., & Fieve, R. R. (1974). Clinical factors in lithium carbonate prophylaxis failure. *Archives of General Psychiatry, 30,* 229.

33. Calabrese, J. R., & Woyshville, M. J. (1995). A medication algorithm for treatment of bipolar rapid cycling. *Journal of Clinical Psychiatry, 56* (Suppl. 3), 11.

34. Prien, R. F., Himmelhoch, J. M., & Kupfer, D. J. (1988). Treatment of mixed mania. *Journal of Affective Disorders, 15,* 9.

35. Post, R. M., Uhde, T. W., Putnam, P. W., et al. (1982). Kindling and carbamazepine in affective illness. *Journal of Nervous and Mental Disease, 170,* 717.

36. Brady, K. T., & Sonne, S. C. (1995). The relationship between substance abuse and bipolar disorder. *Journal of Clinical Psychiatry, 56* (Suppl. 3), 19.

37. Miklowitz, D. J., Goldstein, M. J., Nuechterlein, K. H., et al. (1988). Family factors and the course of bipolar affective disorder. *Archives of General Psychiatry, 45,* 225.

38. Sachs, G. S., Lafer, B., Truman, C. J., et al. (1994). Lithium monotherapy: Miracle, myth, and misunderstanding. *Psychiatric Annals, 24,* 299.

39. Kane, J. M. (1988). The role of neuroleptics in manic-depressive illness. *Journal of Clinical Psychiatry, 49*(Suppl. 11), 12.

40. Baldessarini, R. J., Tondo, L., & Faedda, G. L. (1996). Effects of the rate of discontinuing lithium maintenance treatment in bipolar disorders. *Journal of Clinical Psychiatry, 57*(10), 441.

41. American Psychiatric Association. (1993). Practice guideline for major depressive disorder in adults. Washington D.C.: American Psychiatric Association.

42. American Psychiatric Association. (1994). Practice guideline for the treatment of patients with bipolar disorder. *American Journal of Psychiatry, 151*(Suppl. 12), 1.

43. McElroy, S. L., Keck, P. E., Pope, H. G., et al. (1989). Valproate in psychiatric disorders: Literature review and clinical guidelines. *Journal of Clinical Psychiatry, 50*(Suppl. 3), 23.

44. Solomon, D. A., Keitner, G. I., Miller, I. W., et al. (1995). Course of illness and maintenance treatments for patients with bipolar disorder. *Journal of Clinical Psychiatry, 56*(1), 5.

45. Keck, P. E., McElroy, S. L., Vuckovic, A., et al. (1992). Combined valproate and carbamazepine treatment of bipolar disorder. *Journal of Neuropsychiatry and Clinical Neuroscience, 4,* 319.

46. Keller, M. B., Lavori, P. W., & Kane, J. M. (1992). Subsyndromal symptoms in bipolar disorder: A comparison of standard and low serum levels of lithium. *Archives of General Psychiatry, 49,* 371.

47. Clarkin, J. F., Glick, I. D., Haas, G. L., et al. (1990). A randomized clinical trial of inpatient family intervention. *Journal of Affective Disorders, 18,* 17.

48. Kripke, D. F., & Robinson, D. (1985). Ten years with a lithium group. *McLean Hospital Journal, 10,* 1.

49. Basco, M. R., & Rush, A. J. (1996). *Cognitive-behavior therapy for bipolar disorder.* New York: Guilford.

50. Fawcett, J. (1996). Bipolar II disorder. *Psychiatric Annals, 26*(7), S440.

51. Dunner, D. L. (1993). A review of the diagnostic status of "bipolar II" for the DSM-IV work group on mood disorders. *Depression, 1,* 2.

52. Kupfer, D. J., Frank, E., Perel, J. M., et al. (1992). Five year outcome for maintenance therapies in recurrent depression. *Archives of General Psychiatry, 42,* 769.

53. Frank, E., Kupfer, D. J., Perel, J. M., et al. (1990). Three year outcomes for maintenance therapies in recurrent depression. *Archives of General Psychiatry, 47,* 1093.

54. Fawcett, J. (1994). Progress in treatment-resistant and treatment-refractory depression: We still have a long way to go. *Psychiatric Annals, 24*(5), 214.

55. Seth, R., Jennings, A. L., Bindman, J., et al. (1992). Combination treatment with noradrenalin and serotonin reuptake inhibitors in resistant depression. *British Journal of Psychiatry, 161*, 562.

56. Zajecka, J. M., Jeffriess, H., & Fawcett, J. (1995). The efficacy of fluoxetine combined with a heterocyclic antidepressant in treatment-resistant depression: A retrospective analysis. *Journal of Clinical Psychiatry, 56*(8), 338.

57. Keller, M. B. (1988). Undertreatment of major depression. *Psychopharmacology Bulletin, 24*, 75.

58. Schweizer, E., Rickels, K., Amsterdam, J. D., et al. (1990). What constitutes an adequate antidepressant trial of fluoxetine? *Journal of Clinical Psychiatry, 51*, 8.

59. Fava, M. (1992). High-dose fluoxetine in the treatment of depressed patients not responsive to a standard dose of fluoxetine. *Journal of Affective Disorders, 25*, 229.

60. Hornig-Rohan, M., & Amsterdam, J. D. (1994). Clinical and biological correlates of Treatment-Resistant Depression: An overview. *Psychiatric Annals, 24*(5), 220.

61. Nierenberg, A. A. (1994). Treatment-resistant depression in the age of serotonin. *Psychiatric Annals, 24*(5), 217.

62. Pope, H. G., McElroy, S. L., & Nixon, R. A. (1988). Possible synergism between fluoxetine and lithium in refractory depression. *American Journal of Psychiatry, 145*, 1292.

63. Gupta, S., Masand, P., & Tanquary, J. (1991). Thyroid hormone supplementation of fluoxetine in the treatment of major depression. *British Journal of Psychiatry, 159*, 866.

64. Jacobsen, F. M. (1991). Possible augmentation of antidepressant response by buspirone. *Journal of Clinical Psychiatry, 52*, 217.

65. Weilburg, J. B., Rosenbaum, J. F., Meltzer-Brody, S., et al. (1991). Tricyclic augmentation of fluoxetine. *Annals of Clinical Psychiatry, 3*, 209.

66. Kocsis, J. H., Frances, A. J., & Voss, C. (1988). Imipramine for treatment of chronic depression. *Archives of General Psychiatry, 45*, 253.

67. Stewart, J. W., Quitkin, F. M., & McGrath, P. J. (1989). Social functioning in chronic depression: Effect of six weeks of antidepressant treatment. *Psychiatric Research, 25*, 213.

68. Nardi, E., Capponi, R., Costa, D. A. et al. (1992). Moclobemide compared with imipramine in the treatment of chronic depression: A double-blind placebo controlled trial. *Clinical Neuropsychopharmacology, 15* (suppl.).

69. Hellerstein, D., Yanowitch, P., & Rosenthal, J. (1993). A randomized double-blind study of fluoxetine versus placebo in treatment of dysthmia. *American Journal of Psychiatry, 150*, 1169.

Afterword

As a clinician, you will need to recognize the ubiquitous problem of depression in all of its many presentations. You must decide for yourself how many separate disorders are included within the rubric of "depression." You must learn to appreciate and differentiate the various border disputes surrounding these disorders.

Choose a model that explains depression to you satisfactorally in most cases. Establish a protocol for treating the acute depressive episode. Be sensitive to the nuances of (unipolar and bipolar) course in your patients. Learn to recognize, differentiate, and treat mania and hypomania, as well as you have mastered depression.

Choose a model of short-term psychotherapy to utilize when you believe psychotherapy is indicated. Learn to combine pharmacotherapy and psychotherapy, whether you do both yourself or work closely with a colleague.

Develop a personal algorithm for the treatment of resistant depression and make liberal use of other opinions when necessary. In providing care, determine those areas in which you need help and use colleagues who complement your own expertise as consultation resources. Always be mindful of suicidal ideas and the danger of self-destructive behavior in the depressed patient. Finally, commit yourself to keeping current, whether it be with atypical presentations (e.g., depression's other spectrum), new drug options, or novel approaches to the course of depressive illness.

It is my hope that this guide will lead to an appreciation for the broad range of problems and prospects for treatment that comprise this most common disorder.

Index